Central Banks' Independence in Historical Perspective

Central Banks' Independence in Historical Perspective

Editor
Gianni Toniolo

Walter de Gruyter · Berlin · New York 1988

Editor

Professor Dr. Gianni Toniolo
Dipartimento Di Scienze Economiche
Università Degli Studi di Venezia
Italy

332.11
C3972

Library of Congress Cataloging in Publication Data

Central banks' independence in historical perspective.
  Bibliography: p.
  1. Banks and banking, Central. I. Toniolo, Gianni, 1942-
HGl811.C46 1988   332.1'1   88-30020
ISBN 0-89925-511-6 (U.S.)

Deutsche Bibliothek Cataloging in Publication Data

Central banks' independence in historical perspective / ed.
Gianni Toniolo. - Berlin ; New York : de Gruyter, 1988
  ISBN 3-11-011440-2
  NE: Toniolo, Gianni [Hrsg.]

Copyright © 1988 by Walter de Gruyter & Co., Berlin 30.
All rights reserved, including those of translation into foreign languages. No part of this book may be reproduced in any form – by photoprint, microfilm or any other means nor transmitted nor translated into a machine language without written permission from the publisher.
Typesetting: Wagner GmbH, Nördlingen. – Printing: Karl Gerike GmbH, Berlin. – Binding: Lüderitz & Bauer, Berlin. – Printed in Germany.

To the memory of
Jean Bouvier and *Fausto Vicarelli*
economists, historians and friends

Foreword

Modern central banks came of age in the inter-war period. By then, they valued their independence as an essential feature of central banking. Strong, Norman and Moreau were ready to stand by the freedom of their institutions at any price. And independence from national governments was considered a prerequisite for the admission to the club of central banks: they were unwilling, for instance, to enter into large commitments with the Bank of Italy so long as it remained under the dominance of Treasury.

Yet, modern central banks are *liberti* or, at best, the free offspring of parents that were not born free. European central banks, as they have been known since the 1930s, developed from quasi-monopolistic banks of issue. The latter originated from an implicit contract between the Government and a group of private capitalists in which issuing privileges were garanted in exchange for assistance in the placement of State Bonds (often a formal or *de facto* underwriting) or for direct cash advances. The very existence of such banks depended on the Government's willingness to renew periodically their chartered privileges. Moreover, their prosperity was closely connected with their position as Government treasurers.

It is something of a paradox that, as the major banks of issue lost their private character slowly acquiring – long before nationalization – their present nature of public institutions, independence from Parliaments and Governments was increasingly felt as a crucial feature of their new status. Today, at least in principle, there seems to be little disagreement on the need for an independent central bank. In June 1988, at the Hannover summit, not all the heads of Government were quite sure that they wanted a European central bank but they agreed that, should there be one, it should be independent both from Brussels and from the individual national capitals.

Independence, and the consciousness of its importance, were developed by the men who had to seek the solution for increasingly complex problems of management and control of the monetary and banking system. Its scope changed with time and in relation to the specific social, political, economic and institutional features of each individual country. And it depended on the intellectual and moral stature of those who happened to run the Governments and the Banks.

There is an increasing body of literature dealing with the interplay of Treasury and Central Banks and with the emerging policy results in the relatively novel (for economics) framework of game theory. The papers collected in this book take an entirely different approach which, however, does not necessarily conflict with the research lines now fashionable among economists. On the contrary, they may very well complement and enrich their results not by conveying the banal message that "reality is more complex", which model-builders are right in rejecting, but rather by suggesting ways of improving the assumptions underlying the theory. On the whole, however, this book differs from current research in the field mainly because it deals with the long run. If it is true that independence is one of the main results of the "learning by doing" process which developed the *art* of central banking, it cannot be fully understood outside its historical perspective. The hope of the editor is that these essays might have a message for both the economist and the historian.

The paper by Fausto Vicarelli – whose premature death deprived the Italian economics profession of one of its most prominent members – features as an introduction, although it was originally produced as a general comment on the other papers dealing with individual case studies. Chapter 2 deals with the Fed, an exception in our sample since it did not have to "evolve" but was born as a central bank. Was it also born independent? National emergencies aside, the interplay between monetary policiy and policy *tout-court* is evidence that autonomy was not a once and for all achievement and that it rested not on legal provisions but on the Fed's moral standing which was nothing else than the moral standing of the men who happened to be at its head. The case of the "Old Lady" is recalled in chapter 3 which is mostly concerned with developments of the years 1945 to 1983. The peculiarity of this picture seems to be the fact that on policy issues the Treasury and the Bank tended to be on the same side of the fence facing the opposition of other social and political bodies. Chapter 4 on the Banque de France was one of the last writings of Jean Bouvier, the prominent French historian of banks and finance. The case is perhaps the clearest illustration of an institution fighting for its independence, with various degrees of success, throughout the course of its bicentennial history (it was hard, in this respect, to be born under Napoleon). Here, again, we learn how much men matter. Germany – chapter 5 – illustrates well the evolution of the most important bank of issue, the Bank of Prussia, into a modern central bank. And it shows how much collective memories – both of hyperinflation and of subservience to a dictatorship – mattered in shaping the statutes of an independent Bundesbank. At the same time, looking back at German banking history one might argue that legal provisions guaranteeing independence hold when they are not needed and are useless in times of need: a law, even a Constitution, is subject to *ad hoc* interpretation or, in the last resort, it may be changed to serve political purposes. At the end of the day, *de facto* rather than *de jure* autonomy matters. And the former is a complex mix as difficult to maintain as it is to detect and to study. The final chapter, on Italy after the Second World War, deals particularly with a hitherto rather neglected topic: the independence of the Central Bank as far as its powers of supervision over the credit system are concerned. It is easy to see how topical the issue may be in a country where the large majority of banks are owned, directly or indirectly, by the state or by local public authorities.

The essays collected in this book originated from a Seminar held at the Fondazione Adriano Olivetti on June 7, 1985 and from a Conference organized by the same Institution in Venice on February 13–14, 1986. Most of them were revised for publication and appear here in their final draft. Unfortunately, the papers prepared by Vicarelli and Bouvier, were left in my hands as semi-finished products. The former presented some footnoting and reference problems. The paper by Bouvier confronted the editor with more problems: the presentation was still in colloquial form, the style retained much of its French flavour, footnoting and references were imprecise. I could neither take the risk of betraying a great scholar and an old friend with major editorial interventions on the text nor deprive the book of his important contribution. Interested readers will easily overcome some stylistic difficulties and, at times, enjoy the more colloquial aspects of the paper's presentation. I did my best in reconstructing footnotes and references with the invaluable help of Maria Teresa Pandolfi and Alain Plessis. Some gaps remain, in spite of our efforts, and I take full responsibility for them.

The lively discussion at the Rome and Venice gatherings has not been reproduced here: I thank all the participants for the intellectual enjoyment of the occasions. Sergio Ristuccia, then Secretary General of the Adriano Olivetti Foundation, was the driving force behind the whole enterprise and deserves all my gratitude. I am particularly grateful to Gianni Nardozzi who, besides contributing a paper, was the source of endless intellectual stimuli. Marcello De Cecco provided important comments and suggestions. Without the help of Giovanni Maggia, the present Secretary General of the Foundation, I doubt that this book would have arrived at publication. Maria Cavallini has been a good editorial assistant.

Ca' Foscari, Università di Venezia,   *Gianni Toniolo*
July 1988

Table of Contents

Chapter 1
Central Bank Autonomy: A Historical Perspective 1
Fausto Vicarelli

Chapter 2
The Autonomy of Monetary Authorities: The Case of the U.S. Federal
Reserve System 17
Richard Sylla

1	The Two Banks of the United States, 1791–1836	17
2	The Independent Treasury System, 1840–1914	18
3	The Federal Reserve System, 1914–Present	21
4	The Independence of the Fed	24
4.1	Subservience to the Treasury during World War I	26
4.2	The Great Depression: Failure and Reform	28
4.3	Subservience to the Treasury Again: World War II and After	31
4.4	The Treasury-Fed Accord of 1951	31
4.5	The Controversial 1965 Discount Rate Increase	32
4.6	Partisan Monetary Politics? The 1972 Election	33
4.7	Congressional Oversight, 1975	34
4.8	1979: Changes in Fed Operating Procedures	35
4.9	Pressure from the Supply Side, 1981–1985	36
5	Conclusion	37
References		38

Chapter 3
The Bank of England: Relationships with the Government, the Civil
Service, and Parliament 39
Alec Cairncross

1	Historical	39
1.1	The Period before the Nationalisation in 1946	39
1.2	After Nationalisation	47

1.2.1	1945–51	48
1.2.2	1951–76	53
1.2.3	1976–83	60
2	Analytical	61
2.1	The Legal Position and the Working Relationship	67
2.2	The Working Relationship	69
3	Conclusion	70
References		72

Chapter 4
The Banque de France and the State from 1850 to the Present Day 73
Jean Bouvier

1	The Problems of Being a Historian	73
2	The Manifold and Complex Factors that Determine Relations Between the State and the Banque de France	75
3	New Developments from 1850 to 1936	77
3.1	The Development of State Control in the 19th Century	77
3.2	The Ups and Downs of the Period 1920 to 1936	82
4	Change and Continuity from 1936 to the 1980s	87
4.1	1936–1944	87
4.2	1945–1986	88
4.2.1	Continuity of Mechanism, Logic, and Behaviour	88
4.2.2	The New Statutes of the Banque de France (January 1973)	95
References		102

Chapter 5
Relations between Monetary Authorities and Governmental Institutions: The Case of Germany from the 19th Century to the Present ... 105
Carl-Ludwig Holtfrerich

1	Introduction	105
2	The Historical Evolution	107
2.1	From the Foundation of the Reich to the First World War	107
2.1.1	The Legal Arrangements	108
2.1.2	The Degree of Dependence in Practice	111
2.1.3	Cases of Conflict	112
2.1.4	Debates on the Central Bank's Position vis-à-vis the Government	112

2.2	From the Beginning of the First World War to the End of Germany's Great Inflation 1923	113
2.2.1	The Legal Arrangements	114
2.2.2	The Degree of Dependence in Practice	115
2.2.3	Cases of Conflict	116
2.2.4	Debates on the Central Bank's Position vis-à-vis the Government	117
2.3	From the End of Hyperinflation to the End of the Weimar Republic	118
2.3.1	The Legal Arrangements	118
2.3.2	The Degree of Dependence in Practice	121
2.3.3	Cases of Conflict	122
2.4	The Nazi Period (1933–1945)	133
2.4.1	The Legal Arrangements	133
2.4.2	The Degree of Dependence in Practice	135
2.4.3	Cases of Conflict	137
2.5	From 1945 to the Present	139
2.5.1	The Legal Arrangements	140
2.5.2	The Degree of Dependence in Practice	142
2.5.3	Cases of Conflict	144
2.5.4	Debates on the Central Bank's Position vis-à-vis the Government	148
3	Conclusion: The Prime Motives for the Legal Changes in Relations between Germany's Central Bank and Government and a Summary of Arguments Pro and Con the Bank's Autonomy	150
References		154

Chapter 6
A Central Bank Between the Government and the Credit System: The Bank of Italy after World War II 161
Giangiacomo Nardozzi

Introduction		161
1	Credit Legislation and the Bank of Italy	162
2	The Bank of Italy's Structural Superversion and the Evolution of the Financial System	165
2.1	Alternative Views on the Financial Structure	165
2.2	The Development of the Structure of the Credit System under Menichella	167

2.3	The Rationale of the Bank of Italy's Choices with Regard to the Structure of the Credit System in the Period 1948–59	168
2.4	The Early Sixties and the Start of Carli's Governorship	171
2.5	Carli and the Structure of the Financial System	172
2.6	The Structure of the Financial System and the Relationship with the Government	174
2.7	Monetary Versus "Real" Policy Making	176
2.8	The Change in Strategy During the Seventies	179
3	The Major Monetary Policy Choices	182
3.1	Monetary Policy Between 1947 and 1960	182
3.2	From 1964 to 1973	184
3.3	From 1973 to the Present	186
4	From (Italian) History to (General) Theory	188
References		193
About the Authors		197

Chapter 1
Central Bank Autonomy: A Historical Perspective

Fausto Vicarelli

1. When the economist begins to tackle such an important and topical subject as central bank autonomy, one question immediately arises: can the autonomy or independence of an economic institution be discussed without taking into consideration a theory which justifies its existence and explains the logic of its evolution? Assuming there are grounds for this question, if the answer to it is a negative one, the economist who begins to explore central bank autonomy will encounter certain difficulties since, even today, central banking theory has yet to be developed or, more optimistically, is still in the development phase[1].

Naturally, the contrast between theory and economic historiography typical of the studies on the inter-relations between economic development and the structure of the financial system is encountered here as well. The characteristics of the evolutionary process which has characterized the financial institutions and the capital markets since the industrial revolution have been analyzed at length, particularly in terms of the relations between banks and industry, of economic historiography, which boasts a distinguished tradition of research in this field[2]. The same cannot be said for economic theory, which is not yet able to offer any general explanation for the long term behaviour of financial institutions or their interaction with the development of the capital markets and economic growth.

This situation can be explained by the analytical bond which links economic development and the financial structure on the one hand and the growth of the central bank institution on the other, since the significance of a study of the degree of autonomy of the latter can only be found in a framework of dynamic analysis. There would, in fact, be little sense in carry-

---
[1] Interesting reflections on a possible analytical construction process, beginning with the developments in monetary theory, can be found in Ciocca (1983).
[2] Cf. for example the collection of essays edited by Cameron (1972).

ing out a study of central bank autonomy and of the relationship between economic development and financial structures independently of each other. This would mean supposing that central bank autonomy has no influence on the way in which the financial structure evolves in relation to economic development and that, at the same time, it is immune to the impulses and "pressures" which either explicitly or implicitly arise from the form and substance of this evolution.

Whilst, however, economic historiography on banks and industries has a vast field of research within which to work, with an accompanying certainty in terms of knowledge and interpretation, that which deals with central banking autonomy encounters objective restrictions when it moves from the consideration of historical data to the interpretation thereof. Here, the lack of a theory of central banking has greater consequences in terms of analytical difficulties. The very concept of autonomy takes on different meanings according to the theoretical, and therefore general, view one has of the role of the central bank. As will be shown below, some historical episodes of conflict situations between the central bank and the government referred to in the papers collected in this book may be read as examples of central bank autonomy or as demonstrations of the lack thereof, according to the extent of the range of objectives which the central bank itself sets and against which it measures the degree of its independence.

2. The lack of a complete central banking theory should not, however, allow us to forget the theoretical reflection which has accompanied the process of identifying the role of the central bank, particularly since the late 19th century. Although Bagehot was the one who began this task of systematic consideration, it is Keynes who is the fundamental contributor. As is well known, in *Indian Currency and Finance* Keynes maintained that it was necessary to create a central bank in India contrary to the more widely-held idea that the English gold standard model should be extended to India as well. According to Keynes' arguments, the need of a central bank is reflected both in the lack of elasticity in the money supply and in an inefficient management of reserves on the part of the government.

The fact that in the Indian system it is the State that issues bank notes and that the value of the issue can only vary proportionally with a variation in metal reserves is decisive with respect to this lack of elasticity. An increased volume of means of payment is therefore dependent on the importation of gold reserves and thus requires an increase in domestic interest rates that will attract them from abroad. The existence of a central bank which, with given reserves, can manipulate the issue of bank notes by means of variations in the amount of bills discounted to the banking system would instead allow money supply to adapt to the fluctuations in the demand for means of payment. In as much as regards the management of reserves, the crucial point is that the State is compelled to hold reserves sufficient not only to counter a balance of payment crisis, but also to be able to uphold the banks in the case of an internal confidence crisis. In other words, the government must also hold reserves for the banking system without, however, being able to control the monetary means which come into the banks' possession. Since, moreover, the reserves held by the government are mainly the result of its revenues and payments, that is to say its treasury balance, and thus reflect budget policy, the lack of a central bank results in the creation of a mixture of budget and credit policy, or rather of fiscal and monetary policy. Even when the central bank is a historically-consolidated institution, as it is in England, strict adhesion to the working rules of the gold standard drastically limits its discretionality in the management of the money supply. The protection of exchange parity as a primary aim leads to variations in the quantity of gold reserves and therefore of money in circulation with effects on internal prices, in the presence of either internal or external factors which upset the balance of payments. To give up control of the quantity of means of payment is therefore to consider currency as one considers natural events, and thus means giving up the policy target of stability for its value, as Keynes emphasizes in his *Tract on Monetary Reform*[3].

It is, however, in the *General Theory* that Keynes' contribution to the theoretical basis of "controlled currency" is brought to fruition. The Keynesian view of capitalism as a monetary economy, that is to say as a system in which economic decisions are taken within the context of the strict interrelation of industrial and monetary powers, is, in fact, the most solid base for discretional control of the quantity of currency by an authority above, though not outside, the parties involved and their interests.

The implications of the Keynesian view for the theory and the policies of central banking are more penetrating and pervasive than macroeconomic developments have perhaps shown to date. Since control of the level of economic activity means control of the effective demand, and since interest rates structure and levels are the key control variables, monetary policy limited to fixing the quantity of currency and ignoring the effects which this has on interest rates cannot be effective in controlling economic activity.

It is opportune to note that beneath the Keynesian view lies a conception of an intrinsically unstable system so that the control of the money supply has

---

[3] For more extensive reflection on this subject see Vicarelli (1984).

the stabilizing task of working "against the tide". The monetarist theoretical paradigm, on the other hand, precisely because of its confidence in the intrinsic stability of the industrial forces in the system, shows that monetary control cannot be other than a source of disturbance. The corollary of this is that the only wise policy is to increase the quantity of currency at a constant rate[4]. The conclusion reached by new classical macroeconomics is not substantially different in terms of prescribed policies, although it follows a theoretical path which is as much more refined as it is more detached from the historical realities of the world in which we live in its hypothesis of rational expectations.

3. Minimizing the contrast between the Keynesian and the monetarist views of the role of the central bank to one of intermediate monetary policy objectives (control of interest rates or of money supply), would be misleading. The true contrast is in fact between two different conceptions of the role of the central bank, resulting from two different views of the workings of the capitalist system: in short, a favourable and an unfavourable view regarding "controlled currency".

It is hard for any analysis of the degree of autonomy of the central bank to remain impartial before these two conceptions of central banking. The different views make themselves felt at three levels of problems related to central banks' operations: the criterion by which its conduct is established, the method by which it operates and the extent of the range of problems with which the central bank deals. Consequent effects on the judgements made about the degree of autonomy of the central bank are inevitable.

How would an orthodox monetarist consider the criterion which the central bank should adopt in establishing its conduct? Certain that a clear relationship exists between money supply and price level, he would have no hesitation in indicating the fixing of quantitative targets for money supply in relation to the desired rate of inflation as the only criterion for the conduct of monetary policy. He would reply to any questioning of the validity, or above all the stability of the relationship by confirming the innate capacity of market forces to ensure fundamental stability in the system. The autonomy of the central bank is definitively expressed by its freedom to establish the fundamental criterion for its monetary conduct in its quantitative targets. The degree of autonomy which the bank in fact enjoys is thus related to its capacity to keep to publicly-announced objectives, above all in situations of conflict with government conduct. This capacity is supposed to be the most

---

[4] Cf. above all Friedman (1969).

significant index by which the political independence of the bank can be measured, an independence which is based on its institutional role as guarantor of the stability of currency value.

The conduct of the central bank following the Keynesian view has fewer certainties on which to call, although this does not mean that it is in any way indeterminate. The complexity of the existing links between industrial and monetary forces, even in the short term, does not offer clear and absolute behavioural rules, but only criteria deriving from an analysis of the performance of the system in the period under consideration. The quantity of money is a revealing indicator of the monetary policy pursued – not the only one, to be sure – within a system of financial flows whose complete picture cannot be established without taking into account the levels and the structure of interest rates and, above all, the wider range of objectives of economic policy-makers.

Plurality of objectives and the search for the most appropriate policies characterize this view of the role of central banking. Central bank autonomy, in this context, is related to the bank's autonomous capacity to identify and put into effect the criteria and policy instruments held to be most appropriate for attaining the bank's own objectives. The defence of monetary stability is certainly one of the most important of the objectives assigned to the central bank, but its achievement is hardly ever separated from that of complementary targets such as that of relative exchange rate stability which in an open economy certainly requires consistent fiscal and monetary policies which are beyond the competence of the bank itself. Consequently, no judgement of the level of autonomy can be based on the degree to which given objectives are achieved or, in a wider sense, to the effectiveness of monetary policy. It is not difficult to envisage internal and external circumstances that may make monetary policy ineffective, even in the case of a central bank with complete autonomy of choice of criteria and instruments for monetary action.

4. Reading the papers collected in this book with an eye on the Keynesian interpretation of the action of the central bank makes it clear that the authors are far from the idea that one single strict criterion should inspire monetary policy. Sharing the opinion expressed by Bouvier at various points in his paper on the role of currency protection by the central bank, the authors show a general understanding of the complexity of the economic policy objectives and of the value of considering the tasks of monetary policy within the context of its relation to choices made by other decision-makers. This leads to the rejection of a monetarist inspired view of central banking. At the same time, however, some aspects of the judgement of the degree of central bank autonomy create a certain perplexity as to the interpretative model to which they refer.

In his paper, Sylla mentions the two aspects of the definition of independence offered by J. T. Wooley, with which he would seem to agree: a) the Federal Reserve System (Fed) is independent if it can propose and put into practice a monetary policy that has not previously been approved by the President of the United States, the Congress and all the other interest groups outside the Fed itself and which may not be to their liking; b) the Fed is independent if it is capable of reaching its objectives without the help of action by other policy-makers. Sylla agrees that the satisfaction of both these criteria would give a far too restrictive idea of independence, which could not be supported either by economic theory or by history. He therefore limits himself to the use of the first definition to verify the Fed's independence at certain crucial points in U.S. economic history.

Sylla underlines with great clarity the way in which the Fed's independence has been threatened since it was founded in 1913. It indeed had to relinquish this independence during the two World Wars to avoid worse consequences since the war effort required public sector financing on favourable terms. During the Great Depression in the Thirties, expansionist action by the Fed through open market operations would have been blocked by pressure from the more influential banks who, with a partial and short-sighted vision of the crisis, were concerned about further reductions in the rate of return of the public bonds with which their portfolios abounded. Sylla accepts this recent interpretation of the Fed's role during those periods with caution, but points out Keynes' authoritative favourable view of the Fed's action published in the *Economic Journal* as early as 1932.

The exceptional nature of the wartime events and the uniqueness of the Depression do not permit the verification of the idea of central bank independence adopted by Sylla. In my opinion, two other episodes are much better suited to this purpose. Both of them are dealt with in his paper and refer to events which manifestly indicate a situation of conflict between the Fed and the Treasury.

The first of these incidents regards the change of monetary policy made by the Fed in 1951 after several years of public bond interest rate stabilization. Sylla points out the obvious conflict between a monetary policy that promoted price level stability and one that minimized the Treasury's cost of servicing the public debt developed gradually in the post-war period. He emphasizes the Treasury's accusation of non–cooperation by the Fed in the face of its decision to increase the minimum lending rate. He indicates the positions taken by the President and Congress and notes the terms of the agreement finally signed by the Fed and the Treasury in March 1951. The agreement – Sylla concludes – marked the re-emergence of *the possibility of* an independent central bank monetary policy. The sense of this judgement compared with the definition above leads one to believe that the two bodies disagreed on policy objectives (favouring the financing of the public debt against the control of inflation), and that the agreement sanctioned one at the cost of the other. The text of the agreement, however, asserts that the "common purpose" of both the Fed and the Treasury is "to assure the successful financing of the Government's requirements and at the same time, to minimize monetization of the public debt". For their part, in terms of actual behaviour, the Fed has continued to concern itself with the smooth placement of the public debt, even after this change of direction.

This contradiction can only be resolved by assuming that the conflict grew from a different source: not over objectives themselves, but over actual policy implementation. At the end of the Forties, the Fed was convinced that even small variations in interest rates, in the presence of a very large public debt in the portfolios of the banks, could make monetary policy effective. This theoretical-practical position emerges clearly from the evidence given to the Patman Commission, and is expressed in the theoretical approach according to which – to use Tobin's words –

monetary controls operate far more through the restriction of the availability of credit than through increasing the cost thereof, more through restrictions imposed on loan-makers than through reactions induced in borrowers (Tobin 1953).

The novelty of this way of considering the channel of transmission of monetary policy, with respect both to the neo-classical and to Keynesian conceptions, lies in the idea that credit restriction can be carried out by the central bank without a reduction in banking reserves and consequent increase in interest rates and reduction of the demand for credit from the private sector. This can be accomplished through a direct influence on the banks' supply of credit. This influence, in the presence of an increase in the rate of interest of public bonds brought about by central bank open market operations, works through the reduction of secondary liquidity which for the banking system is the value of the public bonds in their portfolios, and by discouraging the banks from selling the bonds when their market price decreases. In other words, what emerges from the work of the Patman Commission is that the Fed wanted to make funds available to public sector financing while at the same time avoiding higher credit costs destined for the private sector, and ultimately higher interest rates on the public debt. A different interpretation of the philosophy underlying monetary policy leads to an equally-different appraisal of the nature of the conflict between the Fed and the Treasury.

Apart from the specific case of the 1951 episode, there is the more general problem of what reference points should be used when evaluating the autonomy (or independence, to use the term Sylla prefers) of the central bank. If we focus on the objectives, as Sylla claims we should, then central bank autonomy is almost always destined to be sacrificed since the monetary targets can be determined only in a wider economic policy context. A Keynesian could hardly disagree with this point. Yet the fact that monetary policy is a part of economic policy *tout court* is coherent with a high degree of central bank autonomy in the choice of the guide lines for determining its own action, and its independence must be evaluated in relation to this.

The second episode refers to another change of direction which was far more radical. It was made by the Fed in 1979 in its decision to keep to quantitative money supply growth targets. In the light of the policy-mix which took place with the Reagan administration's expansionist fiscal policy, the period since the end of 1971 lends itself to several reflections on the way in which the central bank acts. This is the second of the three problems which are affected by the different views of central banking. Sylla underlines the essential points of the new monetary policy lines of the Fed: nominal interest rates increase to unprecedented levels, the profound 1981–82 recession and the consequent rise in the level of unemployment, the reduction of inflation and the strong economic recovery in 1983–84. Remembering the *Wall Street Journal's* elogy to the courageous anti-inflationary policies of the men from the Fed, Sylla concludes with the statement that, "The story in all likelihood is the crowning achievement of Federal Reserve independence".

An overall, and thus more balanced, judgement of the costs and benefits of U.S. economic policy since the start of the 1980s cannot ignore the national and international repercussions of the tight monetary policy and expansionist fiscal policy. The continuation of very high real internal interest rates is justified by the Fed by the pressure put on financial savings by the large public deficit. The Treasury in reply puts the high interest rates down to the Fed's unreasonable monetary action. In fact, the result has been a massive influx of capital to the United States, an overvaluation of the dollar, a worrying current account deficit in the U.S. balance of payments, the reinforcing of latent protectionist tendencies among the U.S. industrial sectors which have been the hardest hit in terms of competitiveness by the strength of the dollar. Would it not have been possible to obtain the same positive results at a lower price in terms of internal problems and of disturbances in the international monetary system? This questions neither the objectives nor the criteria for the action of the two parties (Fed and Treasury). It rather poses a question concerning the way in which this action was put into practice. Such a way, in a view of central banking that is coherent with the concept of "controlled currency", cannot be other than a dialectic contrast between the two institutions. It is only by means of such a contrast, at an effective level, that a measure of policies sufficient to maximize the benefits and minimize the costs can be determined.

In the actual case considered here, less restrictive monetary policies and less expansionist fiscal policies would very likely have resulted in a stimulus to aggregate demand not different from the one that actually took place, with the advantage of a more balanced dollar exchange rate and balance of payments, and with a lower public sector deficit. The fact that this did not take place means that the dialectic contrast between the two instutions either did not exist or was insufficient, which is synonymous not of autonomy, but of inefficiency.

5. Common to all the papers collected in this book is the emphasis given to the Governor's (or *Chairman's*) personality as a factor determining the actual autonomy of the central bank. Since, in the vast majority of cases in the history of various different countries, the behaviour of the Governor has shown itself to be particularly relevant in times of conflict with the government or with the political powers in general, the implicit recognition of the validity of the dialectic method in the conduct of monetary policy can be seen in the relevance of this figure. Yet, once again, it is not easy to move from the historical interpretation of actual situations to the identification of an explanatory model of behaviour. The legitimate curiosity about the theoretical model underlying this interpretation remains, therefore, unsatisfied.

The need to reflect on the working of the financial systems if not in terms of pure theory at least in a manner somewhat detached from current facts and problems is not the prerogative of academics. In some countries it has given rise to *ad hoc* committees with the task of providing an overview of the structural problems and, often, suggestions for their solution. Between 1931 and 1980 England was able to profit from the results of the work carried out by three prestigious committees (Macmillan, Radcliffe, and Wilson), and one of the best aspects of the paper by Cairncross is certainly its having based the analytical section of its enquiry into the autonomy of the Bank of England on a survey of the conclusions of the various Reports, since they are supposed to mirror the theoretical and practical climate prevailing at the time they were written, and thus to offer a key to the reading of the events which are the subject of Cairncross' story.

The relations between the Bank of England and the Treasury are mainly tackled by the Radcliffe and Wilson Committees. The Radcliffe Report was produced at the end of the Fifties when Keynesian ideas prevailed in England both in terms of economic theory and in terms of its practical application. It emphasizes the need to consider monetary policy as a tile in the broader mosaic of economic policy, and therefore suggests, "constant co-operation, strategic and practical, between the central bank on the one hand and those responsible for alternative or supplementary monetary measures, essentially the Treasury and the Board of Trade on the other". This recommendation, Cairncross comments, excludes both the extreme model of two completely separate and independent institutions, the Treasury and the central bank, and the other model of a central bank which establishes a strict objective such as currency stability on its own account.

The Wilson Report, which was published in 1980, a time in which monetarist ideas had gained the upper hand, particularly in government circles, re-confirmed the independence of the Bank of England and the connections between monetary policy and other forms of macroeconomic policy. This would seem to oppose the mainstream of practical thought which was dominant at the time. The fact is that the correspondence between the behaviour of the English institutions and the general ideas by which it was inspired is not always precisely reflected in the reports. During the Seventies, for example, important changes took place in the criteria underlying the Bank of England's action: in 1971 the decision to abandon the policy of credit control by various forms of rationing widely used in the previous decade; in 1973 the return to administrative restrictions ("the corset"); in 1976 the introduction of quantitative targets of monetary growth. Were these changes brought about by a different view of the role of the central bank or merely by incidental economic necessities? Where they desired by the Bank of England or imposed by the Treasury? These questions remain unanswered.

Holtfrerich's paper offers a comprehensive and well-documented view of the events which led the German Central bank to its present institutional form, concentrating on acts passed in 1951 and 1957 which modified the law set up by the Allies at the end of the Second World War and formally constituted the Bundesbank. The considerable autonomy that characterizes the German central bank – Holtfrerich notes the common opinion that "in Europe the central bank with the greatest degree of autonomy is undoubtedly the Deutsche Bundesbank" – is a means of defence against pressure from political powers that has been given to the controllers of the currency by a public twice profoundly shocked by the experience of drastic inflation.

Holtfrerich, too, analyses various episodes of conflict with the government. More recently these have often concerned the decision to revalue the Mark, which brings him to the conclusion that the position of the Bundesbank was strengthened when floating exchange rates were introduced. Nonetheless, the result of the conflicts, like the aversion towards inflation shown by the German people, is not enough to account for institutional structures which are certainly influenced by an idea of central banking that needs to be explained. As I have already pointed out, defence of the purchasing power of the currency, even though a primary objective of the central bank, leaves a wide range of options for monetary policy compatible with its integration into the wider economic policy goals. This reasoning is, moreover, amongst those put forward in Germany by the critics of the policy line pursued by the Bundesbank during the last twenty years.

6. Is it possible to analyse central bank autonomy without discussing the problem of its relations with the banking system and, more generally, with the structure of the financial system and with its long term evolution? Only the reports by Bouvier and Nardozzi pose this question, both deciding that it is not possible, although they articulate their reply differently. This question concerns the third of the three levels of problem about the conception of central banking to which I have referred above: the extent of the range of problems with which the action of the central bank deals.

A view of central banking coherent with the concept of "controlled currency" cannot limit the tasks of the central bank to money management, but must extend them to directing the financial structure to the needs of economic development and include the role of guarantor of the overall stability of the financial intermediation system. The first of these two tasks divides into promoting the operational and allocation efficiency of the banks, defending the autonomy of the banking system against industry, studying and encouraging an appropriate balance between the influence of the intermediaries and of the capital markets. The second task is centred around the role of lender of last resort.

It is not easy to place the above-mentioned tasks of central banking in a Keynesian perspective and, given the developments in monetary theory during the last half century, their coherence with the idea of "controlled currency" is still a hypothesis to be proved rather than a proposition to be reconfirmed. This is not the place to tackle the problem, but perhaps some brief notes are needed to explain why such a wider view of central banking has been somewhat neglected[5].

---

[5] For an analysis of this subject see Vicarelli (1979) and Vicarelli (1983).

Despite the fact that in his *Treatise on Money* Keynes gave great importance to the finance structure and the characteristics of its institutions, sketching oligopolistic market forms and credit rationing phenomena as "normal", post-Keynesian thought developed along different analytical lines, inspired mainly by the early contributions by Hicks[6]. Briefly, the characteristics of such developments may be identified as: an idea of money and of credit as variables in a system of financial flows in which the relationship between debtor and creditor is expressed in terms of supply and demand of financial assets and liabilities in perfectly competitive markets; the importance of interest rates as an expression of the relative scarcity of funds; the irrelevance of the various possible combinations of the two forms of company financing, risk capital and bank loans, the treatment of financial institutions as exogenous variables.

The effects of these analytical developments could not fail to make themselves felt in the analysis of the central bank's activity. If the financial markets are perfectly competitive, control of the monetary base is sufficient to control the flow of assets and liabilities and to determine an interest rate structure consistent with the agents' behavioural functions. On the other hand, the atomistic view of the markets and agents there in excludes by definition the existence of strategic behaviours which could justify the interest and the concern of the authorities for the consequences of such behaviours on the system.

The actual situation is different, however, and the economic events of the last twenty years have revived the question of whether interpretations that had been considered obsolete, such as the contrast between industrial and financial capital, *à la* Hilferding, could in fact retain a fair degree of validity. A large number of banks have gone bankrupt, just as they did in the Twenties and Thirties, again threatening the stability of the financial system. Paradoxically, disregarding any consistence with theoretical creed professed or vaunted, the central banks of the countries that have embraced monetarist doctrines have carried out massive rescue operations, sometimes extended to organizations which are only slightly connected with the banking system. Unfortunately, none of the papers, not even those that on several occasions discuss the central banks' rescue operations, aks questions about the philosophy which was at the base of the rescue operations themselves.

It is important to recognize that when the problem of central bank autonomy is discussed taking into account such vast fields of action, it is difficult to remain within the boundaries of economic analysis and to avoid entering into

---

[6] Especially Hicks (1935).

evaluations which are purely political. In Bouvier's paper, this happens at various points, particularly when, in his discussion of the debate that took place before the nationalization of the Bank of France in 1945, he outlines the position taken by the *"Comité provisoire d'organisation professionnelle des Banques"*, dominated between 1941 and 1944 by the large deposit banks. The large banks sought gradual privatization of the public and semi-public banking sector with the obvious aim of controlling the commercial banks through the *"Comité"*. Paradoxically, this total corporate economic control – which was opposed by the Bank of France in the name of the "interêts généraux de la nation" – was defeated only after the Liberation with de Gaulle at the head of the government, by an economic policy inspired by a dirigistic, anti-capitalist philosophy.

Even more clearly makred by considerations of a political nature is the paper by Nardozzi. In my opinion, its main analytical quality is that it places the analysis of the relations between the central bank and the banking system in a fundamental position for the understanding of the relationship between the central bank and the government. Nardozzi opportunely emphasises the innate limits of an analysis of central bank autonomy based, in the wake of prevailing literature, on aspects of the central bank-government relationship which arise out of the management of the money supply. He explains the direction of his study through references to historical peculiarities in the Italian banking law which, drafted at a time when the entire structure of the financial system was being questioned, gave priority to the institutional relations between the central bank and the intermediation system. However, for the reasons given above, this direction of study has a more general validity that goes beyond the historical peculiarities of Italy in so far as the management of money supply is only one element of central banking. As Nardozzi himself observes, the structure of the banking system helps to determine the availability of and the choices between the policy instruments, and this in turn reflects upon the positon of the central bank in its dialectic relationship with the government.

In his analysing the autonomy of the Bank of Italy, Nardozzi distinguishes between three periods. The first, under Menichella's governorship, saw the central bank engaged in action aimed at "modelling" the credit system. According to Nardozzi, the results of this action can be summarized as follows: containing the expansion of the national level banks; developing local and savings banks; creating the special credit system. The plan underlying the action by the Bank of Italy is said to have been the shape of the system of financial intermediation in a way consistent with the real accumulation drive then taking place in the country. Not unconnected with this plan was the desire that low interest credit, which was to be given mainly to finance investment in the South, retained its exceptional nature and did not become synonymous of long-term credit. Encouragement of the creation of a strong bond market and the reinforcement of the Stock Exchange for the needs of large companies were aimed at avoiding, or at least minimizing, this danger.

In the Fifties the Bank of Italy reputedly enjoyed great autonomy, politically based on its role in the great design for Italian economic development. Complete independence in the control of currency and of credit were nothing more than a necessary consequence of this more fundamental autonomy. In the Sixties, under the governorship of Carli, it became more difficult for the Bank of Italy to direct the financial system. Carli apparently aimed to develop the markets, particularly the money market, but encountered the opposition of the banking system on this issue.

What was Carli's aim in reinforcing the role of the markets? On this point, Nardozzi's paper tends towards an interpretation in which the subjective element of political evaluation of the facts wins out over the hypotheses drawn up from purely analytical models. He believes that Carli's philosophy was determined not by his intention to contain banking intermediation, but by his desire to defend the Bank of Italy's autonomy with respect to the government: "Never so much as during this period has the structural policy of the Bank of Italy towards the financial system been so tied to the way in which it considered the problem of its autonomy from the government". Since this autonomy was threatened by possible government interference in credit management, this could no longer be entrusted, as it had been in the Fifties, to *moral suasion*. Recourse to the market was therefore necessary for the control of the banking system which could no longer be entrusted to administrative measures.

Nardozzi's hypothesis begs a more detailed historical precision in its analysis. One possible objection that arises when looking more closely at the facts is that the interest rate stabilization policy carried out by the Bank of Italy during the late Sixties with the consent of the banking system virtually created a channel for priviledged access to credit by the government. Banks were induced to increase the share of bonds in their portfolio – assets that had no risk of insolvency and yielded considerable returns – thus shifting their investments from the private sector to the public sector in its widest sense[7]. If Nardozzi refers to government interference in the overall allocation of credit, the conduct of the Bank of Italy does not seem to have been guided

---

[7] For a deeper analysis of the long term strategy of the Bank of Italy cf. Marconi (1979).

by the strategy he attributes to Carli. If he is thinking of political interference directed towards the control of individual banks, then the connection with market expansion as an instrument of protection from this danger is not clear. The events of 1979, with the political attack on Governor Baffi and on Deputy-Director General Sarcinelli, would seem to be more in accord with this thesis.

The third period that Nardozzi discusses, from 1976 to the present day, is characterized at a structural level by the creation and strengthening of the money market, fed almost entirely by short and very short-term Treasury bonds; by a medium-term exchange policy aimed at relaxing foreign restrictions through the re-constitution of currency reserves and through revitalization of the productive sector; by the re-acquisition by the Bank of Italy, through the "divorce" from the Treasury, of a margin of autonomy in money management abandoning its role of residual purchaser for Treasury bills; by giving up administrative ("ceilings") credit controls.

Though these changes in general guidelines or policy instruments cannot be evaluated without reference to the economic situation in the period in which they took place, it is difficult to deny that there has been a general orientation towards the creation of a larger role of the market. Nardozzi gives a precise reply to the question of whether this orientation reflects a Bank of Italy strategy by saying that,

The orientation towards the market which has characterized the most recent and current tendency of the Bank of Italy does not seem to be the product of trust in superior capacities attributed to it to direct the economy, so much as of the absence of a long term political plan with which to measure itself.

An evaluation of this statement implies again comparing actual facts with the wider view of central banking referred to above. In this view, it will be recalled, the orientation of the financial structure towards the needs of economic development is among the aims of the central bank. Yet Nardozzi would reply, if I correctly interpret his reference to recent statements by Ciampi, that a coherent design for economic development is more the desire of the Bank of Italy than the will of political powers. If this were really the case, the situation would be rather anomalous. Perhaps Nardozzi is too pessimistic.

References

Cameron, R. (1972): *Banking in the Early Stage of Industrialization,* New York: O.U.P.

Ciocca, P. (1983): Fra 'scienza' e 'arte' – l'economia politica della moneta e le banche centrali, *La moneta e l'economia: il ruolo delle banche centrali,* Ciocca, P. (Ed), Bologna: Il Mulino.

Friedman, M. (1969): *The Optimum Quantity of Money and Other Essays,* Chicago: Aldine.

Hicks, J.R. (1935): A Suggestion for Simplifying the Theory of Money, *Economica.*

Marconi, M. (1979): Lineamenti di un trentennio di politica monetaria, *Capitale industriale e capitale finanziario: il caso italiano,* Vicarelli, F. (Ed), Bologna: Il Mulino.

Tobin, J. (1953): Monetary Policy and the Management of the Public Debt: the Patman Inquiry, *The Review of Economics and Statistics.*

Vicarelli, F. (1979): Introduzione, *Capitale industriale e capitale finanziario: il caso italiano,* Vicarelli, F. (Ed), Bologna: Il Mulino.

Vicarelli, F. (1983): *Credito, Dizionario di Economia Politica,* Lunghini, G. and D'Antonio M. (Eds), Torino: Boringhieri.

Vicarelli, F. (1984): *Keynes The Instability of Capitalism.* London: Macmillan.

Chapter 2
The Autonomy of Monetary Authorities: The Case of the U.S. Federal Reserve System

Richard Sylla

The issue of the autonomy of the monetary authority is, and long has been, the subject of much discussion and debate in the United States. For seven decades the U.S. monetary authority and central bank has been the Federal Reserve System created by act of Congress in 1913. The Constitution of the United States, written in 1787, gave Congress the power "to coin money" and "regulate the value thereof". In creating the Federal Reserve System one and one-quarter centuries later, Congress both exercised and delegated its constitutionally mandated monetary powers. Congress's exercise of power in 1913 calls for no comment. But its delegation of monetary authority to a new Federal Reserve System that in many respects was intended to be *independent* of private financial business interests, of duly constituted governmental (executive and legislative) authorities, and of partisan political interests is a remarkable outcome.

1 The Two Banks of the United States, 1791–1836

In the perspective of U.S. history, the creation of the Federal Reserve System can be viewed as a compromise between two earlier central banking traditions that were implemented and then rejected on the grounds that they were not sufficiently independent of particular economic and political interests. The first tradition is that of the corporate central bank, publicly chartered but privately owned, similar to the venerable Bank of England during its first two and one-half centuries of existence. In the early decades of the American republic, Congress on two occasions chartered for twenty years Banks of the United States, the first operating from 1791 to 1811, and the second from 1816 to 1836. Like the Bank of England, the two Banks of the United States were by far the largest banks of their time and place, and also like the Bank of England, on which they were modeled, they were the government's bankers while at the same time carrying on a private banking business. Unlike the Bank of England, their initial charters were allowed to lapse rather than be renewed. This happened because at the time of the charter renewal debates Americans on balance doubted that a large and privileged corporate bank with a special relationship to the federal government was a good and proper institution. Because of their size and special relationship to the government, the two federal banks had substantial powers to regulate other banks; at the same time, the federal banks competed with the private banks for nongovernmental business. Some (primarily Jeffersonian idealists) saw the regulatory power possessed by a large corporation as inconsistent with democratic and republican principles; others (primarily bankers and businessmen) saw it as contrary to their individual economic interests. These two elements of anti-Bank opinion – political idealism and economic self-interest – came together to defeat renewal of the two charters. As a result, the United States from 1836 to 1914 lacked a central bank that evolved with its financial system, in contrast to the general experience of the leading European nations.

2 The Independent Treasury System, 1840–1914

The second central banking tradition tried and rejected in the United States was that of having the government's fiscal authority, in this case the United States Treasury, also serve as the central bank. This tradition began briefly in 1840–1841, and then more lastingly in 1846, with the establishment of the so-called Independent Treasury System, which continued to operate until 1914 when the Federal Reserve System assumed many of its functions. The Independent Treasury System began as a deliberate attempt to isolate the finances of federal government from the banking system of the United States. To that end the government established subtreasuries in a number of cities to receive and hold the government's revenues (at the time, mainly recepts from import duties) on which the Treasury would then draw to make governmental payments. Toward the end of the nineteenth century, however, the odd and naive idea that the federal government's fiscal operations could be carried on independently of the nation's banking and financial systems was increasingly seen to be a practical impossibility. The public debt of the United States had greatly increased in the Civil War of 1861–1865, and in the following decades high import duties combined with the nation's rapid economic growth created substantial revenue surpluses that, had they been allowed to accumulate in the subtreasuries, would have brought about a deflationary monetary contraction in the U.S. economy.

For some two decades after the Civil War, the problem of surplus federal revenues building up in the Treasury had a simple solution. The Treasury used the surplus revenues to redeem and retire the public debt. These actions were tantamount to open-market purchases of securities to offset the otherwise deflationary effects of surplus revenue accumulation. As such they embodied what later came to be viewed as an important central banking function. But these early open-market operations, erratic and unpredictable, were not carried out with an intent to stabilize the U.S. economy, and they may at times have had an opposite effect.

By the turn of the century, however, it was abundantly evident that officials of the U.S. Treasury formally recognized that they possessed central banking powers that could be used to stabilize the financial system and the economy. Treasury interventions in the money markets then became explicit and regular. In the fall of 1902, for example, in response to a severe money market stringency that saw banks' cash reserves drop to a twenty-year low in relation to deposits, the Secretary of the Treasury, Leslie M. Shaw, came to the aid of the market. His policy measures included prepaying interest on outstanding government bonds, purchasing bonds at high premiums (an open-market operation), and increasing bank cash reserves by depositing government funds in national banks. A banking panic that otherwise might have occurred was avoided.[1] A few years later, in 1906, Secretary Shaw affirmed the central banking powers of the Treasury and suggested that they be increased:

If the Secretary of the Treasury were given $100,000,000 to be deposited with the banks or withdrawn as he might deem expedient, and if in addition he were clothed with the authority over the reserves of the several banks, with power to contract the national-bank circulation at pleasure, in my judgment no panic as distinguished from industrial stagnation could threaten either the United States or Europe that he could not avert. No central or Government bank in the world can so readily influence financial conditions throughout the

---

[1] In a recent article Allen (1986) argues that Shaw's interventions had either no effect or a perverse effect. Money market banks anticipated deposits of Treasury funds at times of stringency, and therefore took fewer precautions against drains of their own reserves. This is consistent with the so-called rational expectations view of macroeconomics and economic policy.

word as can the Secretary under the authority with which he is now clothed (Friedman/Schwartz 1963: 149–50).

Such sweeping claims, backed as they were by actions, soon aroused the always latent American distrust of the centralization of power in government. One of Shaw's successors, William G. McAdoo, who was Treasury Secretary when the Federal Reserve Act was passed in 1913, later described Treasury central banking as follows:

An enormous amount of idle money was held in the United States Treasury. At times the Treasury deposited funds, in varying amounts in certain national banks to help business, but this was erratic and whimsical. Many banks received no government deposits at all, and large sections of the country were neglected. The entire system was the victim of a kind of irregular and vicious centralization... The money power of the country passed into the hands of a few financiers and big bankers, and the Treasury itself, through politics and manipulation, acted in sympathy with them (Clifford 1965: 48–49).

The business and financial communities expressed similar sentiments. As one leading periodical, *The Commercial and Financial Chronicle,* commented in 1914,

A few years ago, when the United States Treasury was burdened with excessive revenues and the money market depended on the whim of the Secretary of the Treasury, practically all public men, of whatever shade of political belief, were agreed that the government ought to be taken out of the banking business (Clifford 1965: 50).

These comments pertaining to the 1900–1914 period make several points clear. First, the U.S. Treasury recognized that it possessed extensive central banking powers, and, moreover, it used these powers. Second, both government officials and members of the business and financial communities were skeptical about these developments, fearing that at best the Treasury's central banking actions would be "whimsical and erratic" and that at worst they would favor some financial, economic, and geographical interests over others. Less clearly expressed at the time was the fear that the Treasury as a central bank would tend to have a long-run bias toward "easy money" and inflation, although there is evidence that such a bias was on the minds of those who led the fight for a central bank and the Federal Reserve Act. The great deflation of the late nineteenth century had produced, first, the Greenback Party of the 1870s and then the Free Silver/Populist movements of the 1880s and 1890s. By making the expansion of the money stock the key element of their programs, these movements had politicized U.S. monetary policy to the point where it became economically disruptive. The politico-economic crisis came to a head in the 1890s and proved profoundly disturbing to a new American elite composed of leading bankers, financiers, and managers of the large manufacturing corporations that were first appearing in this critical period of U.S. economic history. It was this elite, as historian James Livingston has demonstrated in a recent and important book, that spearheaded the movement for a central bank and monetary reform that would consciously strive to depoliticize issues of money and banking (Livingston 1986). When the U.S. Treasury began its large-scale interventions in the money markets after 1900, its activities served to reinforce the distrust the new elite had for politicized momentary policy. The corporate elite would become increasingly influential in U.S. economic policy as the twentieth century progressed. And it would become the primary defender of an independent central bank when the United States, unlike in 1900–1914, became a nation with high individual and business taxes, large government expenditures, and a huge national debt that the Treasury, even though it then was no longer the central bank, wanted to manage at low interest costs and stable market prices.

3 The Federal Reserve System, 1914–Present

In any event, in the wake of the great financial panic of 1907, when American leaders turned to the task of creating a wholly new central bank, the second U.S. central banking tradition, that of letting the U.S. Treasury, the nation's fiscal agency, exercise central banking authority, was explicitly rejected. Rejected also was a return – suggested by some – to the first tradition, that of a privately owned central bank operated and controlled by bankers. The Federal Reserve Act of 1913 made bows in the direction of each of the two traditions, but its interesting features were altogether new. In the first place, it created not a central bank but a central banking system with twelve regional Federal Reserve Banks, each operating and having authority in a defined geographical area of the United States, with a coordinating Federal Reserve Board in Washington, D. C., the nation's capital. The regional Reserve Banks were designed to prevent the central banking system from being dominated by either the nation's financial center, New York City, or its political center, Washington, D. C. The capital of each of the twelve Reserve Banks was subscribed by the member banks (all federally chartered "national" banks, and those state-chartered banks that chose to join the System), who in return were to be paid only a prescribed dividend, not a proportionate share of their Reserve Bank's earnings. The member banks could elect six of the nine directors of each Reserve Bank; only three of these directors could be bankers, the other three to be representatives of the commercial, industrial, agricultural, and other nonbank interests of the region. The remaining three directors of each Reserve Bank were appointed by the Federal Reserve Board in Washington, D. C. Together the nine directors appointed the officers of their Reserve Bank, the chief of whom was called the Governor. The regional Reserve Banks were given a partial monopoly of the nation's note issue and became fiscal agents of the federal government, banks of rediscount and reserve for the member banks, and lenders of last resort in their regions. Member banks had to hold their legally prescribed reserves as deposits in their Reserve Bank; in return they could rediscount their eligible commercial paper at the Reserve Bank.

The Federal Reserve Board consisted of five members appointed for staggered ten-year terms by the President of the United States, plus two *ex officio* members, the Secretary of the Treasury and his subordinate, the Comptroller of the Currency. Thus, the Board, unlike the Reserve Banks, was a governmental organization. Its purpose was to oversee and supervise operations of the Reserve Banks, to regulate relationships between them and between the Reserve Banks and the government, and, in general, to bring about a uniform banking and monetary policy in the United States.

In retrospect, the original Federal Reserve System created in 1913 and implemented in 1914 was riddled with structural weaknesses as an institution. The authority of the Board in relation to that of the regional Reserve Banks had not been clearly drawn. A Governors' Conference composed of the twelve Governors of the regional Reserve Banks was organized shortly after the System commenced operations. It tended to be dominated by the Federal Reserve Bank of New York, and it operated more or less independently of the Federal Reserve Board until the Board asserted more authority in 1923. Disputes arose as to whether the Banks or the Board had ultimate power over open market operations and rediscount rates. There were also worries, understandably given that World War I greatly increased the fiscal requirements of the U.S. Treasury, that the Secretary of the Treasury exerted too much dominance over the Board and perhaps the whole Federal Reserve System.

The independent central banking system that had looked good on paper in 1913 never looked so good or independent during its early years of operation. Its structural and operating weaknesses, always evident to close observers of the system, contributed mightily to the economic and financial debacle that was the Great Depression of 1929–1933. Out of that experience came a series of fundamental changes in the legislative underpinnings of the System. These changes centralized authority in the System and, in retrospect, strengthened its independence from special economic and political interests.

The legislative changes of the 1930s, chiefly in the Banking Act passed by Congress in 1935, were most notable for increasing the authority of the Board in Washington over both the Reserve Banks and the member banks of the System. Some changes were more symbolic than substantive. These included changing the old name, Federal Reserve Board, to Board of Governors of the Federal Reserve System, whose head was henceforth called "Chairman", and the conferral on the Board of Governors of the power to approve (or not) the chief executive officer of each Reserve Bank, who henceforth was called "President" rather than "Governor". The more substantive changes gave the Board of Governors authority to alter the legal reserve requirements of member banks, to set maximum interest rates that banks could pay on time deposits, and to set margin requirements on loans to purchase securities. Perhaps more important, the authority to determine open market operations was conferred on a new twelve-person Federal Open Market Committee consisting of the seven members of the Board of Governors and five regional Reserve Bank presidents who served on a rotating basis. Previously open market policy had been the province of the regional Reserve Bank Governors, and the individual Reserve Banks had discretion in determining *their* open market operations. The new Open Market Committee was clearly a governmental agency pursuing national goals in a unified manner, in contrast to its predecessors.

Although most of the changes of the 1930s were designed to centralize authority in the Federal Reserve System and to give the Board of Governors new powers over the Reserve Banks and member banks, thereby reducing the influence of bankers (who at the time were widely regarded as responsible for both the onset of the Depression and its severity), two changes made the Board more independent as well of executive governmental authority. The two *ex officio* members of the Board, the Secretary of the Treasury and the Comptroller of the Currency, were removed and replaced by two additional Board members specifically appointed, as the other five members always had been, by the President of the United States. This reduced direct Treasury influence on Board actions. The other change was to increase the terms of Board appointees to fourteen years, a change that made it difficult for any single President to make the Board of Governors sympathetic to executive will by appointing a majority of the Governors.

The legislative changes of the 1930s might seem to give lie to the notion of Federal Reserve independence from other duly constituted governmental authorities. They demonstrate that Congress could fundamentally alter the manner in which the System was consituted and how it was to carry out its functions whenever Congress deemed such legislative action to be proper. As a matter of fact, however, no significant structural or operating changes for the Federal Reserve System have been mandated by Congress since the mid-1930s. This is not to deny that the System's independence has been questioned and possibly even compromised in the ensuing half century. Since the 1930s, wars, inflations, allegations of partisan political motivations, assertion of greater Congressional oversight, and numerous changes in operating procedures have forced the Federal Reserve Systems to tread delicately where matters of independence and autonomy have been concerned. These episodes in the history of "the Fed" (as the Federal Reserve System is often called) are discussed more fully in the remainder of the paper. In the mid-1980s, however, the structural and operating independence of the U.S. central banking system does not appear to be under serious attack, and, indeed, the Chariman of the Board of Governors of the Federal Reserve System is sometimes said in the press to be the second most powerful person in the U.S. government, after only the President of the United States. Whether the current high prestige and autonomy of the Fed will continue depends in large measure on the general performance of the U.S. economy, affected as it is by economic policies over which the Fed has some – but by no means total – influence and control. Central bank *independence* thus creates for the Fed both an opportunity and a dilemma.

4 The Independence of the Fed

"An independent Federal Reserve System is the primary bulwark of the free enterprise system and when it succumbs to the pressures of political expediency or the dictates of private interest the ground work of sound money is undermined."

So in 1952 wrote William McChesney Martin, Jr., then Chairman of the Board of Governors of the Fed (Clifford 1965: 23). Martin's words were – and remain – a classic statement of the American philosophy of central banking. The central bank works to promote a broad societal goal ("free enterprise") through particular means ("sound money") in an institutional setting that by design is independent of forces ("political expediency" and "private interest") that might undermine implementation of the means and, therefore, promotion of the goal.

In what sense is the Federal System independent? In a recent and perceptive study of the Fed, John T. Woolley, a political scientist, identifies two meanings pertinent to investigations and discussions of independence. Can the Federal Reserve, without prior approval of the President or the Congress of the United States, or of any interest group outside the Fed itself, implement and sustain a monetary policy not preferred by the President, the Congress, or other interests? The answer to this question for the most part is, yes, the Fed does possess this *political* independence. Political independence is the kind of independence that was designed into the Fed by its founders more than seventy years ago and that has lasted to the present day. But the qualification, "for the most part", is necessary because the history of the Fed shows, as will become evident, that even this fundamental concept of independence can be, or can be threatened to be, set aside at particular times.

The second meaning of independence concerns the ability of the Fed to achieve its goals independently of the actions of others. For example, can the Fed achieve the monetary-policy objectives of price level stability and "low" interest rates in the face of huge budget deficits resulting from a President's unwillingness to increase taxes and a Congress's unwillingness to cut governmental spending? The answer of both macroeconomic theory and recent U.S. history seems to be, no. If the Fed attempts to keep interest rates low when budget deficits are large, the resulting monetary expansion will prevent the objective of price level stability from being reached; if, on the other hand, the Fed restrains monetary growth to prevent inflation, the budget deficits likely will cause real interest rates to stay high. Thus, as far as achieving goals is concerned, the Fed cannot do so independently of the policies and actions of others. In John Woolley's terminology, the Fed does not possess *functional* independence. Monetary policy and fiscal policy in practice are interdependent rather than independent of one another (Woolley 1984: Ch. 1).

The answers to the questions arising in the foregoing discussion of independence suggest that although the Fed cannot achieve all of its *objectives* independently of what others in economic policy and economic life are doing, it can implement policy *measures* of which others – the President, members of Congress, and so forth – disapprove. That leaves open the questions of whether and how often the Fed actually does implement an independent policy. Opinion on these questions varies considerably. Some outside observers and the Fed itself believe that Fed independence is real and desirable. Another view – a middle-of-the-road-view – is that although the Fed can be independent, it is most effective in achieving its goals when it is a "team player" in the making of economic policy. That is, the Fed is most effective when, in a spirit of cooperation with the administration (President, Treasury, and so on) it uses its power and influence to shape overall macroeconomic policy, and when the policy decisions are made, the Fed goes along with them, even if its recommendations are not entirely adopted in the policy package. This view ascribes to the Fed an independent *voice* in economic policymaking but not an independent policy. Still a third view regards Fed independence as not reality at all, but rather myth – and, to some partisan groups, a very useful myth. In this view the federal administration or the Congress (or possibly some nongovernmental interests such as bankers) direct Federal Reserve policy, which the Fed itself merely implements. When the U.S. economy is performing well, the administration or the Congress takes the credit for wise policies; when the economy does not perform well, the myth of Fed independence becomes politically useful because an "Independent" Fed can be made a "scapegoat" for the policy failures of others as well as for the economy's weak performance (Woolley 1984: 14–15).

Even if one grants, as most do, that the Federal Reserve System has the power to act independently as a central bank, it is evident that opinion is divided as to whether it does in fact act independently. There are, I think, three basic reasons for the wide range of opinion. First, there are several important and powerful interests outside the Fed that have the ability to exert pressure on the Fed and to influence its actions. These include the President (federal administration), the Congress, the banking community, and the economics profession. Second, when the Federal Reserve acts – or fails to act – it is extremely difficult to understand or explain with any great degree of certainty *why* it acted as it did. This is the always difficult problem of understanding the motivations of historical actors and actions. Third, the history of the Fed appears to demonstrate that at various times one or another of the several external interests have dominated Federal Reserve actions, as well as instances of the Fed behaving independently. I turn now to an examination of some significant events in the historical development of the Fed that give perspective to the issue of central bank independence.

4.1 Subservience to the Treasury during World War I

For purposes of establishing the independence written into its Congressional charter in 1913, the Federal Reserve System came into existence at a most inopportune moment in history. By the time the System was organized and had become operational a year later, the guns of August 1914 in Europe had launched the Great War. Although the United States did not enter the conflict until April 1917, the effects of the outbreak of war in Europe were felt immediately across the Atlantic. Gold flowed into the United States from war-ravaged Europe and the Fed was powerless to offset its effects on the U.S. price level. To have "sterilized" the gold flow by modern means, the Fed would have had to sell securities from its portfolio or to raise reserve requirements. But since it was newly founded it did not yet have securities to sell, and it did not yet have the power to raise reserve requirements. As a result, from June 1914 to March 1917, the U.S. money stock rose 46 percent and U.S. wholesale prices 65 percent.

After the United States entered the war, the Fed became, in the words of Friedman and Schwartz, "the bond-selling window of the Treasury" (Friedman/Schwartz 1963: 216). The mechanism was simple. The Treasury sold its loans to the public, who borrowed to finance the bond purchases from private banks, who in turn rediscounted the bond loan paper at the regional Federal Reserve Banks. In this the Fed was subservient to the demands of the U.S. Treasury, but only after it had tried to exert some independence. At the time the United States entered the war, the Fed objected both to the low rate of interest the Treasury placed on its loans and securities and to the amount of debt financing, the Fed arguing for relatively more reliance on taxation. Perhaps because it anticipated such a problem, Congress had passed a wartime law, the Overman Act, which authorized the President

... for the national security and defense, for the successful prosecution of the war ... to make such a redistribution of function among executive agencies as he may deem necessary, including any functions, duties and powers hitherto by law conferred upon any executive department, commission, bureau, agency, office or officer ... (Clifford 1965: 100).

The law was considered to apply to the Federal Reserve, and with it the Secretary of the Treasury was able to overcome the Fed's reservations about low interest rates and excessive borrowing by threatening to take over the entire System. So much for the Fed's early attempts at independence. The lesson to be drawn is clear. In a grave national emergency, the Congress and the President together can – and will – create legislation to set aside the independence of the central bank. But the Overman Act was allowed to lapse after the war, showing that an independent central bank was valued – apart from grave emergencies.

4.2 The Great Depression: Failure and Reform

During the 1920s the Federal Reserve System was freed from its wartime role of subservience to Treasury financing requirements. The American economy performed well, on the surface at least, and the Fed made progress in working out the techniques of independent monetary control. Friedman and Schwartz call the 1920s the "high tide" of the Reserve System, and give substantial credit to its *de facto* leader, Benjamin Strong, Governor of the Federal Reserve Bank of New York until his death in 1928 (Friedman/Schwartz 1963: Ch. 6). On close examination, however, the Fed was wracked by internal conflicts that stemmed from an institutional structure that divided authority between the Federal Reserve Board in Washington, D. C. and the regional Reserve Banks, especially the Federal Reserve Bank of New York and Benjamin Strong. In the atmosphere of financial speculation that increased over the decade, the approach of the Reserve Banks and Board differed. The Reserve Banks preferred to counteract speculation by raising discount rates, whereas the Board preferred so-called direct pressure (what later would be called "moral suasion" by its backers and "jaw-boning" by its detractors), that is, lecturing the member banks on proper behavior rather than sending a firm message through discount rate changes. These conflicts *within* the Fed during the fair weather of the 1920s did not augur well for the foul weather that came in the 1930s.

The economic and financial collapse of 1929–1933 confirmed the auguries. The Fed rather passively stood by as the economy slipped into serious depression in 1929–1930, and it did very little to counteract the two waves of bank failures that broke out in the fall of 1930 and in the spring and summer of 1931. Then, in response to external gold drains precipitated by the European crisis beginning with the Austrian Kreditanstalt failure in May 1931 and climaxing with Great Britain's abandonment of the gold standard in September 1931, the Fed sharply raised its discount rate in the context of an already weak U.S. economy. More banks failed, and in 1932 the U.S. unemployment rate reached 25 percent. In the spring of 1932, the Fed belatedly began a program of massive open market purchases to reflate the economy, but it abandoned this program a few months later. This set the stage for more bank failures and the ultimate collapse of the U.S. financial system that culminated in the so-called Bank Holiday of March 1933, when all the nation's banks were ordered closed by the new president, Franklin D. Roosevelt.

Scholarly debate continues to the present day over the reasons for the Fed's failure to counteract what, in part as a result of the Fed's failure, became the greatest collapse in modern economic history. The Fed may have been attached to faulty theories such as the real bills doctrine, and it may have failed to distinguish between nominal interest rates (which were low) and real interest rates (which, given the price level collapse, were high). It may have been plagued by weak and divided leadership. It may have paid too much attention to gold movements and misinterpreted their significance. And it may even have felt that inaction was needed to force wages down to match the price decline, and that a purging of the economic system was necessary every so often for its long-run health. This is not the place to pursue these fascinating and controversial views that appear in the literature on the Fed and the Great Depression.

One issue that has quite recently come to the fore is worth pursuing because it bears on the issue of independence. Accounts of the Great Depression often argue that if only the Fed had taken firm action in 1930 – or in 1931 or 1932 – the slump would not have been as catastrophic as it in fact became. As a matter of fact, the Fed on one occasion – April to August 1932 – did carry out a program of large-scale open market purchases to inject reserves into the U.S. banking system. Friedman and Schwartz argue that the program began under pressure from Congress and that it ended soon after Congress adjourned in July 1932 (Friedman/Schwartz 1963: 322–23, 384–85). But why, in the deepening stages of the worst depression in history, did the Fed abandon what in retrospect was a proper course of action? In a recent and intriguing analysis, Epstein and Ferguson argue with some evidence that influential bankers caused the abandonment of the open market purchases because the program threatened to turn their already meager earnings into actual losses (Epstein/Ferguson 1984). The reasons are twofold. The depression itself had forced nominal interest rates, particularly on safe assets such as government securities, to unprecedentedly low levels, often a fraction of 1 percent. And, second, the banks, in the face of weak and risky loan demand, had shifted their asset portfolios into precisely these same government securities. The Fed's open market purchases thus threatened bank earnings by pushing the already low yields on government securities still lower while at the same time their operating expenses did not change. Hence, according to Epstein and Ferguson, the banks, which could exert a great deal of influence on Feld policy through their influence on – and, indeed, presence on – the boards of directors of the regional Reserve Banks, torpedoed the open market purchase program to maintain their short-run earnings. If so, it was a very short-sighted action on the part of the banks, as subsequent events were to demonstrate.

Could the perceived self-interest of banks – even if their perceptions were wrong – actually have determined Fed policy in the depression? The verdict is not in; the Epstein-Ferguson analysis is fresh, and it has not yet been subjected to the scrutiny that in time will be given it. One bit of their evidence is worth noting, however, because of the authority of the source. Close on the heels of the Fed's abandonment of its open market purchase program, J. M. Keynes wrote that "in the United States the fear of Member Banks lest they should be unable to cover their expenses is an obstacle to the adoption of a wholehearted cheap money policy" (Keynes 1932: 421–22). Keynes, it may be presumed, had an informed insight into the events of 1932 in the United States.

Whether American bankers did or did not exert a pernicious influence on Federal Reserve policy in the Great Depression, they lost a good deal of their capacity to exert such influence in subsequent years as a result of the New Deal banking reforms of 1933–35. These, as noted, centralized System authority and power in the new Board of Governors and reduced the authority of the regional Reserve Banks. The architect and moving force in these reforms was Marriner Eccles, a confidant of President Franklin D. Roosevelt, who was appointed to the Federal Reserve Board in 1934 and went on to a long and distinguished career as Chairman of the Board of Governors until 1948. The independence of the Fed was reinforced by the 1930s reforms, but the member banks lost much more of their former influence in the central bank than did the President, the Treasury, and the Congress. Indeed, although the two Treasury officials were taken off the Board of Governors, two separate laws of the New Deal period extended the President's and the Treasury's authority in monetary policy. The Thomas Amendment to the Agricultural Adjustment Act of 1933 gave the President, acting through his subordinate, the Secretary of the Treasury, the power to engage in open market purchases of government securities by issuing Treasury currency for that purpose whether or not the Federal Reserve System approved! Further, the Emergency Banking Act of 1933 gave the Administration almost complete control over banking and central banking in emergencies:

> During such emergency period as the President of the United States by proclamation may prescribe, no member bank of the Federal Reserve System shall transact any banking business except to such extent and subject to such regulations as may be prescribed by the Secretary of the Treasury, with approval of the President (Clifford 1965: 145).

These laws are reminiscent of the Overman Act of World War I, which gave the administration similar powers over the central bank. They demonstrate how easily the independence of the Federal Reserve system can be circumscribed given an atmosphere of crisis.

4.3 Subservience to the Treasury Again: World War II and After

With the experience of World War I as precedent, the Federal Reserve openly cooperated with the Treasury in World War II. Only the mechanism of cooperation differed. The Treasury's need to finance huge war expenditures, mostly by borrowing, was again paramount. In World War I, the Fed cooperated by readily discounting the loan paper of member banks arising from loans to customers for the purchase of government debt. In World War II, the Fed bought government debt directly, in the process creating reserves that the banks could employ to buy more government debt. Again the Fed argued that the interest rates the Treasury desired for its debt were set too low, and that more reliance ought to be placed on taxation. The Treasury was able to win these arguments without having to reinstitute a law along the lines of the Overman Act that was in effect during World War I.

In April 1942, the Fed announced that it would peg the rate of interest on 90-day Treasury bills at three-eights of 1 percent per year by buying or selling bills at that rate whenever they were offered. A pattern of rates for other maturities, ranging up to 2.5 percent on long-term bonds, was also established. To enforce these rates the Fed had to purchase massive quantities of government securities, leading to the rapid growth of bank reserves and the money stock. Inflation was supressed by wage and price controls during the war itself. As the controls were removed after the war, the price level rose. The Fed might have acted against some of this inflation but it did not, in part because it was regarded as inevitable, in part because of the fears of renewed depression after the war, and in part because of its commitment to keep low the Treasury's interest costs on a greatly enlarge public debt by supporting the interest rate structure on government securities. Although some terms of the support program were modified, the Fed was *de facto* the price-supporting agency of the Treasury.

4.4 The Treasury-Fed Accord of 1951

The obvious conflict between a monetary policy that promoted price level stability and one that minimized the Treasury's cost of servicing the public debt developed gradually in the postwar years. It came to a head and burst into the open in 1950 when the Korean War began. The price level raced upward, and the Fed, committed to supporting government security prices, was more or less powerless to fight inflation. When it tried to do so by raising the discount rate and reducing bank reserves, the Treasury found it difficult to borrow. It protested against the Fed's noncooperation. The President sided with the Treasury in the conflict, but Congress increasingly sided with the Fed. The open debate led to less heated discussions and finally to the celebrated Accord of March 4, 1951, stating:

The Treasury and the Federal Reserve System have reached full accord with respect to debt-management and monetary policies to be pursued in furthering their common purpose to assure the successful financing of the Government's requirements and at the same time, to minimize monetization of the public debt (Clifford 1965: 230).

The Accord freed the Fed from its commitment to support government security prices, although the Fed did not explicitly admit as much for another two years. As Friedman and Schwartz argue, the Fed may have come, through long experience, to regard supporting government security prices as *one* of its functions, and only gradually abandoned (perhaps never entirely) that point of view.

In any event, the Accord marked the re-emergence of *the possibility of* an independent central-bank monetary policy. In subsequent years the Fed pursued a policy described as "leaning against the wind", and the possibility created by the Accord became a recognized reality during the post-Accord Fed chairmanship of William McChesney Martin, Jr. Central bank monetary policy, after years of subordination to nontraditonal ends, once again became the subject of lively practical and academic interest. In 1956, President Dwight D. Eisenhower said, "The Federal Reserve is not under my control, and I think that it is proper that Congress did set it up as an independent agency" (Harris 1964: 160). Six years later, in 1962, President John F. Kennedy supported Eisenhower's first point while challenging his second point. Kennedy asked Congress for a

revision of the terms of the Chairman (of the Fed)... so that a new President will be able to nominate a Chairman of his own choice at the beginning of his term... The principal officer of the system must have the confidence of the President... (Harris 1964: 114).

Kennedy's request was not implemented by Congress. The proposal has continued to surface in political and academic discussions of American central banking since 1962, but it has not been seriously considered by Congress.

4.5 The Controversial 1965 Discount Rate Increase

In 1965 stimulated by the highly publicized tax cuts of 1964 and an accommodating monetary policy, the American economy approached full employment for the first time in years. To these stimuli were added rapidly growing federal expenditures to finance President Lyndon Johnson's Great Society social programs and the United States' increasing involvement in Vietnam. The year, in retrospect, also marked the beginning of the great inflation that plagued the American economy until the 1980s, As the year progressed, the Federal Reserve expressed increasing concern over inflation, and its officials talked of the need to increase interest rates. In retrospect, the Fed may have been too accommodating in 1964 and 1965. By late 1965 both the money stock and market interest rates were increasing sharply, a sign that demand for money was outpacing supply, and the Fed had been increasing the supply to moderate the increase in interest rates. The administration, however, saw matters differently. In its view, the Fed was being too tight and interfering with reaching the cherished goal of full employment. When the Fed in December belatedly (in terms of fighting inflation) raised the discount rate from 4 to 4.5 percent, the Johnson Administration publicly and in strong terms erupted with criticism of the central bank, and Congressional hearings on the breach in economic policy followed. A mild and appropriate assertion of Fed independence provoked a strong, negative response from the administration. One cannot help but wonder whether the memory of this experience made it difficult for the Fed to take a strong anti-inflation stance in the years that followed.

4.6 Partisan Monetary Politics? The 1972 Election

From April 1972 to January 1973, the U.S. money stock increased at an annual rate of over 11 percent, well above its rate of increase in preceding months. In November 1972, President Richard Nixon won re-election in a landslide. The architect of the monetary expansion, which in the context of the wage and price controls imposed by Nixon in 1971 produced strong real growth in the economy before the election followed by rising inflation in 1973–1974, was Nixon's friend, Arthur F. Burns, Chairman of the Fed. In 1960, Burns (then a former Chairman of President Eisenhower's Council of Economic Advisers) had warned Nixon (then Vice President and Republican candidate for President) that unless monetary policy were eased, the economy would be at the bottom of a recession just before the 1960 elections. The Eisenhower cabinet discussed the problem at Nixon's request but took no action (Tufte 1978: 45–52). Nixon lost the 1960 election.

These events led to charges after 1972 that Federal Reserve policy in that year was designed by Burns to ensure Nixon's victory by creating a booming economy at the time of the election. The facts just stated would seem to support the contention. As Woolley notes in his recent study of monetary politics, however, the case for partisan political motivations at the Fed in 1972 is not nearly so obvious as the bald facts make it seem (Woolley 1984: Ch. 8). Liberal economists and opposition Democrats in Congress, worried about unemployment and aborting the economic recovery of 1972, at the time had called for an easy money policy. The charges of partisan motivations in Fed policy came long after the election and the subsequent inflation, not before November 1972. Moreover, Woolley argues, the Fed's 1972 expansion was designed to preserve the Fed's autonomy rather than representing a surrender or compromise of its independence. Controls over interest rates had not been a part of the 1971 wage/price control program: the exemption of interest rates from controls had been a cornerstone of the Fed's position regarding the program. The threat to bring interest rates under the control program was real, according to Woolley, and the Fed created all the money it did in 1972 to prevent interest rates from rising to the point that controls on rates would have been legislated. That the Fed's policy tended to promote Nixon's re-election was only incidental, according to this analysis. The entire episode, and the varying ways in which it has been analyzed, demonstrate the great difficulties involved in assessing central bank autonomy. Did the Fed abdicate or preserve its independence in 1972?

4.7 Congressional Oversight, 1975

In 1975, the U.S. economy was in deep recession and inflation was not under control – a conjunction of economic conditions commonly called "stagflation". In addition, many members of the newly elected Congress were swept into office on a tide of reaction to the Nixon Watergate scandals, and the view was widespread that the Fed had manipulated the economy to re-elect Nixon in 1972, in contrast to the situation in 1972 itself (when such a view was not apparent). The time seemed ripe for Congress to exert greater control over the Fed, as was its prerogative.

The attempt was forthcoming (Woolley 1984: Ch. 7). One bill, HR 212, specified the rate of growth of the money supply that the Fed was to achieve and proposed that the Fed allocate credit to "national priority uses". The Fed opposed the bill. Two weaker bills were then introduced: HR 3160, requiring he Fed to lower interest rates, and HR 3161, giving the President rather than the Fed the power to allocate credit. The Fed opposed these bills as well. Eventually, and partly embodying Fed proposals, the House of Representatives passed not a bill but a resolution (House Concurrent Resolution 133). HCR 133 called on the Fed to lower interest rates, to announce targets for future rates of money stock growth, and to appear before Congress every six months to explain its targets and other policies. The resolution, with its emphasis on monetary growth targets, marked official recognition of the monetarist thinking that was increasingly gaining support in the economics profession, but the older Keynesian concern with interest rates was not slighted. Congress, like the economics profession, did not speak with one voice. Moreover, the Fed's monetary growth targets could be expressed as ranges, and there was no requirement that the targets, even as ranges, be hit. Congress's attempts to oversee and control the policies of the central bank were watered down to a demand that the Fed come in at regularly scheduled intervals and discuss policy. The Fed breathed a sigh of relief and has had no trouble at all in complying with the resolution. The incident shows that a crisis would have to be serious indeed before Congress could threaten the autonomy of its creature, the Fed.

4.8 1979: Changes in Fed Operating Procedures

By 1979, U.S. inflation rates had moved into the double-digit range, the dollar was plummeting in value on foreign exchange markets, and Americans were losing confidence in the ability of their economic policymakers to prevent a runaway price level from leading to an eventual economic collapse. Many reasons were given for the inflation, which appeared to be feeding on itself as increases in the price level created expectations of further, larger increases and a flight from holding money. Many analysts were convinced that the Fed was largely to blame. Although it had announced money growth targets at Congress's prodding since 1975, it seldom hit the targets, erring instead on the high side. The problem was that the Fed continued its time-honored practice of focusing on interest rates. As inflation increased, nominal interest rates rose, and the Fed, in attempting to moderate the rise in rates, created excessive additions to the money stock that merely caused more inflation.

At an unusual Saturday meeting on 6 October 1979, the Fed, on the initiative of its new Chairman, Paul Volcker, adopted a dramatic change in its operating procedures. Henceforth, the Fed would target on specified rates of growth of the money stock rather than on interest rates, which would be allowed to find their own levels as money demand interacted with the money supply, controlled by the Fed. The intellectual origins of the Fed's shift in emphasis could be found in monetarism, although monetarists were quick to denounce the shift because money growth in practice zigzagged up and down in the ensuing years instead of following the steady growth prescribed by the monetarists. In consultations prior to the Fed's adoption of the Volcker proposal, the Carter administration went along to avoid a confidence-eroding public battle in an already strained atmosphere.

The Fed's policy, in retrospect, had the desired anti-inflationary effect. Interest rates in the United States soared to unprecedented levels, and the U.S. inflation rate dropped by more than ten percentage points between 1980 and 1983. The classic prescription of tight money worked, and it worked in the classic way: a deep recession, concentrated in 1981-1982, saw the U.S. unemployment rate climb to nearly 11 percent (from less than 6 percent in 1979). When the economy recovered from the recession in handsome fashion from 1983 to 1985, inflation remained at a relatively low level compared to that of the 1970s. The Fed stimulated the recovery by easing money dramatically in 1982, at which time, in a further policy shift that stepped back a notch from monetary targeting, it gave renewed emphasis to moderating fluctuating interest rates. During the recovery, nominal and real interest rates remained quite high, in part because of the Reagan administration's tax cutting measures, which served to raise the federal government's fiscal deficit to record levels.

The Wall Street Journal (December 7, 1984), referring to this episode in the Fed's history, described it as "the story of how a handful of appointed officials, operating with extraordinary independence, squeezed most of the inflation out of the American economy". This story could well be considered the crowning achievement of Federal Reserve independence. Few economists believed it possible – or desirable, given the costs – that the inflation of the late 1970s could be brought down so far in three years. And it is unlikely that a central bank under the control of elected officials would have been allowed to pursue what was widely viewed as a draconian monetary policy.

4.9 Pressure from the Supply Side, 1981-1985

The U.S. economic recovery slowed in the last half of 1984, and some economists began to forecast a recession in 1985. Adherents of supply-side economics, the view that cuts in marginal tax rates promote prosperity by generating incentives to produce, blamed the Fed for the economic slowdown. These adherents, who numbered in their ranks high officials of the Reagan administration and influential members of Congress, contended that the Fed was not allowing the money stock to grow fast enough to maintain the recovery they attributed to the Reagan tax cuts taking effect in 1981, 1982 and 1983. As a result of slow money growth, real interest rates remained at high levels, discouraging domestic investment and raising the foreign exchange value of the dollar to levels that made large sectors of the American economy uncompetitive in world markets. In their more fervid moments, the supply-siders said that if the Fed aborted the recovery, it would be time to re-examine the issue of Fed independence. In rebuttal, the Fed pointed to the fiscal deficit as the culprit behind high real interest rates and the overvalued dollar.

The year 1985, in the event, did not bring the recession that some supply-siders had predicted. Instead, the Fed began to ease its monetary policy, and the monetary aggregates increased at high rates during 1985 and 1986. U.S. interest rates and the internationl value of the dollar declined considerably in these two years. Monetarists predicted higher inflation and renewed their call for a monetary growth rule, but once again they were proven wrong. Aided by a large decline in world petroleum prices, the United States in 1986 had its lowest price inflation in a quarter century. The American economy continued to grow at moderate real rates. Despite the continued criticism of supply-siders, monetarists, some officials of the Reagan Administration, and even some Reagan appointees on the Federal Reserve Board, Chairman Paul Volcker continued to be – or to appear to be – the one steady and trusted hand at the helm of U.S. economic policy until he resigned in mid-1987.

5 Conclusion

The foregoing survey of key episodes in the history of the Federal Reserve System indicates, I think, that the independence of the American central bank is real, but also that it is fragile. Independence can be compromised by elected officials of the government and possibly, though not evidently since the reforms of the 1930s, by private economic interests. Moreover, independence can be set aside in times of grave national emergency, as experience during the two World Wars of this century amply illustrates. paradoxically, the independence built into the Federal Reserve System by the laws that established it and govern its operations does not appear to be a result of these laws, which can be ignored or changed without great difficulty. The Fed's independence depends more on the character and strength of its leaders, the outstanding examples being Benjamin Strong in the 1920s, Marriner Eccles in the 1930s, William McChesney Martin, Jr., in the 1950s and 1960s, and Paul Volcker in the 1980s.[2]

---

[2] This conclusion was reached in the 1984 and 1985 drafts of this paper, and the latter was presented at the conference in Venice in February 1986. Much the same conclusion is reached, I am pleased to report, by Kettl (1986). I recommend Kettl's book to all who are interested in the independence issue, and especially to those who are unconvinced by

In the American context, the best way to attack discretionary monetary policy and central bank independence is to note that the Federal Reserve has not always – or even usually – had effective and wise leadership. The best way to defend central bank independence is to note that sometimes the Fed has had such leadership, and that the alternatives, ranging from total control by elected officials to the total control of a monetarist rule or prescription, would likely prove inferior to informed and nonpartisan discretion. If the independence of the Federal Reserve System is to remain a viable concept, it will be because central bankers through their actions earn the right to it, not because it is conferred upon them by mutable laws.

References

Allen, Andrew T. (1986): Private Sector Response to Stabilization Policy: A Case Study, *Explorations in Economic History,* 23; 253–68.
Clifford, A. Jerome (1965): *The Independence of the Federal Reserve System,* Philadelphia: University of Pennsylvania Press.
Epstein, Gerald and Thomas Ferguson (1984): Monetary Policy, Loan Liquidation, and Industrial Conflict: The Federal Reserve and the Open Market Operations of 1932, *Journal of Economic History,* 44; 957–83.
Friedman, Milton and Anna J. Schwartz (1963): *A Monetary History of the United States 1867–1960,* Princeton: Princeton University Press.
Greider, William (1987): *Secrets of the Temple: How the Federal Reserve Runs the Country,* New York: Simon & Schuster.
Harris, Seymour E. (1964): *Economics of the Kennedy Years,* New York: Harper and Row.
Kettl, Donald F. (1986): *Leadership at the Fed,* New Haven: Yale University Press.
Keynes, John Maynard (1932): A Note on the Long-Term Rate of Interest in Relation to the Conversion Scheme, *Economic Journal,* 42; 421–22.
Livingston, James (1986): *Origins of the Federal Reserve System: Money, Class, and Corporate Capitalism 1890–1913,* Ithaca: Cornell University Press.
Tufte, Edward R. (1978): *Political Control of the Economy,* Princeton: Princeton University Press.
Woolley, John T. (1984): *Monetary Politics: The Federal Reserve and the Politics of Monetary Policy,* Cambridge: Cambridge University Press.

---

the argument of my paper. A more recent book of Greider (1987), however, takes a negative view of Fed independence. Greider views the Fed as a non-elected body with an anti-inflationary bias that restrains economic growth in order to preserve the value of financial assets, most of which are owned by wealthy people. The working classes, he thinks, would benefit if the Fed were to be brought under the control of the Treasury, which presumably would promote a more inflationary, growth-oriented monetary policy. Greider is not a scholar, however, and his economic analysis is simplistic if not suspect. Nonetheless, his book is a thorough and stimulating work of political economy.

Chapter 3
The Bank of England: Relationships with the Government, the Civil Service, and Parliament

Alec Cairncross

1 Historical

1.1 The Period before Nationalisation in 1946

The Bank of England was founded in 1694 as a joint-stock company by Act of Parliament. The Government of the day had experienced difficulty in the floating of loans and it was to raise and lend money to the State that the Bank came into existence. In return, it was granted privileges in its Charter to issue bank notes, remaining for many years the sole banking institution in England and Wales (but not Scotland) with more than six partners to enjoy this right.

The Bank acquired a monopoly of the note issue in the London area and in 1833 its notes were made legal tender. Banks of issue with more than six partners could not be founded in England until 1826 and were at first debarred from operating within 65 miles from London. In 1833 this restriction was withdrawn in respect of banking business but only on condition that there was no issue of notes. In 1844 the Bank Charter Act confined the right of issue to banks which already had notes in circulation and fixed a maximum for each of them. When such banks were converted into limited companies or came to have more than six partners in some other way, such as amalgamation, their note-issuing rights ceased and the Bank of England was allowed to add two-thirds of the lapsed issue to its fiduciary issue, fixed in 1844 at £ 14 m. This allowed a gradual transfer of surviving rights of issue to the Bank of England, a process completed in 1921. The Bank was not permitted, however, to issue notes for under £ 5 (a restriction that did not apply to the Scottish chartered banks) and it was not until the amalgamation in 1928 of the Bank's note issue with the issue of Treasury notes made during the first world war that the Bank became the sole bank of issue in England and Wales.

Thus it is only in the present century that the Bank has acquired a monopoly over the note issue. The abandonment of the link between notes and gold is even more recent. From 1844 until the second world war all Bank notes in excess of a fiduciary limit had to be backed in full by gold and for most of that period the fiduciary issue was small and inelastic. In those circumstances the growing currency requirements of the country had to be met through the use of gold sovereigns or notes that were effectively gold certificates; and this left correspondingly less gold to provide a liquid reserve of foreign exchange. The gold reserves of the Bank, over and above what was needed as backing for its note issue, were extremely small and obliged the Bank to find ways of protecting them that were inconvenient to business and not well understood (Sayers 1936). In the years before the first world war there was widespread concern that the reserves would prove inadequate in a crisis and the London clearing banks felt the need to build up reserves of their own. On the other hand, the Bank of England had difficulty in meeting the cost of a higher reserve; and in an effort to maintain its income had been forced to seek business in competition with other banks, using for this purpose, so they claimed, the reserves which they were obliged to deposit with the Bank in order to give it the grip on the financial system which its responsibilities required (De Cecco 1974: chapter 7; Sayers 1976: 1–3, 60–65).

The Bank's links with the government were close in comparison with other financial institutions. It enjoyed from the start a privileged position in conducting deposit banking, shielded from competition and acting as the government's financial agent and adviser. It carried out on the government's behalf both routine operations, such as receiving taxes or paying interest on the national debt, and operations of a very different kind such as supervising the issue of new loans and, in more recent years, managing the Exchange Equalisation Account. In course of time it also became increasingly involved in advising on matters of high policy and in giving effect to the policy when decided.

The distinguishing feature of a central bank is not, however, that it is a government bank or a bank of issue but its relationship with the rest of the banking system. As Sayers puts it:

The business of a central bank, as distinguished from a commercial bank, is to control the commercial banks in such a way as to promote the general policy of the State. There are three fundamental points implicit in this: first, a central bank does not, as a commercial bank does, exist to make maximum profits for its owners; second, it must have some means of controlling the commercial banks; and, third, it is subordinate to the State (Sayers 1958: 64).

It goes without saying that the Bank of England was not founded as a central bank. It began as a private bank, pursuing its own commercial interests, with no powers over other banks and subordinate to the State only in the sense that it had to conform to its Charter, keep within the law, co-operate with the government in its business dealings with it and carry out the government's instructions when acting as its agent. Its influence on the banking system arose initially from its greater size, resources and prestige so that it was able to provide a leadership that other banks could not aspire to. As time went on, however, it could no longer dominate other banks by its sheer size since, unlike continental public banks, it confined its activities almost entirely to the capital city and even in London the greater part of ordinary banking business was in the hands of other banks. The Bank had few provincial branches while independent banks outside London flourished with the industrial revolution, bank partnerships gave way to joint stock companies and amalgamations created commercial banks with larger resources than the Bank itself. The attempt in the Bank Charter Act of 1844 to reinforce the authority of the Bank by giving it monopolistic powers over the note issue proved unavailing. Control over the note issue was of limited help when the business of the country was increasingly conducted through the use of cheques. The Bank Act had to be suspended twice within fourteen years of its enactment and the Bank at first drew the moral that it should hold itself aloof from much current business for fear of being caught up in any future crisis. This carried it along a path that diverged increasingly from the continental pattern. It also confronted the Bank with a double problem: how to exercise control over the banking system given the limited scale of its operations and how to ensure an adequate income for itself (Sayers 1976: 1–3).

The income of the Bank was derived from its banking business, which included in the late 19th century not only government business but business for banking customers – the London clearing banks, the merchant banks, British overseas banks and some foreign banks. The discount market formed another group of customers and there were also private customers, including both corporate bodies and private individuals. The period of cheap money in the 1890's and a parallel squeeze exerted by the Government on the Bank's remuneration for its services forced the Bank to cut its dividend to 8 per cent in 1895 and obliged it to pursue a more vigorous lending policy until the outbreak of the first world war. From 1922 until 1946 it was possible to pay an unvarying dividend of 12 per cent and business involving competition with commercial banks faded out. The interests of stockholders had had little or no influence on the Bank's operations from the beginning of the century and the Bank's concern to earn an adequate income was no longer pursued after the first world war by encouraging private customers.

The problem of control had been resolved mainly through the development by the Bank of the use of Bank rate as an instrument for regulating the flow of credit. This allowed it to exercise control by acting as lender of last resort. The technique did not involve collaboration with the joint-stock banks or direct pressure on them but made use of the discount market and of open market operations to make bank rate effective. The Bank did not buy bills and hardly ever sold them. Well before 1890 it had developed the practice of selling Consols spot and repurchasing them forward. It also sold government stock outright or borrowed against it or borrowed from important customers such as the Indian Government. The underlying strength of sterling and the balance of payments before the first world war, and Britain's rôle as a major exporter of capital, allowed the Bank to exert great leverage on the financial system by comparatively small changes in interest rates.

By 1914 the Bank of England had largely fulfilled the first two requirements of a central bank in that it did not seek to earn maximum profits and had established control over the monetary system, although that control was somewhat precarious given the limited size of the Bank's "free" reserves of gold and its increasing dependence on at least the tacit support of the clearing banks. What of the third requirement – subordination to the State? As Sayers points out,

the authority of the State over the central bank is always necessarily absolute. All that is open to question is the extent to which the sovereign body should detail its commands to the central bank – for the monetary laws are such commands (Sayers 1958: 65).

It is possible – and this was the situation in 1914 – for the State to limit itself to prescribing the value of the monetary unit in terms of a fixed weight of gold, leaving the central bank to do the rest, with perhaps some relaxation of the prescription on request from the central bank in special circumstances. Or the central bank may be reduced to "a mere engine for facilitating the financing of State services" (Sayers 1958: 66). There are fashions in these matters that sometimes find expression in bank charters and revisions in them. But whether the Bank has a written constitution or not, the extent to which the State asserts detailed control over it may vary widely.

In the case of the United Kingdom, the position in 1914 was that the Bank and the Treasury were still very much at arms length in their relationship with one another. The Bank had their marching orders – to preserve convertibility of the currency at a fixed rate – and it was only in emergency, when they felt hesitant over their ability to carry out these orders that they turned to the Treasury. They had shown great skill in devising appropriate techniques of control. But they were saddled with a law that fastened on the wrong instrument of control – the note issue – and froze unnecessarily a large part of their gold reserve; they had less gold than their responsibilities required; and they could exert only indirect pressure on the commercial banks when these banks were in command of resources far exceeding those at the Bank's disposal.

The limitations to the Bank's authority over the commercial banks were illustrated during the banking crisis of 1914. The commercial banks were uneasy about the adequacy of the Bank's gold reserves and although unwilling to challenge the Bank openly were making claims that amounted to a bid for a voice in decisions that had traditionally been the undisputed prerogative of the Bank. The Bank's power to build up its gold stock had come to depend on the goodwill of the larger banks since it could acquire gold only by making Bank rate effective and for that purpose it was obliged to borrow in the market, at first the balances of countries like Japan and India but increasingly from the joint stock banks themselves. Although other action was open to the Bank it was of a kind the Bank was reluctant to take. On the other hand if it were left to the larger banks to build up their own stock of gold they would have the power to dispute (and delay) its use. The banks were also disinclined to make it easier for the Bank to bear the cost of acquiring more gold by putting larger balances at its disposal, recalling how larger balances after the Baring Crisis had gone with keener competition in banking services from the Bank itself. Some of the bankers called for a Royal Commission and there were those who wanted increased gold holdings in their hands to be coupled with a share with the Bank of England in control over the enlarged reserve (De Cecco 1974: chapter 7; Sayers 1976: 60 ff.).

When the crisis came in 1914, the Treasury was firmly on the side of the Bank. The government had increased its own balances with the Bank as a contribution to easing the financial problem; no Royal Commission had been appointed; the Chancellor's principal advisers (reinforced by Keynes) were out of sympathy with the spokesmen of the clearing banks; and the Governor (Cunliffe) had the ear of the Prime Minister and Chancellor. The clearing bankers had offered, in accordance with their plan, to make contributions from their own holdings of gold to an emergency pool that would be put at the disposal of the Bank of England. But they coupled this with a proposal to suspend gold payments and it was on the latter proposal that the main battle was fought. Cunliffe wanted none of their gold and reacted strongly against the proposal for suspension without arguing the matter. The arguments were supplied by Blackett and Keynes in the Treasury and were accepted by the Chancellor. Thus the original plan of the clearing banks was left in limbo and Cunliffe emerged triumphant with the full confidence of the Prime Minister and Chancellor (Sayers 1976: 69–74).

The limitations to the Governor's own authority emerged a few years later when he fell foul of the Treasury, in 1917. The quarrel between Cunliffe and Bonar Law (who became Chancellor in December 1916) remained highly secret for many years: it was at bottom a clash of personalities rather than of policy and had no lasting effect on the relationship between the Bank and the Treasury. From May 1915 onwards Cunliffe had tried to insist on dealing direct with the former Chancellor, Lloyd George, who was now Prime Minister, and by-passing his successor, first McKenna and then Bonar Law. This created friction not only with the Chancellor but also with the top civil servants on the foreign exchange side, Sir Robert Chalmers and Maynard Keynes.

Things came to a head when Cunliffe returned from a long absence in the United States and found to his annoyance that Chalmers and Keynes were apparently disregarding the interests of the Bank and had given instructions for the disposal of gold held for the United Kingdom by the Canadian Government in Ottawa and pledged in part as security for debts contracted in New York. The borrowed dollars were all to meet Treasury requirements but some of the debt stood in the name of the Bank and on hearing that the loan would not be renewed, the Governor felt entitled to instruct the Canadian Government to provide an equivalent amount of gold to liquidate it. When he learned of the earlier Treasury instructions he took action, without consulting Ministers, Treasury officials or his own Committee of Treasury, to instruct the Canadian Government to refuse to deliver any more gold until it had been paid for the liquidation of the debt in the name of the Bank, i.e. to ignore the Treasury's instructions. He also called on the Chancellor to dismiss Chalmers and Keynes. The Chancellor, not surprisingly, was very angry and protested to Lloyd George who, in a stormy interview with the Governor, was reported by the latter as threatening to "take over the Bank". It took over a month before some accomodation was reached between Cunliffe and Bonar Law but at the end of the day neither had resigned nor been dismissed[1].

Immediately after the interview at No. 10 Downing Street between the Prime Minister and the Governor, the latter was asked to sign a statement in

---

[1] This account is based on that in Sayers (1976), vol 1, pp 99–107.

the Prime Minister's own handwriting (but drafted presumably, in the Treasury). He was asked to promise

that during the War the Bank must in all things act on the directions of the Chancellor of the Exchequer whenever in the opinion of the Chancellor national interests are concerned and must not take any action likely to affect credit without previous consultation with the Chancellor (Sayers 1976: 99–107).

Cunliffe refused to sign, confident that his colleagues would support him, as indeed the Committee of Treasury did next day when they decided unanimously "that it was impossible for the Bank thus to renounce its functions". It was only after lengthy negotiations stretching over a month that Cunliffe was persuaded to give a written undertaking that:

so long as I am Governor of the Bank I shall do my utmost to work loyally and harmoniously with you and for you as Chancellor of the Exchequer and, while I shall continue, if you allow me, to tender you such advice as I consider it my duty to offer, I fully realize that I must not attempt to impose my views on you (Sayers 1976: 107).

Although the incident had no enduring repercussions on Bank/Treasury relations, it is of some significance as the one example quoted by Dalton in the nationalisation debates in 1945–46 of the dangers to which the state would be exposed if the Bank of England remained in private hands.

In one respect Cunliffe's spell as Governor marked an important departure in Bank-Treasury relations. In the nineteenth century a Governor served for two years only, after membership as Deputy Governor, also for two years, of the Committee of Treasury. Thus the direction of the Bank changed at frequent intervals and was in the hands of Governors with limited prior experience of the workings of the Bank. Cunliffe, almost by accident, held office for five years – longer than any of his predecessors. After a brief period under Cokayne the Bank acquired a Governor in Montagu Norman who remained in office for twentyfour years. The continuity that this afforded made it possible for the Bank to take a longer view, to build up a more expert staff and give it more responsibility, and to assume new functions, domestic and external.

Thus it was not until Norman's Governorship that the ascendancy of the Bank of England over the banking system was unquestioned and its evolution into a central bank was complete. For much of its earlier history the Bank was not conscious of any responsibility for control over the monetary system nor did the government think in these terms.

So far as the government was concerned, it was the note issue, not deposit banking, that dominated its thinking until the present century. It made use of the Bank of England in the management of its debt and in such borrowing operations as it found necessary, allowing the Bank certain privileges in return. But except in the safeguarding of those privileges, the government took little part in the relations between the central bank and the rest of the financial system, although it was on those relations that the central banking functions of the Bank of England rested. Nor, between 1815 and 1914, did the government greatly complicate the task of the Bank by its own borrowing operations: the national debt, four times as large as GNP in 1815, did not increase in absolute terms over the century and fell to less than half GNP by 1914. There were very few occasions on which the government and the Bank were at cross purposes or when the one felt obliged to bring pressure on the other: these usually arose over the need to relax the restrictions imposed in 1844 on the note issue. But in any event the government was not equipped to cross swords with the Bank of England: there were at most only two or three people in government service who were thoroughly familiar with monetary problems and it was only in a crisis or in matters of debt management that contact between the two bodies extended much beyond exchanges between Chancellor and Governor.

As for the Bank of England, it took some time before it awoke to its duties as lender of last resort. It saw itself until late in the 19th century as a bank competing with other banks, albeit with an interest in maintaining a healthy financial environment and with a duty to assist in maintaining the government's credit. The Bank felt bound to show leadership in a financial crisis but this was by no means the same as exercising control over the monetary system. As we have seen, even when it accepted this rôle it did not find it easy to establish its authority for lack of the necessary resources. It had to work out for itself, without government guidance and with little assistance from the government, the methods appropriate to its rôle. But of course the methods appropriate before 1914 needed re-examination in the very different conditions that followed.

The war of 1914–18 obliged the Bank and the Treasury to work closely together and collaboration continued under post-war conditions. In the inter-war period, although there were acute controversies over successive acts of policy – the return to the Gold Standard in 1925, the devaluation of 1931, the functioning of the Exchange Equalisation Account after 1931 – there is no evidence of a sharp division of view between Bank and Treasury over the policy adopted. The Bank accepted explicitly that in monetary matters the government must have the last word. As Montagu Norman put it in evidence in 1926: –

I look upon the Bank as having the unique right to offer advice and to press such advice even to the point of nagging: but always, of course, subject to the supreme authority of the Government[2].

But there was in fact no great need for nagging, or at least for the government to assert its authority, because, as Gregory has pointed out, "those responsible shared much the same social philosophy and the same intellectual background" (Gregory 1955: 10). The Bank of England was part of the Establishment; and the urge to formal control that gains strength in countries where the seat of government is at some distances from the industrial and commercial capital was absent in London.

1.2 After Nationalisation

The post-war period falls into three fairly distinct phases. First came a period under the Labour Governments of 1945–51 in which the wartime policy of cheap money was prolonged and Bank rate was held constant at 2 per cent. So far as monetary policy was used at all it took the form of credit rationing in compliance with requests to the clearing banks from the Chancellor or the Governor. In the second phase, which began shortly after a Conservative Government took office in October 1951, the use of Bank rate was resumed and a rather more active monetary policy was adopted. For a time great weight was placed in public pronouncements on the contribution of monetary policy to the management of the economy but the Bank of England itself was more sceptical. The Government suffered some disillusionment in 1955 when the Chancellor reduced taxation and hoped to find a sufficient offset in a tighter monetary policy. By the time the Radcliffe Committee reported four years later, opinion had moved away from reliance on monetary policy and it continued to play only a subordinate part for many years. Over the whole of the period after 1951, monetary restraints tended to be employed as part of a package of measures at times of crisis and were then relaxed in stages, independently of other measures. Although rates of interest were variable, the main thrust of policy was delivered through credit rationing and administrative controls.

Within this second phase come the familiar episodes of stop-go, leading up to the devaluation of 1967, and followed by the big expansion in the money supply in the boom of 1972–74. The acceleration in inflation in the early Seventies changed the atmosphere in which monetary policy took shape and led to a third phase of policy characterised by the use of monetary targets. In this phase, inflation was identified with an excessive growth in the money

---

[2] Cited by R. S. Sayers (1957), p. 35.

supply, the money supply itself became the centrepiece of monetary policy and monetary policy overshadowed all other aspects of economic policy. Broadly speaking this has been true since 1979 and, with some qualifications, even since 1976 when monetary targets were first introduced.

1.2.1 1945–51

The first phase opened with the nationalisation of the Bank. This might suggest that the Bank had been at loggerheads with the government or that it had conspicuously failed to carry out its duties as a central bank efficiently and responsibly. But in fact the Bank had worked in close collaboration with the Treasury for many years (and particularly in war-time) and it was difficult to point to any example of refusal to comply with a government request. No real change was effected by expropriation of the Bank's proprietors, who had no influence whatever on the operations of the Bank or on the choice of Governors and had received an unchanged dividend for over twenty years. Even members of the Cabinet like Lord Pethick-Lawrence-Marshall's favourite pupil of fifty years previously – admitted that it "would not make a pennyworth of difference".

The Labour Party's insistence on taking over the Bank of England – the Act took legislative precedence over all other measures of nationalisation – derived largely from ideological considerations. Control of credit in the public interest was taken to be indispensable in a Socialist country and, that being so, the power to exercise control must rest visibly with the government. The Bank, as the spokesman of the City, seemed unlikely to entertain radical views or share the predilections of a Socialist government. It may have appeared prudent, therefore, to bring it under control before it sought to thwart or delay measures upon which such a government would feel obliged to insist. There was also deep suspicion in the Labour Party of any agency involved in high finance and vague distrust of the Bank for the part it was thought to have played, first in the return to gold in 1925 and even more for its share in the alleged "bankers' ramp" of 1931 (i.e. the Bank's failure to raise sufficient funds abroad on acceptable terms) when the Labour Government fell from office.

In the debates on the Bill, the Chancellor of the Exchequer, Hugh Dalton, was content to argue that nearly all central banks were publicly owned and maintained, quite mistakenly, that in 1932 only the Bank of England and the Reichsbank were in private hands. (H of C Debates 1945a: Vol. 415)[3]. The

---

[3] H. of C. Debates, vol. 415, col 45, 29 October 1945. Dalton was relying on Kisch and Elkin (1932) who found "only two important Banks which, at least on paper, are inde-

truth was very different: in the early 1930's government-owned central banks existed in only ten countries including the USSR (Gregory 1955).[4] Dalton also laid stress on the need, for purposes of economic planning, to have control over the allocation of credit between different uses and groups of user. Such control had been exercised by war-time Chancellors, first in 1941 by Sir John Simon and later in the war by Sir John Anderson, when they made requests to the banks to give priority to some types of requirement and deny credit altogether to others (H of C Debates 1945b: Vol. 417). Conservative speakers were alarmed both by the enhancement of the government's peacetime control over the banks that this implied and by the context of economic planning in which these powers were to be brought into use. They were only partially reassured by a provision in the Bill excluding the use of the powers it conferred to discriminate against particular banking customers as distinct from categories of customer and a further provision that gave bankers the right to make representations when subject to a direction from the Bank.

So far as the constitution of the Bank was concerned it was to remain under the direction of a Governor and Deputy Governor as in the past, assisted by a "Court" of sixteen directors, of whom not more than four were to be executive (i.e. full-time) directors. This took the place of a rather larger Court of 24 members (excluding the Governors). Governors and directors were all to be appointed by the Crown: in practice this meant by the Prime Minister "acting on the advice of the Chancellor of the Exchequer after consultation with the Governor or, in the case of the Governor's appointment, with the senior non-executive directors" (Wilson Committee 1980: para 1265)[5]. The term of office of the Governors was to be five years, of the directors, four years and all of them were to be eligible for reappointment. The Governor may resign but the Government has no power under the Act to dismiss him in mid-term (Wilson Committee 1980: para 1272).

---

pendent of their respective Governments" (Kisch and Elkin 1932: 18). This is not quite the same as (to quote Dalton) "in greater or less degree, State institutions". Kisch and Elkin, moreover, were at pains to emphasise that in times of crisis neither the Bank of England nor the Reichsbank enjoyed real independence. The German Bank Act of 1924 might open by declaring that "the Reichsbank is a bank independent of Government control" but "in practice the situation works out as in England. At a time of anxiety... the Bank is in effect the servant and instrument of the State" (Kisch and Elkin 1932: 19).

[4] Monetary Policy and the Management of the Public Debt: Joint Committee on the Economic Report, Part I, 82nd Congress, 2nd Session, pp. 146–195, quoted by Sir T. E. Gregory (1955: 7n).

[5] Report of the (Wilson) Committee to review the functioning of financial institutions (Cmd 7937), 1980, para 1265. It is unlikely that such consultation took place in 1983.

Much of the debate in Parliament centred on the powers of direction written into the Bill. These empowered the Treasury, after consultation with the Governor, to issue a direction to him; they also empowered the Bank to make a request or a recommendation to the commercial banks (which remained privately owned) and, if authorised by the Treasury, to enforce the request or recommendation by a direction. The Treasury, however, was given no power to issue a direction to the commercial banks; it could only bring pressure on the Bank of England to do so. Directions were to remain secret unless the government decided otherwise. The power to issue them did no more than assert the Government's authority as proprietor. A similar clause was written into all subsequent nationalisation Acts and gave rise to the same kind of controversy. In the case of the Bank of England, the power of direction has never been used and it is unlikely that it ever will be. The right of the government to insist on the adoption of the monetary policy it favours has not been questioned. But beyond the enactment of powers of direction, nothing in the legislation indicated, for the benefit either of the Bank or of the public, what the division of responsibility was to be between the Bank and the Treasury, what kind of policy prescription should be followed, or how monetary policy was intended to take shape under the new arrangements. The natural presumption that very little would change proved to be correct.

In the years of Labour government from 1945 to 1951 there was in fact little discernible change in the relationship between the Bank and the Government (nor indeed in any other Bank relationships). Contact between the two continued to be confined almost entirely – on matters of policy at least – to the Chancellor and the Governor although the Bank was increasingly involved at the official level (e.g. in the negotiations under Keynes that led up to the loans from the United States and Canada and the Financial Agreement with the United States of December 1945). The Bank was particularly concerned with the various monetary agreements concluded with other countries in 1946–47 as a preliminary to convertibility, with exchange control, and with plans for dealing with the large sterling balances that had accumulated in war-time. These were all matters in which the Bank acted as agent for the government in association with the Treasury, offering independent advice and from time to time taking an initiative that was not altogether to the Treasury's liking[6].

---

[6] For example the Treasury thought the Bank over-hasty in its efforts to conclude monetary agreements in advance of July 1947 when convertibility was due to begin (Ellis Rees 1962, in PRO T 267/3).

In particular, the Bank took issue with the Treasury over the convertibility of sterling, the blocking of sterling balances and the Bretton Woods Agreement. They were opposed to the pledge to make sterling convertible within a year (or even with the five years that the Bretton Woods Agreement would have allowed); they had no faith in the early achievement of free, non-discriminatory, multilateral trade foreseen in the Bretton Woods Agreement; and they nevertheless hoped to maintain and even extend the use of sterling without blocking the balances accumulated in war. These views were not shared by Keynes, the dominant figure in the Treasury until his death in 1946, although there were some in the Treasury who entertained doubts akin to those of the Bank. In the event the government was not much influenced by these doubts in 1945–47. The Bank did not press their views, nor was there always a single view. For example, there were some in the Bank who would have liked to see sterling devalued as early as the middle of 1947; but two years later the Governor, when consulted, was resolutely opposed to devaluation while the Treasury had come to be in favour of it.

So far as domestic monetary policy was concerned, the running was made by the Chancellor in person over the first two years. Dalton, who was Chancellor until November 1947, was determined to bring down the long-term interest rate to 2½ per cent and could claim that at least his initial moves had the support of Keynes (in March/April 1946) and of Catto, whom Dalton had confirmed as Governor when the Bank of England Bill became law. There is no evidence that the Bank in those years pressed for tighter money (Cairncross and Eichengreen 1983: 120). Nor is there much sign of disagreement on monetary policy between the Bank and the Treasury before 1948.

Both in the Bank and the Treasury the view seems to have been taken that with so large an overhang of money accumulated in war-time there was little point in making use of higher interest rates to check spending since only a very large increase would have had much effect. The Economic Section (then in the Cabinet Office, not the Treasury) did look to monetary policy to check the boom but seems to have had in mind restrictions on bank advances rather than higher interest rates. Once a budget surplus emerged in 1948 the Financial Secretary of the Treasury, Douglas Jay, urged on the Bank the view that the surplus should be reflected in a corresponding slowing down in the growth of the money supply or an actual fall. In the course of the protracted discussions that followed it became clear that the budget surplus which Jay had in mind was very much larger than the *cash* surplus after meeting the borrowing requirement of the nationalized industries. The scope for using the cash surplus to check the growth of the money supply would also be further reduced if it were applied to redeeming debt in the hands of the public rather than floating debt in the hands of the banks.

On this there was general agreement. What caused disagreement was that the Bank seemed content to rely on fiscal policy to keep the growth in the money supply under control while the Treasury was alarmed by the expansion in bank advances to the private sector and the failure of the Bank to control it. It looked to them as if the Bank had abandoned all responsibility for the growth of the money supply. The Treasury contemplated a ceiling on bank advances which the Bank thought 'most unwise'. Lord Catto, the Governor, viewed such a proposal 'with the utmost alarm: it is not practical', he told the Chancellor, 'and would lead us into a mess of violent deflation'. It was only through the borrower that disinflationary pressure should operate. Nor should such pressure take the form of higher interest rates which would, in any event, do little to deter industrial borrowers if kept within normal limits. The idea of a ceiling on bank advances was dropped.

In the discussions before devaluation in 1949 the Bank had remarkably little influence on events. The Governor (now C. F. Cobbold) was strongly against devaluation and pressed, like some of the top Treasury officials, for a cut in public expenditure which stood no real chance of acceptance by the government. He wanted a deferment of further nationalisation plans and a new agreement with the United States and Canada to "take some of the rest of the world's demand for dollars off our back" by assuming some of the burden of sterling liabilities. When it appeared that the government would refrain completely from any cut in public expenditure the Governor threatened to refuse outright any effort to restrict credit or raise interest rates. The one way in which he may have had some success in influencing the final decision was through his insistence on the danger that one devaluation might be the prelude to a second and the need, therefore, for a larger devaluation than would be sufficient if all necessary accompanying measures were taken.

The devaluation was more or less forced on the Chancellor, not by the Bank of England but by his Ministerial colleagues and more particularly by three younger members of the government of whom the two who pushed for devaluation, Gaitskell and Jay, were not even in the Cabinet. That they obtained agreement to devaluation was largely because the official advice from the Treasury, initially divided, crystallised in favour of the move shortly before Gaitskell was brought in to help the Prime Minister when the Chancellor, Stafford Cripps, went off for a month to a clinic in Switzerland.

From 1947 to 1951 the influence of the Bank on government policy was at a low ebb. In the convertibility crisis of 1947 Dalton complained that he was getting little help from Catto and two years later was reflecting in his diary that it had been a mistake to appoint Cobbold to succeed him. Cripps in turn showed little disposition to consult the Bank. He rejected proposals in 1949 to raise Bank rate or make it effective, contenting himself with a letter to the Governor asking for "every endeavour to ensure that inflationary policies are held in check". When Cobbold sent him an extraordinary protest from Lord Linlithgow, representing the London clearing banks, against government-imposed restrictions on credit or a ceiling on bank advances, Cripps retorted that he "could not accept the view that the volume of money was at the discretion of the Clearing Banks" (Cairncross 1985: 443). As for Gaitskell, both in 1950 as Minister for Economic Affairs and in 1950–51 as Chancellor, he either ignored, overrode or rejected bank advice. He made no attempt to consult the Bank in early 1951 when there was talk of revaluing the pound; in the negotiations in May/June 1950 for the setting up of the European Payments Union, he took a line very different from that favoured by the Bank in earlier discussions; and throughout his year as Chancellor (1950–51) he resisted repeated efforts by the Bank to get him to raise Bank rate.

1.2.2 1951–76

The second phase, which may be said to have lasted from 1951 until 1976, opened with a remarkable episode in which the Bank and the Treasury, although very much on the same side of the argument, were completely defeated. The Conservative government which took office in October 1951 was sympathetic to the views of the Bank of England and took early action, in what had developed into an exchange crisis, to revive the use of Bank rate. The Bank put forward a scheme early in 1952 which was given the code name ROBOT to indicate the greater degree of automaticity that it involved. The scheme provided for the abandonment of a fixed parity and the blocking of sterling balances on a comprehensive scale. It commended itself to Ministers, including the Prime Minister, because they liked the idea of "freeing the pound"; to the Treasury because they saw little chance of holding to the existing parity as the reserves drained away and were impressed by the competitive power of American exports at current exchange rates; and to the Bank because it wanted early convertibility of sterling and saw no other way of getting rid of the bogey of "cheap sterling" (i.e. sterling available abroad at less than the official rate). Although the scheme was not broached until late in February it was intended to announce it in the Budget which was brought forward by a week to 4 March for that purpose. Thus very little time was afforded either for consideration of the scheme or for reviewing in detail how the blocking of sterling balances was to be organised. Yet it was a scheme that flouted the IMF's insistence on fixed parities, would have destroyed the European Payments Union, and might have seriously disrupted relationships with Commonwealth and other holders of sterling balances.

The scheme was strongly supported by the Chancellor and by some other Ministers, especially Lyttelton, the Colonial Secretary, and opposed, equally strongly by Lord Cherwell, Paymaster General and a close friend of Churchill's. Cherwell, briefed by Donald MacDougall and Robert Hall, was successful in preventing an immediate decision in February; and when no announcement of the scheme was made in the Budget, speculation against sterling fell away and the pound strengthened[7]. Although the Treasury continued to take a pessimistic view of prospects and the Bank was more insistent than ever on the awkwardnesses of inconvertibility, interest in the scheme dwindled, less drastic proposals were meditated and when it was reconsidered in June by a group of Ministers – not even the full Cabinet – it was again decided not to proceed with it.

From the autumn of 1952 the aim of convertibility was pursued along other lines as "a collective approach". The pound remained subject to speculative attacks partly because of doubts as to Britain's power to sustain convertibility at the existing parity and partly because of rumours of a renewed effort to achieve it. The Bank's anxiety to make the pound convertible and put an end to cheap sterling laid it open to the suspicion that it either fed those rumours or at least did not kill them and so was responsible for the very loss of reserves that it could point to as evidence of the weakness of current policy. (Dow 1964: 88). In the middle of one of those attacks, in February 1955, the Bank was allowed to support the rate for transferable sterling, which made the pound to all intents and purposes convertible without any binding commitment to maintain this position and without any parallel action in support of convertibility by Britain's trading partners.

In informing the Cabinet of the move, the Chancellor said that it 'was not designed as a further step towards convertibility of sterling' although it would in course of time make it easier to achieve convertibility. He would appear to

---

[7] Although the scheme was supposed to be top secret, Ministers were known to be contemplating something of the kind and some of them may have talked, as Ministers do. It was widely believed that the Bank not only did little to conceal its own views on convertibility but made no secret of its support for a scheme on the line of Robot, with damaging effects on market expectations. As became even more evident in the next few years, the views of the Bank, and the activities and negotiations giving expression to these views, coloured market opinion when market opinion was itself an important element in policy-making.

have assumed that it would still be possible to withdraw support if necessary and no doubt this was formally true provided the apparatus of control had not been completely dismantled. But the practical and psychological obstacles to such a course were very great and it would not appear that the Bank, committed as it was in favour of early convertibility, did justice to these obstacles in putting the case to the Chancellor. By the time Heathcoat Amory became Chancellor in 1958 it was accepted that there could be no return to the previous régime. Here, as in the resumption of the use of Bank rate in November 1951, the Bank of England was tendering advice successfully to a Conservative government that would undoubtedly have been rejected by a Labour government.

There was an example later in 1955 of a serious misunderstanding between the government and the Bank. It would seem that monetary policy was given the credit by the Chancellor (and the public too) for putting an end to the exchange crisis of 1951–52, damping down the pressure of demand associated with rearmament, and making possible a smooth and rapid growth in output over the next three years. It was to monetary measures that he turned again in the early months of 1955 when the symptoms of excess demand reappeared: a renewed deficit in the balance of payments, a strain on the exchange rate and more rapidly rising wages and prices. Bank rate was raised in January and again in February. In his budget speech in April the Chancellor claimed that these measures had been effective and went on to justify a reduction in income tax in terms of his reliance on "the resources of a flexible monetary policy" but perhaps also with an eye on the General Election due in May.

For the next three months, however, there was little sign of the tightening of monetary policy to which the government stood committed. It was not until late June that the Treasury woke up to the fact that any guidance to the commercial banks issued by the Bank of England had clearly been inadequate. Bank advances had risen in the first quarter by £ 127 m. and in the second quarter by £ 162 m., financed through the sale by the banks of short-dated Government securities. There then ensued one of the most remarkable episodes in post-war relations between the government and the banking system.

Perhaps the most curious aspect of the affair was that although the government was seeking to enforce a credit squeeze on the commercial banks, communication between the two required the intermediation of the Bank of England which objected strongly to direct contact without its participation. The commercial banks insisted that a credit squeeze must apply all round; and since a large part of the increase in advances in the second quarter of

1955 was to the nationalized gas and electricity industries, they proposed, with the agreement of the Bank of England, to require those industries to keep within their overdraft limits and cut their borrowing as soon as possible. The industries concerned, however, had turned to the banks only because conditions on the stock exchange had obliged them to defer the issues required in order to finance their investment programmes – programmes, as the Treasury indignantly pointed out, that had been publicly approved by the government. The Treasury also suspected that the banks had not only the sympathy but the encouragement of the Governor and that they had not been adequately briefed by the Bank of England as to the rigour with which the credit squeeze should be applied. When Treasury officials were finally allowed to speak to commercial bank representatives they found them unaware that they were expected to press credit restriction to the point at which redundancies would result.

The banks for their part were willing to do as the government wished provided a public statement was made by the government that the banks could quote to their customers. The Governor opposed the inclusion in any such statement of any figure for the size of the cut to be made in advances – the Treasury wanted 7½ per cent in three months – and when the Chancellor wrote to the Governor on 25 July he contented himself with a request for 'a positive and significant reduction in advances'. In reporting the banks' agreement, the Governor emphasized that their representatives had expressed a desire to see similar restraint in the public sector. The Chancellor had given an assurance about public expenditure but the bank chairmen remained sceptical and one of them, in a letter which the Governor took care to draw to the attention of the Treasury, accused the Chancellor of having gone back on what he told the bankers. (In point of fact, the increase in public investment in 1955 'which was the nub of the controversy' increased very little compared with investment in the private sector, and at constant prices was actually falling.)

The Chancellor, although much annoyed, pursued a conciliatory policy. In due course the banks settled on making a 10 per cent cut in advances by the end of the year and were remarkably successful. The reduction, however, came too late to allow the Chancellor to avoid fresh measures. In October he found it necessary to introduce an autumn budget that raised taxation by about as much as it had been cut in April.

A month later the Chancellor had another surprise when he discovered in November from a speech by the Governor at the Mansion House that the Bank's view was that it was a mistake to rely heavily on dear money to get rid of excess demand. At that point, as in the 1980's, the traditional rôles of

Bank and Treasury seemed to have been reversed and it was the Treasury, not the Bank, that was pressing for a disinflationary monetary policy.

It was no doubt partly these events that give rise to the appointment early in 1957 of the Radcliffe Committee to which the Government looked for advice on how the monetary system actually worked. This was dealt with at some length in the Committee's Report. But in the meantime another matter of importance to the relationship between government and Bank had arisen. After the rise in Bank rate from 2 per cent to 7 percent in September 1957 it was alleged that there had been a breach of security from which a profit had been reaped through transactions on the stock exchange. These allegations had been examined by a Tribunal of Inquiry which threw a flood of light on the way in which decisions were taken when Bank rate was changed. In particular it directed attention to the rather ambiguous position of non-executive directors of the Bank of England who might be consulted by the Governor before a change was made and yet were supposed to conduct their private business – for example, as merchant bankers – without drawing on any knowledge of the Governor's intentions.

The rôle of the non-executive directors was dealt with in Chapter IX of the Radcliffe Report and so also was the relationship between the Bank and the government. We shall be discussing the Report below but for present purposes we need only note that it was widely interpreted as implying that "money does not matter" when this was not at all what the Report actually said (Radcliffe Report 1959: para 514)[8].

Policy in the 1960's was dominated by the weakness of the balance of payments and the eventual devaluation of the pound in 1967. The experience of these years is chiefly of interest in illustrating how policy on interest and exchange rates remained the province of the Prime Minister and Chancellor, to the exclusion of their colleagues (except, for a time in the mid-1960's, the Secretary of State for Economic Affairs). Other Ministers who held different views were unsuccessful in raising the matter in Cabinet between the time when the Labour Government took office in October 1964 and the crisis of July 1966. When defeated in Cabinet, they remained out of touch and had no influence on the final decision to devalue, taken by the Prime Minister and Chancellor and then agreed to in full Cabinet.

The Bank of England was fully in accord with the refusal to devalue until some weeks before it happened, though it was not at all happy at the rôle it

---

[8] "Our conclusion is that monetary measures cannot alone be relied upon to keep in nice balance an economy subject to major strains from both without and within. Monetary measures can help, but that is all" (Radcliffe Report, Chapter IX, para 514).

was required to play. In the early stages in October 1964 its advice on Bank rate was ignored with unfortunate effects on international confidence in the pound and it had then to engage in a massive support operation, offering what reassurance it could to the contributing central bankers for responsible efforts by the British government to maintain the parity[9]. The Governor (Lord Cromer) was out of sympathy with the measures taken and argued as his predecessor (Cobbold) had done in 1949 for deflationary action through cuts in public expenditure. This created friction between him and the government and at the end of his term of office in July 1966 his appointment was not renewed. Instead, the government elevated the Deputy Governor, Leslie O'Brien, in spite of an earlier understanding that in taking office as Deputy he would be debarred from the succession.

The Treasury was in a position not unlike that of the Bank in that devaluation had been ruled out so firmly that it was supposed to be "unmentionable" and if pressed on the Chancellor was tantamount to calling for his resignation. At no time from October 1964 onwards was either the Bank or the Treasury asked for a position paper on the exchange rate; they were obliged to wait on events while devising what expedients they could to defend the parity. Both had become convinced of the inevitability of devaluation before the decision was finally taken. Both were also agreed that the measures to restrain demand that accompanied devaluation were insufficient, as indeed became all too evident.

The monetary policies pursued over this period had relied heavily on control over bank credit and had put the banks at a disadvantage in competition with other financial intermediaries. The authorities had also tended to rely on rationing rather than price adjustments in the form of higher interest rates. In 1971, however, the Bank of England proposed, in a document entitled "Competition and Credit Control", to abandon lending ceilings and guidance on the allocation of credit within the ceilings.

The change in policy initiated by this document was not buttressed by a greater readiness to let interest rates fluctuate as a means of exercising control over credit. Nor did it in practice lead to the recapture by the clearing banks of the business they had lost to the "fringe" banks and other competitors in the years when their hands were tied by credit ceilings. Instead, the whole credit system expanded faster than ever. In just over two years, from the publication of "Competition and Credit Control" in September 1971 to the end of December 1973, total sterling bank advances to UK

---

[9] For a full account see Cairncross and Eichengreen, (1966: 166 ff.).

resident borrowers expanded nearly one and a half times. The clearing banks raised their lending over that period by 112 per cent while "other" banks probably more than trebled theirs. The result was an explosion in property values since much of the lending was concentrated on the property and financial sector, which by the end of 1973 owed more to the banks than the whole of British manufacturing industry (Reid 1982: 60–61).

When the boom collapsed in December 1973 it threatened to bring down with it a large swathe of the secondary banks from which short term funds were being withdrawn at an alarming rate. A State of Emergency had just been declared as a confrontation with the miners approached; world oil prices were about to be trebled; bank rate had risen from 7½ per cent in July to 13 per cent in November; and on 17 December, in an emergency budget, drastic cuts in plans for government spending were announced, fresh restrictions on the banks were introduced – the so-called 'corset' – and a development gains tax on property disposals was foreshadowed. The impact on property companies and the banks financing them was devastating.

The evidence suggests that both the Treasury and the Bank of England would have welcomed earlier action to raise interest rates, but that they were overridden by the Prime Minister (Edward Heath). What is not clear is whether the expression of their views was confined to the gentle hints that appeared in print or took more forcible shape behind the scenes. The Bank seems to have refrained from any public statement of undisguised concern. Lord O'Brien, who was Governor until the middle of 1973, said afterwards of the Prime Minister that he "was not easily deflected from what he felt he wanted to do". The Chancellor of the Exchequer, Lord Barber, seems to have meditated resignation but concluded from the example of Lord Thorneycroft in 1958 that it would only serve to remove from the Cabinet one cautionary voice (Reid 1982: 72, 76).

The rescue operation that was put in hand once the run on the banks began in December 1973 was organised entirely by the Bank of England, not the Treasury. The Treasury may have been kept informed by its "East End branch" of what was going on but the Bank was

> left to get on with combatting the emergency very much on its own, with little questioning or close watching from the Treasury or the Government. The Bank's intervention was so firm, prompt and discreet that it effectively muffled the threatened crisis (Reid 1982: 19).

It was intervention on the grand scale. The "Lifeboat" which it organised with the clearing banks to finance the many support operations and stand-by credits that proved necessary involved at peak a commitment of no less than

£ 1285 m. of which the Bank had promised to put up one tenth and in the end took an even larger share.

1.2.3 1976–83

In 1976 a new phase began with the introduction of monetary targets. An exchange crisis obliged the government to seek financial support from the IMF (and from the EEC) and to accept the need for deflationary measures, both fiscal and monetary. The money supply had been expanding at nearly 30 per cent per annum in the middle of the year and in order to regain control Bank rate was raised to 15 per cent. From 1976 onwards the government announced a monetary target, at first for £ M 3 but later for other monetary aggregates: at first also for the year ahead but in 1980 for the next four years as part of a Medium Term Financial Plan. Although the growth of the money supply rarely fell within the target range and (after 1980) the range itself did not stay put, the device served two important purposes. It drew attention to the increased importance attached by the government to limitation of the growth of the money supply; and it provided the Bank of England with a measure of the severity of the monetary policy called for by the government.

During this period also Parliament took an increasing interest in monetary affairs. The system of Select Committees instituted in the late 1960's began to be used to bring forward witnesses from the Bank of England; and the range of questions that could be put to these witnesses (including, very often, the Governor) was greatly extended from 1980 onwards. One of the last acts of the Labour government of 1974–79 was to set up a committee of inquiry under the former Prime Minister, Harold Wilson, and this examined at some length the respective rôles of the Treasury and the Bank of England in framing and carrying out monetary policy. The conclusions of the Committee are discussed below.

The most recent development in the relationship between the Bank and the government arose in 1983 when it became clear that the government did not intend to renew the appointment of Gordon Richardson who was thought to be willing to continue for another term and was widely regarded as a popular and successful Governor. It came as a surprise when it was announced that he was to be succeeded by Robin Leigh-Pemberton who was then Chairman of one of the four large clearing banks, the National Westminster Bank, a post that would previously have excluded him from consideration. He had no previous experience of central banking (which is by no means the same thing as banking) and had made a number of statements on economic policy that were in keeping with the views of the Conservative

Party but very much out of keeping with those of the opposition parties. There was an unusual amount of criticism of his nomination, even by some who were well-disposed towards the government, partly because it seemed to indicate a desire on the part of the Prime Minister, no admirer of Gordon Richardson, to make sure of willing acceptance and implementation of her views on monetary policy. The Labour Party's shadow "Chancellor of the Exchequer", Peter Shore, wrote to the Governor-designate asking for an assurance that if a Labour government came to power he would co-operate loyally with it in carrying out the government's monetary policy. Leigh-Pemberton gave that assurance. This did not, however, prevent a statement some months later, in February 1984, by Roy Hattersley (who had succeeded Peter Shore as Shadow Chancellor) denouncing the Prime Minister for breaking "the convention which once kept public appointments above the political battle" and warning the Governor that "since he was appointed without reference to the Opposition his term as governor is unlikely to be renewed by a Labour Government". The Governor's appointment was for five years and a general election was bound to be held within that five years – in all probability near the end of it – so that if a Labour Government were elected it would presumably do no more than make a fresh appointment dating from the termination of the existing one. But the significance of these events extends much further than that and brings the Governorship quite unnecessarily into the political arena.

2 Analytical

We now turn to the reports of three successive committees of inquiry – the Macmillan Committee reporting in 1931, the Radcliffe Committee reporting in 1959, and the Wilson Committee reporting in 1980 – to see how they viewed the rôle and relationships of the Bank of England.

The Macmillan Committee did not, like the Radcliffe and Wilson Committees, devote a separate chapter to the rôle and constitution of the Bank but included a brief factual account in Chapter IV of Part I (Historical and Descriptive) and a lengthier treatment of Bank policy and relationships in Chapter III of Part II (Conclusions and Recommendations). Much of the discussion in both passages relates to the note issue and the extent to which gold should be set aside as backing for the currency and, in effect, excluded from the working reserve of foreign exchange. This part of the Report has lost interest in circumstances in which the link between gold and the note issue is of very little practical importance, as was true from 1931 onwards, or is no longer made, as has been true since 1946.

The Committee started off by describing the Bank as:

almost unique as a Central Bank in that it is a private institution practically independent of any form of legal control save in regard to its powers of issuing bank notes and granting loans to the State.

One of its witnesses, Sir Ernest Harvey (then Deputy Governor) told the Committee that, with these exceptions and the requirement to issue a weekly account, and apart from a statutory obligation to refrain from trade in commodities, "the Bank of England is practically free to do whatever it likes". Any restrictions on the Bank's operations were of its own devising.

The Committee appeared to be content that this should be the situation. Even Ernest Bevin, included as a prominent trade unionist, after proposing in a Reservation that the Bank should be transformed into a public corporation, added that "it should remain free from political influence". He would have been content with a minimum of change so long as the Governors were appointed by the Crown, an Advisory Council established and Bank stock replaced by fixed interest bonds.

Yet in its "Concluding Note" the Report included a passage that pointed in a very different direction. "It is of the greatest importance", ran the penultimate paragraph, "that other domestic action, not of a strictly monetary character, should be taken as an essential condition to the monetary authority being in a position to employ effectively the methods of monetary policy". But such action, or some of it, lay outside the Committee's terms of reference and raised "matters of active political controversy". It could not, therefore, be explored in the main report. Nevertheless, even if it led into non-monetary ground, it was felt by some members of the Committee to be "part and parcel of their view of the monetary situation as a whole" and since they felt bound to do full justice to their views, they had insisted on setting them out in a series of Addenda on controversial issues such as devaluation, tariffs, wage-cuts, and so forth. How in those circumstances monetary policy could be kept "free from political influences" must have puzzled the reader.

The Report had little to say about how this problem should be handled as between the Bank and the government. It seemed to assume that while the non-monetary alternatives of policy were inherently political, the monetary ingredient in policy could remain nonpolitical, or at least that whatever advice the Bank of England tendered could be regarded as politically neutral. The Report confined itself to a discussion of the instruments of policy at the Bank's disposal, how these instruments could be strengthened and what changes the Bank might be wise to make in its use of them. Various proposals were made for an enlargement of the Bank's resources including an increase in the Bank's capital. There should be an improved flow of statistical information into the Bank and, in published form, from it. The Bank's relations with the money market and the accepting houses were thought to be "close and successful". It was only relations with the clearing banks that were unsatisfactory: there was still a degreee of aloofness and remoteness when the policy of the Bank could only be made fully effective with their cooperation. More frequent and regular meetings were suggested. The banks should be taken into the confidence of the Bank of England to ensure harmony between their policy (for example, in attracting deposits from abroad) and that of the Bank. Above all, they should be left in no doubt whether the Bank favoured a relaxation or contraction of credit conditions.

The Radcliffe Committee, for reasons already explained, took more interest in Bank-Treasury relations; the chapter on the subject that appeared in their report was written by the chairman personally. It dealt at some length at the request of the Chancellor with the question of part-time directors in the light of the report of the Bank rate Tribunal after the alleged "leak" in 1957. Part-time directors were at that time in a majority on the Committee of Treasury (the Governor's "Cabinet"), since of the five members of the Committee elected by the Court to serve along with the Governor and Deputy Governor, not more than one could be an executive director and at least four were therefore part-time. Those who were not on the Committee of Treasury took part in other standing committees dealing with some aspect of the Bank's affairs but unless consulted by the Governor in his discretion on a current problem took no part in the discussion of central banking issues since the Court's rôle in dealing with such issues was purely formal. How far the Governor took the Committee of Treasury into his confidence depended to some extent on individual practice but most Governors would wish to have the Committee firmly behind them in pressing advice on the Treasury. The Committee was essentially advisory, and accepted that responsibility rested on the Governor "for initiating and formulating advice or proposals tendered to the Central Government on behalf of the Bank. (Report on the Working of the Monetary System 1959: para 759).

The Report of the Committee rejected suggestions that there should be no part-time members of the Court or that partners in businesses operating in the money or capital markets should be debarred from membership. Part-time directors should continue to act as special consultants to the Governor and take part in supervising the general administrative activities of the Bank without participating in actual policy decisions on monetary policy. Their detachment from such decisions would be clear if the recommendations of the Committee on working arrangements were accepted for they wanted Bank rate to be "a decision of the Chancellor, conveyed as such" (Report on the Working of the Monetary System 1959: para 759).

In addressing themselves to the issue of Bank/Treasury relations, the Committee argued that in post-war years,

> both parties have been trying to evolve and practise an allocation of their respective functions which, while recognising the clear implication of the 1946 Act that the will of the Government, formally expressed in the form of a direction, is paramount, yet accepts the advantages of retaining in the Bank a separate organisation with a life of its own, capable of generating advice, views and proposals that are something more than a mere implementation of its superior's instructions (Report on the Working Monetary System 1959: para 761).

Since the problems were constantly changing, it was unlikely that there could ever be a permanently satisfactory balance. The Act of 1946 did not attempt to provide one. But the Bank seemed to be reading into a clause in the Act provision for a line that might be drawn between "the affairs of the Bank", for which the Bank should take "first" or "direct" responsibility and other activities that could be represented as purely "agency" functions. Bank rate and the management of the money market might be put under the first heading while exchange control and the operation of the Exchange Equalisation Account came under the second. The Committee repudiated such a distinction. The Bank did not operate the only controls affecting the monetary system and in the process of coordination there had to be

> a constant co-operation, strategic and tactical between the central bank on the one hand and those responsible for alternative or supplementary monetary measures, essentially the Treasury and the Board of Trade on the other. More than that, monetary policy, as we have conceived it, cannot be envisaged as a form of economic strategy which pursues its own independent objectives. It is a part of the country's economic policy as a whole and must be planned as such (Report on the Working of the Monetary System 1959: para 767.)

Thus it was inappropriate to try to insulate one part of monetary policy from the rest, or monetary policy from economic policy, as both the Treasury and the Bank appeared ready to agree. By implication it was impossible to accept the view, put by some witnesses to the Committee, that in the public interest the central bank should be assured complete independence from political influence. Such a view either contemplated two separate and independent agencies of government, each capable of pursuing its own conception of an appropriate economic policy, or alternatively it assumed that it was right for central banks to have a single, fixed purpose, the stability of the currency – a purpose both limited in scope and impossible of attainment without concurrent action by the central government (Report on the Working of the Monetary System 1959: para 768).

This did not mean that the Bank should be reduced to the status of "a rather exceptional government department". Its relationships as a market operator and controller and its connections with overseas central banks and international agencies made it more of a business enterprise than a branch of the civil service. The Bank must be fully capable of forming and presenting ideas of its own. However, it must not appear to bear responsibilities that were properly those of the government and obscure the underlying reality by preserving outworn forms. The true responsibility for decisions on Bank rate for example lay with the Chancellor, not the Bank and they should be made in his name and on his authority. The public announcement, however, should make plain to the public that the Governor had been fully consulted before the decision was made; and the views of the Bank as expressed by the Bank should continue to be given "very great weight".

There followed two specific recommendations, neither of which came to anything. One was that changes in Bank rate should take the form of a direction by the Chancellor to the Bank. This was said to be necessary under existing legislation in order to convey the exercise of the Chancellor's authority although in fact changes in Bank rate had on occasion been announced by the Chancellor personally in the House of Commons. The second was that a Standing Committee on monetary policy should be set up with four representatives of the Bank including the Governors four representatives of the Treasury and two of the Board of Trade. The Chairman would nominally be the Chancellor but in practice the chair would usually be taken by the Economic Secretary to the Treasury.

It is not altogether clear what the Committee was to do by way of "coordination of monetary policy as a whole". It was not to interfere with existing personal exchanges between Bank and Treasury but could have proposals referred to it by the Chancellor, especially on "longer term issues" requiring a fuller and more deliberate consideration. Something of the kind might have been created had the membership been less ambitious; but it was difficult to see the Governor coming on a regular footing to a committee presided over by a junior Minister, not of Cabinet rank, and even the Deputy Governor might have found difficulty in extending his responsibilities to longer-term issues of monetary policy. In any event official contacts multiplied from then onwards without a formal committee and specific issues could be made the subject of study by *ad hoc* groups.

The Wilson Committee also devoted a separate chapter of its report to the Bank of England. This took the same view as the Radcliffe Committee of the case for making the Bank more independent of the central government and giving it explicit statutory policy objectives of its own. The Committee saw no necessary connection between the degree of independence of a central bank and the pursuit of an effective monetary policy. Nor did it see

anything about monetary policy to distinguish it sufficiently from other forms of macroeconomic policy to justify taking it out of the hands of elected governments (Report of the Committee to Review the Functioning of Financial Institution 1980: para 1278).

On the other hand, it wanted the Bank to be retained as a separate organisation with a life of its own, not integrated to the government machine, and was opposed to making the Governor and other members of the Court "more overtly political appointees, changing with each change of government" (Report of the Committee to Review the Functioning of Financial Institution 1980: para 1276).

The Wilson report underlined a number of changes over the previous twenty years, most of them tending to broaden the influence of the Bank. The Banking Act, 1979, for example, makes the Bank responsible for the prudential supervision of the banking system. It is, however, the Chancellor who is responsible to Parliament for the operation of the Act and the Bank is required to report to him annually on its activities under the Act and on the principles by which it is guided in granting or withdrawing authority to take deposits. (Report of the Committee to Review the Functioning of Financial Institution 1980: para 1269). The Bank has also become more closely involved in the non-statutory aspects of the securities market through the Takeover Panel which it helped to set up in 1968 and the Council for the Securities Industry which it promoted in 1978. It has been very active in discussions on industrial finance and created a separate unit in 1976 to deal with the subject. The rapid changes in financial structure that have been in progress in the City over the past decade involve the Bank in several different ways. They also involve the Treasury, although less directly, and institutions in the financial sector have now readier direct access to Ministers and officials where in the past communication used to be channelled largely through the Bank.

On Bank/Treasury relations the report pointed to other developments. These included a strengthening of the Bank's economic and statistical expertise that has made the calibre of the economic staff "at least as good as that of the Treasury's, as well as being comparable numerically" (Report of the Committee to Review the Functioning of Financial Institutions 1980: para

1282) an under-statement on both points. The staff of the Bank is also now represented on a wide range of interdepartmental committees so that its involvement in economic policy generally goes further than before. The Bank is also more open about its activities, publishing an informative *Quarterly Bulletin* from 1960 onwards and a number of research papers beginning more recently while the Governor and other directors make their views known in frequent speeches. The Governor and bank officials appear before standing government committees: in the 1970's before a sub-committee of the now defunct Select Committee on the Nationalised Industries which produced reports on the Bank in 1970 and 1976; and in the 1980's before the Committee on the Treasury which can question the Governor over the whole range of the Bank's activities in the same way as it can question the Chancellor.

These developments were welcomed by the Committee as increasing the accountability of the Bank to Parliament and the public and helping to stimulate constructive debate. But they warned against any expectations of dramatic change since on controversial issues the Bank would be unwilling to risk damaging consequences in financial markets and would feel obliged to defend government policy.

Finally, the Committee touched on the familiar issue of non-executive directors recognising that, as the Governor put it,

they are not part, in the direct sense, of the policy formulation of the Bank. The advice which is given to government by the Bank is the product of the work of the full-time staff of the Bank, including the Governors. They are not part of that (Report of the Committee to Review the Functioning of Financial Institution 1980: para 1296).

The Committee's conclusions were similar to those of the Radcliffe Committee except that they wanted to limit non-executive directors to a maximum period of service of eight years and representation of a wider range of backgrounds and interests without turning non-executive directors into delegates.

2.1 The Legal Position and the Working Relationship

It may be useful to round off this sketch of Bank/Treasury relations with a summary of the legal basis of the relationship. As the Bank pointed out in a memorandum on the subject in 1980, it is a relationship that "owes little to specific legislative provision" (Bank of England 1980). The Bank went on, therefore, to outline their view of the working relationship and this, too, may be usefully summarized.

The principal piece of legislation is the Bank of England Act 1946 already discussed. For many years prior to the Act the Bank had

seen it as its duty to direct its operations to the service of the public interest and to subject itself to the ultimate authority of Government in matters of monetary and economic policy (Bank of England 1980: para 2).

That position was given statutory expression in the provisions of the Act vesting in the Crown, "on the recommendation of the Prime Minister after consultation with the Chancellor of the Exchequer", the power to appoint the Court of Directors including the Governor and Deputy Governor. The fact that the appointments are for a fixed term confers in itself a degree of independence.

The Treasury also has powers to issue directions to the Bank after consultation with the Governor. But as Dalton explained during the Second Reading debate on the Bill, this power was not designed to permit "any day-to-day interference by the Government or the Treasury with the ordinary work of the Bank" but to make it plain that in the event of disagreement, the Treasury had the last word.

No reference appears in the 1946 Act to the most important part of the Bank's work which lies in the execution of monetary policy, domestic and external, and the formulation, in conjunction with the Treasury, of the future lines of policy.

The most important later piece of legislation is the 1979 Banking Act, which for the first time in the United Kingdom provided a legal definition of a bank and gave the Bank of England clearly defined statutory powers and duties of supervision (which it previously lacked) in relation to the banking system. In particular it is now the appointed authority for the purpose of licensing recognised banks as deposit-takers.

Other activities of the Bank governed by statute include its note-issuing powers, its management of the Exchange Equalisation Account on behalf of the Treasury, and its duties as banker to the Government and as the Government's agent in managing the National Debt. The legislation, however, merely sets out the formal position with little or no indication of the working relationship. The Exchange Control Act of 1947 also remains on the statute book although the Bank of England's apparatus of control was abolished in 1979 by a General Exemption Order made under the Act.

2.2 The Working Relationship

In explaining how things work out in practice, the Bank laid stress on its role in the provision of policy advice and as executant of policy (Bank of England 1980: paras 12–19). While Ministers are responsible for economic policy, they base it on 'studies, forecasts, advice and proposals... from a wide range of sources'. To this process the Bank claims to make a distinctive contribution as a 'separate and independent source of advice', not only on domestic and external monetary policy but on 'financial and related economic policy', too. The Bank's advice is made available to Ministers both at official level in day-to-day contacts between the Bank and the Treasury or in official interdepartmental committees and at Ministerial level through the regular contacts between the Governor and the Chancellor or, on occasion, in discussion between the Governor and the Prime Minister or other Ministers. The Bank's distinctive contribution to policy

derives from its operational involvement in the financial markets, and its consequential close relationships with and knowledge of the financial institutions, and from its specialisation in monetary economics and statistics. The Treasury's distinctive contribution stems from its responsibilities for overall co-ordination of macro-economic objectives and the relationship of that policy to the Government's wider objectives (Bank of England 1980: para 14).

The Bank regards itself as bearing the primary responsibility for carrying out the monetary aspects of economic policy through direct credit controls (if any) and operations in the financial markets. It feels free to offer advice on fiscal policy because of its close links with the supply of money; and to control the money supply by operations in the money markets and gilt-edged market. Within the framework of policy agreed with the Treasury, the Bank takes responsibility for market tactics, keeping the Treasury informed of developments. Important changes of direction are discussed in advance; changes in the Minimum Lending Rate, for example, require the approval of the Chancellor after discussion with the Governor.

In debt management, it is the Bank that initiates proposals for consideration by Treasury Ministers, on 'the amount, timing, and terms of new issues of Government stock'. The subsequent issue operations are also conducted by the Bank and it conducts the weekly tender for Treasury bills, deciding itself on the size of the issue.

Finally, in the foreign exchange market the Bank decides the day-to-day tactics while the strategic decisions on intervention policy are discussed with the Treasury and settled at Ministerial level (with the Prime Minister intervening from time to time) between the Chancellor and the Governor.

This account of the working relationship, while it is a good deal more illuminating than anything in the legal provisions, does not tell us how far the Bank's advice is heeded and how far others in the Treasury or elsewhere have their way. Nor can we tell how far there are disagreements or how deep the disagreements go. For that we have to rely on what leaks into the press or emerges from Parliamentary inquiries after dramatic episodes and financial crises. In Britain the monetary authorities, like other government agencies, try to present a picture of perennial unanimity which is obviously a travesty. But although a skilled financial journalist can usually form a shrewd idea of the course of the debates which rage at least as furiously inside as outside, it will only be after the public records are thrown open that we shall know with any certainty how successful the Bank was in tendering advice to the Government and what that advice was. What we do know is that no Governor has ever resigned and no Chancellor has ever issued a directive. It can also be said that the Government has never ceased to attach considerable weight to the views expressed by the Governor (except perhaps on the matter of public expenditure) and that the Bank now enjoys far more opportunities of developing its views of the economic situation in public (although not perhaps its policy recommendations) than ten or twenty years ago.

3 Conclusion

Every monetary system has its own peculiarities, often the product of historical accident or of some special feature of the economic system into which it has to fit. The Bank of England from the start had close associations with government and its ascendancy over the banking system rested heavily on the privileges it enjoyed for the first century and a half of its existence. When Bagehot wrote in the 1870's the Bank still regarded itself as a bank like other banks, although with a different kind of client, and only gradually awoke to the responsibilities of central banking. The government framed the law within which it operated but left it free to operate so long as it complied with the law (or, in extremity, suspended the law). To Parliament and the public these operations were for the most part wrapped in mystery.

With the emergence of a managed economy it was felt that the Bank's functions were too important to allow of such freedom. Monetary policy became subservient to other aims of policy or alternatively itself came to be regarded as fundamental to economic policy. Either way, the government was unwilling to leave the Bank with full discretion. Latterly it sought to establish a new *modus vivendi* through monetary targets that combined a government-imposed objective with tactical freedom for the Bank in its pursuit. Monetary targets, however, have to run the gauntlet of domestic wage-push and international interest-rate pressure, over neither of which the Bank has much purchase; and even governments are liable, with experience, to become less single-minded in their emphasis on monetary objectives. The usual situation tends to recur in which more is asked of the Bank than it feels it can deliver.

This situation exists elsewhere too. But the peculiarity of British arrangements is that policy-making is highly centralised while its implementation relies heavily on informal understandings. London is at once the political, industrial and financial capital and those who exercise authority in their different spheres live and work in close physical proximity to one another. Within the political system the Cabinet enjoys an extraordinary authority that in ordinary times is not much limited by the need for Parliamentary support. The Treasury dominates the civil service as in few other countries. The Bank of England occupies an equally dominant position in the City. The tradition is for the government to speak with one voice; and although disagreements now overflow increasingly into the press, there are strong pressures to compose differences in front of the public.

The record suggests that when there has been disagreement over monetary policy, the Bank of England and the Treasury are, as likely as not, on the same side of the argument. This may be true even of the Chancellor and the Governor. The Prime Minister has the last word and Prime Ministers usually have strong views which they do not lightly abandon. They are no more likely to give way to a Governor than a Chancellor and have on occasion overridden both. Nor is it easy to see why as a matter of principle Governors of Central Banks should be put in a position to defy Prime Ministers. The Chiefs of the Defence Services would not claim as much and in Britain Governors have long ceased to do so. Where the issue is one of principle – for example, does an effort to control inflation take precedence over an effort to expand employment? – it is for the public or their elected representatives to decide. Where it is one of technique the Governor should be free to speak out even if this shows him to be at odds with the government. The really difficult situation is where what one party thinks is a technical issue is for the other an issue of principle: as, for example, when the Government regards the level of public expenditure as exclusively its affair while the Governor regards it as the source of all the trouble.

The British experience has been that there is no alternative to a close working relationship with each preserving its independence of judgment but with responsibility for major decisions resting inevitably on the government of the day.

References

Bank of England (1980): The Relationship between the Bank of England and the Treasury, *Memoranda on Monetary Policy,* Treasury and Civil Service Committee of the House of Commons, Session 1979–80, H. C. Paper 720.
Cabinet Minutes (1955): February 22.
Cairncross, A. (1985): *Years of Recovery,* London: Methuen.
Cairncross, A. and B. Eichengreen (1983): *Sterling in Decline,* Oxford: Basil Blackwell.
De Cecco, M. (1974): *Money and Empire,* Oxford: Blackwell.
Dow, JCR (1964): *The Management of the British Economy 1945–60,* Cambridge: Cambridge University Press, for National Institute of Economic and Social Research.
Gregory, (Sir) T. E. (1955): *The Present Position of Central Banks,* London: University of London, The Athlone Press.
House of Commons Debates (1945a), vol. 415, col 45, October 29.
House of Commons Debates (1945b), vol. 417, col 983, December 17.
Kisch, C. H. and W. A. Elkin (1932): *Central Banks,* London: Macmillan, 4th edition.
Radcliffe Report (1959), see Report on the Working of the Monetary System.
Rees, H. Ellis (1962): *The Convertibility Crisis of 1947,* in PRO T 267/3 (unpublished).
Reid, M. (1982): *The Secondary Banking Crisis 1973–75,* London: Macmillan.
Report of the Committee to Review the Functioning of Financial Institutions (1980), London HMSO Cmnd 7937.
Report on the Working of the Monetary System (1959), London HMSO Cmnd 827.
Sayers, R. S. (1936): *Bank of England Operations 1890–1914,* London: P. S. King and Son.
Sayers, R. S. (1957): *Central Banking after Bagehot,* Oxford: Clarendon Press.
Sayers, R. S. (1958): *Modern Banking,* Oxford: Clarendon Press, 4th edition.
Sayers, R. S. (1976): *The Bank of England 1891–1944,* Cambridge: Cambridge University Press.
Wilson Committee (1980), see Report of the Committee to Review the Functioning of Financial Institution.

Chapter 4
The Banque de France and the State from 1850 to the Present Day*

Jean Bouvier

1 The Problems of Being a Historian

In July 1936, with Léon Blum at the head of the government, the State took exclusive control of the Banque de France, thus, in effect, nationalising it. Nine years later, during the government of General de Gaulle, the Banque was formally nationalised by the law of December 2nd, 1945.

At first sight the period from 1936 to 1945 would seem to represent a decisive break. Prior to 1936 the bank of issue, at the head of which private interests were very well represented, enjoyed, in theory at least, a certain freedom of manoeuvre vis-à-vis the Ministry of Finance and the government. After 1945 the "Banque", as it was commonly known, became, or was forced to become, an annex of the "Rue de Rivoli", where the Ministry had its main offices.

But let us now have a close look at the very difficult problems facing the historian and that he finds himself ill-equipped to solve. Did the nationalisation of the bank of issue mean total submission to the State as early as the second half of 1936? Was the Banque no longer "independent", no longer even "autonomous"? Did the Banque de France become merely an appendage of the Treasury, and is this still the case? Have the Governors been the mere executors of a monetary (and economic) policy decided at the Rue de Rivoli for the past fifty years? And nothing more? Does the Banque carry any real, autonomous weight in the taking of important monetary decisions? Is the Banque still capable of using its "droit de remontrances"? Have matters "economic" and matters "political" finally come to dominate matters "monetary"?

---

* Translated by Rosalind Greenstein.

If the historian recognises that he is somewhat helpless in the face of such questions it is because of the very demands and exigencies of his craft. Ever since the mid-1950s the historian has advanced with great difficulty, as the tools of his trade are singularly lacking. The historian is the only one to "go down the pits", to work only on "raw materials", that is to say to work on oral and written *archives;* Archives that are *internal* to the State, to the firms, the families. That is his territory, those are his rules. But when he wants to study the relations between the Banque de France and the State since the mid-1950s he finds that he cannot use the archives of the Ministry of Finance, nor can he work in those of the Banque de France, for the law does not allow him to do so. All that remains is repeat – badly – what jurists or economists or even certain talented journalists have written. These writings are, of course, sound and useful pieces of work. As an example let me quote *L'Histoire de la Banque de France et de la monnaie sous la IV° République,* an excellent book by Henri Koch (1983), who made a brilliant career at the central bank and was in charge of the *Service des Etudes* from 1967 to 1973. So, for the long period leading up to the 1950s, I shall base my essay on the writings of historians who had the State archives and the archives of the Banque at their disposal. I shall also use the *Souvenirs* of Moreau and the few rare memoirs of certain "decision makers" of the 19th and 20th centuries. These works cover certain periods of the one hundred years from 1845 to 1945: the Second Empire, the field of Alain Plessis' work (Plessis 1982, 1983, 1985a); several episodes relative to the birth of the *Crédit Agricole,* dealt with by André Gueslin (1978); relations between the State and the Banque de France between the two wars, studied in the works of Jean-Noël Jeanneney (1976)[1]; current research by J. C. Debeir (1980) and some personal publications[2]; finally the studies carried out by Claire Andrieu on the Banking Act of June 1941, the bank nationalisations of 1945 and some aspects of monetary policy since 1945 (Andrieu 1981, 1984). In addition, M. Lévy-Leboyer and myself have followed the subsequent developments concerning banks in volumes 3 and 4 of *Histoire économique et sociale de la France* (Braudel/ Labrousse 1976–82).

---

[1] His doctoral thesis (Jeanneney 1976) was followed by an analytical work (Jeanneney 1977).
[2] In particular Bouvier (1973); my "Presentazione" (Bouvier 1986). Also two papers on the policy of the Banque de France between the two world wars (Bouvier 1982, 1984).

2 The Manifold and Complex Factors that Determine Relations Between the State and the Banque de France

In France the relations between the authorities and the bank of issue throughout the 19th and 20th centuries have been a combination of deep complicity and a basic *long-term* consensus over monetary strategy. "Defence" of the franc, protection of its "worth", "stability", in other words the control and slowing down of currency circulation; are all values and procedures that define the relation between the State and the Banque as one of solidarity. But at the same time, in the *short term,* relations between the two are fraught with tension, disagreements, and occasional crises. The tensions and disagreements are hidden and only come to light through the study of the internal archives of the Banque de France and the Treasury. The crises, on the other hand, are visible and shake public opinion. The most famous crisis was that of summer 1936, at the time of the *de facto* nationalisation (or so-called "reform") of the Banque during the Popular Front. It is when these short-term episodes occur that, like a guiding thread over the years, the theme of the "independence" or "autonomy" of the Banque de France appears, the two words being used indifferently[3] despite slight differences in meaning.

The causes of these episodes are many and various and of differing importance. They include the institutional ties between State and Bank; the respective decision-making powers of the bank of issue and the Ministry of Finance concerning monetary matters; the internal power structure of the Banque de France itself where, at least up to June 1936, could be found both representatives of the government and representatives of the private economy. The latter, who had a dominating position on the *Conseil de Régence,* were the most powerful private bankers of the Parisian *"Haute Banque"*[4]. The tensions and crises are also a result of the normal conflicts of tradition and logic of the different "organisations": the Treasury and the Ministry of Finance on the one hand, the machine of the Banque de France on the other. It is a well-known fact that in the history of the "machinery" of the State there has always been a chronic "covert" or "overt" war between the different administrative authorities. Each one wants to extend its own authority and put

---

[3] We can see this in "Central Bank Independence", the study by Banaian/Laney and Willet (1983).

[4] The big commercial banks (deposit bank, "banques d'affaires") were only rarely represented on the *Conseil de Régence*. This is a problem in itself. During the 19th century the same thing occurred at the Bank of England.

its own people in the right places. But more important still, is the chronic opposition that has appeared between the preoccupations of the public authorities, who claim they are the natural defenders of the most general interests of the economy as a whole, and the reflexes of the bank of issue which reasons systematically and first and foremost in monetarist terms. This is what Alfred Sauvy has called "the conflict between money and business", a conflict which, if we think about it, is always latent. Alain Plessis has given us a good illustration of how this worked at certain moments of the Second Empire, for example when the government wanted to boost the economy and so forced the Banque de France to lower the rate of discount, something that the Banque was reluctant to do as a lower rate would probably inflate the issue of banknotes and, in addition, threaten the profits of the Banque. To add spice to the discussions between State and Banque the former wanted to increase taxes on the profits of the Banque, while the latter, on the contrary, objected to the encroachment of the central authorities precisely in this matter. Up to 1936, every time the exclusive right to issue notes came up for renewal (1840, 1857, 1897, 1920, 1928), discussions were heated, but it was the State that had the last word. Since relations between institutions and bodies are always an expression of the relations between individuals, the historian is hardly surprised at the importance of the character and behaviour of these individuals when trying to understand the relations between the Banque and the State. The personality of such and such Minister of Finance, of such and such Governor of the Banque, of this Director of the Treasury, of that *Régent,* how well they understand each other and the esteem they may or may not have for each other must all be taken into consideration. We only have to read the *Souvenirs* of Emile Moreau (1926–1928) to see how the clash of personalities between the Governor and Poincaré, President of the Council and Minister of Finance, sometimes blew up and fueled the differences of opinion over monetary matters.

There remains a purely political element which may show more clearly the diversity of the reasons I have just given and which, when added to them, makes them all the more dramatic. I am referring to two periods in the interwar years when the "left" was in power: 1924, with the *"Cartel"* and 1936, with the *Popular Front*[5]. At such moments the theme of the "independence" of the bank of issue became its duty, a sort of moral duty, to stand up to the State in the name of the "defence of the home currency". The word independence suddenly reappeared, as a truly political weapon, and was used

---

[5] The *Cartel des Gauches* (1924–1926): radical governments with socialist support. The *Popular Front* (1936–1937): socialist and radical government with communist support.

against the new trends in the economic and social policies of the radical government of spring 1924 to summer 1926 and the socialist and radical government of spring 1936. These governments were forced by the economic, social and political situation to increase public spending and to introduce reforms. They were criticised for spending too much, for not caring enough about a "healthy franc". A spirit of revolt, an anti-government opposition even, began to form within the Banque, especially when the Governor and the principal *Régents* were in perfect agreement (1924 to summer 1926 under Governor Robineau). The spirit of revolt easily gained momentum and support in right-wing political circles, in newspapers and economic reviews and in the employers' organisations. The banner of the "independence" of the Banque de France was planted firmly right in the centre of the social-political battlefield. The monetary stake, which was only too real, was no longer a cause but a pretext. It is just such a situation that, from the left-wing point of view, justified the State taking over exclusive control of the Banque in 1936 and 1945.

Hence a remark only a historian would make: it would be difficult to build a "model", with permanent parameters and links, of the relations between the State and the bank of issue. Alain Plessis has shown that, as early as 1850–1870, "the balance of power" between the different authorities at the head of the Banque "was not stable" (Plessis 1980: 1104). Against the permanent and "objective" backdrop of a fundamental common interest (the "defence of the franc"), different successive situations have occurred, the various determining factors changing in size, shape and importance. Let us now have a look at some of them.

3 New Developments from 1850 to 1936

3.1 The Development of State Control in the 19th Century

The Banque de France is a hermaphrodite: a private company whose *Conseil de Régence* is the seat of two branches of power; on the one hand the Governor, a top civil servant appointed by the Ministry of Finance (aided by two Deputy Governors) and on the other hand twelve *Régents,* nine of whom are elected by the two hundred biggest shareholders from among the *"Haute Banque"* and international trade (heavy industry is under-represented). The remaining three *Régents* are regional civil servants of the Ministry of Finance. The Banque obeys both the "logic of the private sector" (Plessis 1982: 46) and that of a "public service". Its ultimate goal is that of the general interest. It is at the service of the State and the economy. It is directed, said Alphonse de Rothschild on February 2nd, 1865, by "two distinct elements" (Plessis 1982: 46), one of which is "the representative of the government and the State" (Plessis 1982: 50) and the other that "of the shareholders and commercial interests." There is, therefore, "a combined action of the *Régents* and the Governor", according to an unofficial text of 1854 (Plessis 1982: 50) in the case of disagreement the only possible appeal is, in fact, to the Ministry of Finance. This disequilibrium in favour of the State was reinforced by the fact that the regulations allowed the Governor to easily obtain the absolute majority in the Conseil and also gave him the right to veto their decisions. "He has the real executive power" wrote Alain Plessis. "... His mission is to have control over each and every act of the Banque de France... in the name of the higher general interests of the State" (Plessis 1982: 49). When the government and the *Régents* reach a consensus, the internal functioning of the Banque is harmonious[6]. The basic consensus is that the two powers see the Banque as "the stronghold of monetary stability... the defender of savers and a guarantee of order" (Plessis 1982: 63). That is the real underlying meaning of the Gold (and Silver) Standard.

In the case of disagreement the tensions immediately appear within the *Conseil*. The chronic source of disagreement since the 1850s has been to decide which should be put first, "the economy" or the "currency". For a dilemma has existed and still does exist, *in fact*, regardless of the *theoretical* solutions that have been proposed over the years. In the 19th century all the banks of issue (with that of England in the lead) "willingly hid behind an attitude of reserve, even of strain, whenever there was the likelihood of extending credit facilities or increasing the number of banknotes in circulation" (Plessis 1982: 60). The favourite words of Governor Rouland during the 1865 "Enquête" into "monetary and fiduciary circulation", relative to the discount on trade bills and advances on securities operated by the Banque de France were: "great caution", "moderation", "constraint" (Bouvier 1973: 87 and 90). And Alphonse de Rothschild agreed: "We must take all possible precaution as far as credit is concerned"[7], since confidence in banknotes is only a matter of "moderation" (Bouvier 1973: 87 and 90 in the number issued. All things being unequal, are we that far away from the 20th century

---

[6] On February 2, 1865 Governor Rouland mentioned "the perfect harmony of outlook and doctrine" of the two powers (Plessis 1982: 51).

[7] Quoted by Jean Bouvier (1973: 87 and 90).

debates on monetary policy, the century of unconvertible notes, "bank money" and inflation[8].

From time to time in the 19th century, in certain economic and political circumstances, the government wanted to "boost" the economy by lowering the Banque de France rate of discount. It would occasionally come up against the opposition of the *Régents and* the Governor together or just the *Régents* alone. If at this point the State was politically strong and stable, it would force its monetary strategy on the Banque and make it lower "the price of money". This was the case in 1852–53, at the beginning of the Second Empire. Alain Plessis has studied this aspect of the relations between Napoleon III's government and the Banque de France very carefully (Plessis 1982: Vol 3). We see a bank of issue, which was far from enjoying permanent independence, vis-à-vis a government that was determined to accelerate growth by more dynamic credit. As the *Régents* did not always agree among themselves: the top industrialists, beginning with Eugène Schneider, supported the government policy of a lower bank rate, while the *Régent*-bankers rejected this idea. So, within the *Conseil de Régence,* the State was able to find some allies among the representatives of certain economic circles.

In the (unpublished) presentation of his thesis (Plessis 1980: 7) Alain Plessis says of the period from 1852 to 1870:

it is surprising to note, in a so-called liberal period, just how much the Banque de France, a private undertaking which was fiercely proud of what it thought of as its *independence,* was subject to frequent intervention amounting to a constant control, on the part of the Ministry of Finance in particular and the public authorities in general.

The opposition between a "liberal" 19th century and a 20th century with State controlled monetary policy "is not so clear cut as has been said" (Plessis 1980: 1526). Under the Second Empire (and at least up to 1936 and even later) the bank of issue was a place of potential confrontation between the State, the management of the Banque and the principal banking and industrial interests (the latter sometimes disagreeing among themselves). To this must be added the weight of public opinion through, for example, the positions of the Chambers of Commerce, who were in favour of a low rate of discount. It is, of course, true that the government received constant financial help from the Banque, in different forms. In the 19th and 20th centuries the Banque has garanted more short and long-term loans more often to the state than to the economy. The Banque "is the biggest holder of State rentes

---

[8] In the conclusion of his work, Henri Koch (1983: 370) wrote, "At first sight the franc seems to have been sacrificed to expansion, matters monetary to matters economic".

in the country" (Plessis 1980: 1525)[9]. When the State is in financial difficulty the Banque intervenes to an enormous extent. In 1862 there was even a time when half the banknotes in circulation were loaned to the government! But the State imposed its requests for help. In the 20th century the same thing has happened often. The State has its own reasons: financial problems, cash flow problems, problems of global economic policy. When the government lowers the bank rate, or stops it from rising too fast, the goal is to affect the distribution of credit. But it is also a way for the State to sell Treasury bonds more cheaply to the Banque and the big commercial banks. On the other side the motives of those *Régents* who represent private interests[10] formed a real "tangled web" (Plessis 1980: 1531). The *Régents* were in favour of high bank rates, which were a source of high profits for the Banque, because they were *also* the largest shareholders. But at the same time they had to be sure not to forget the industrial and trade circles who were so quick to criticise the Banque. On top of this each *Régent* had to bear in mind the interests of his own company, bank or industry. Some of them, Eugène Schneider under the Second Empire, for instance, had also to take their political connections with the régime into account[11]. Finally, if we wish to understand the position of a *Régent* in a given situation, we must study the "subjective elements" (Plessis 1980: 1531), i.e. interpersonal relationships.

The formula used by Faucher in his article in the *Revue des Deux Mondes* of December 15th, 1853 could be usefully applied to the century-old long-term situation: "The Banque de France has been a victim of, rather than a moving force behind, the different advances and reforms." From 1852 to 1914 it was as a result of pressure put on it by the State that the Banque increased the number of its branches; that *all* the decreases in the rate of discount were decided; that the Banque was obliged, from March 1852 on, to accept new securities to guarantee its advances, beginning with the railway bonds (help in the financing of investments in the railways); that, from 1858 to 1861, it sold these bonds directly, even though this was strictly illegal; that, in 1867, it helped (though much against its will) the *Crédit Mobilier* of the Péreire brothers, and then in 1889 saved the *Comptoir d'Escompte de Paris* from bankruptcy; that, in 1897, despite the fact that it ran very much against the grain, it opened a system of permanent advances to the official *"Caisses"*

---

[9] The Banque still holds State rentes.
[10] Nine out of twelve ortwelve out of fifteen, if we count the three *censeurs*, who do not take part in the vote and who act as auditors *(commissaires aux comptes)*.
[11] Eugène Schneider was president of the *Corp Législatif* at the time. James de Rothschild, an "Orleanist" at heart, accepted the new imperial régime out of simple realism.

of the new *Crédit Agricole*[12]. In times of great moment it was the State that decided. Thus, in October 1856, when the *Régents* were split as to whether or not to suspend gold payments during a period of monetary crisis and panic (collapse of the bullion reserve), it was the Government which forced the Banque to maintain convertibility. So sometimes the State puts pressure on the Banque within the frame of legal texts (the statutes of the Banque, decrees, laws authorising the renewal of the exclusive right to issue notes): in particular the governments extend their power each time this right comes up for renewal. At other times the State imposes its point of view less formally, through personal contacts, meetings between men from the Ministry of Finance, the governing body of the Banque and the main *Régents*. We can find countless examples of this in the *Souvenirs* of Emile Moreau, where all the internal mechanisms of the 19th century were still functioning well in the period from 1926 to 1928.

We can therefore say that, well before 1914, the Banque de France was not *independent* in the strict sense of the word. But it had a certain changing margin of *autonomy* and thus of influence, especially with some of the most powerful *Régents* whose views the Governors could not ignore in the case of disagreement, and with whom persuasion and compromise were often necessary. It also had to be remembered that the *Régents* could find allies among the top civil servants of the Ministry of Finance. It was, indeed, exceptional to see a Governor clash directly with the most powerful *Régents* and force them to comply without taking their opinions into account. This could only happen under exceptional circumstances, with a Governor of exceptional character: this was the case with Emile Moreau, who stood up to François de Wendel and Edouard de Rothschild from 1926 to 1928. If the Governor was relatively unassuming or malleable (like Rouland at the end of the Second Empire or Robineau from 1920 to 1926) he could become the *Régents* man and thumb his nose at the Minister of Finance himself as did Robineau to Joseph Caillaux during the summer and autumn of 1925. But the autonomy of the Banque could also be exercised under very different conditions. For instance, in the throes of a general recession, the *Régents* and Governor could impose their points of view on the government, as in spring 1848, when they increased direct taxes by 45% (a very rare case, however). Or, during a period of economic growth and good relations with the State, an able Governor such as Pallain (1900 to 1914) could promote a new strategy. In the case in point the *Régents* were deprived of all initiative and it was the

---

[12] A new *mutualiste* banking network set up under the auspices of the State.

governing body of the Banque with the support of their own top civil servants who promoted the extension of "direct discounting" for traders and industrialists, a strategy that was to last until the second world war, to the detriment of private local bankers in the main, but also of some regional banks[13]. Thus the Banque became more and more both the "bank of banks" and, at the same time, an ordinary commercial bank, its goal being to increase its profits.

However, it was during the inter-war period that the Banque de France was able to bring its powers of influence and opposition into full play and to show its "independence" under a left wing government.

3.2 The Ups and Downs of the Period 1920 to 1936

I have already referred, in the preceeding pages, to the post first world war period, and hinted that the changes in the relations between the Banque de France and the State during the 20th century, since the decade from 1936 to 1945, have not really marked a radical departure from the past, from the 19th century. As Alain Plessis so rightly put it, this decade

> does not mark a radical break... as if the Banque de France were only then becoming the State bank... From the points of view of money and credit there had not been any true liberalism during the Second Empire (Plessis 1983: 97).

On this level the 1920s are no doubt a continuation of the situation prevailing before 1914. The *Souvenirs* of Emile Moreau (an exceptional document) and also the thesis on François de Wendel by Jean-Noël Jeanneney very clearly illustrate the theme that is of interest to us here, in particular for the two-year period from June 1926 to June 1928. But this is neither the time nor the place to go into this period in detail[14]. The real change, as far as the state of the economy and the currency were concerned, was in the appearance of an obvious contrast between, on the one hand, the preservation of the 19th century structures and institutional forms of the central monetary decision-making body, shared between the State and the Banque de France (a private company) and, on the other hand, the unexpected and lasting monetary innovations of the 20th century: inflation, budget deficits, monetary speculation, "hot money" and devaluations. The contrast is therefore between old unchanged institutions and new problems. However, on the political side the

---

[13] Alain Plessis (1985b), paper presented at the 5th Congress of the *Association française des historiens économistes,* Paris, June 1983.

[14] See my "Presentazione" (Bouvier 1986).

gradual consolidation first of the radical and socialist "left", then of the socialist and communist left, between the two wars, led to a serious social fear in business circles and the middle classes, when the left was in power: 1924–1926 and 1935–1938.

It was in just such a general context that before the summer of 1936 the Banque de France was able to become more *autonomous* vis-à-vis the State. I say *autonomous* deliberately, rather than *independent*. The Banque saw itself as a breakwater, resisting the tide of innovations (both monetary and social); it saw itself as the guardian of "traditions" and an underlying economic and social equilibrium, linked to the logic of the "gold franc". As the successive governments from 1919 to 1926 (right wing from 1919 to the spring of 1924, then the left wing "Cartel" from 1924 to the summer of 1926) staggered from deficit to deficit while, at the same time, the franc continued inexorably on its downward slide on the exchange market, the Banque de France rediscovered its influence over the State, through its ever-increasing and varied help to the Treasury. Every year up to 1926, and sometimes several times in one year, the mechanism of "indirect advances" from the Banque to the State came into play: the Banque made massive credits available to the big commercial banks (the "exceptional discounts"), so that they could buy huge quantities of government stocks (Treasury rentes, bonds and debentures). In this situation the Banque, as the creditor that has come to the rescue, was able to influence State budgetary, financial, monetary and economic policies. And it took full advantage of this, both under the right and under the *"Cartel"*, with a change at the end of July 1926, when Poincaré came to power as President of the Council and Minister of Finance. Before this date the Banque de France had formed a solid block, since there was total agreement between Governor Robineau and the majority of the *Conseil de Régence,* which was dominated by Edouard de Rothschild and François de Wendel. The *Revue des Deux Mondes* stated very clearly, as early as February 1921, that Robineau had started to use the *droit de remontrances* against the government again, with the "solid support of the *Conseil de Régence*"[15] in order to exert pressure in favour of an open deflationary policy (of the budget, of prices, of incomes). He maintained this position right up to 1936. After July 1926, with the strategy remaining unchanged, the distribution of powers was modified (State, Governor, *Régents*) by the arrival of Emile Moreau at the Banque, after Joseph Caillaux had at last dared to dismiss Robineau and at the very moment that Poincaré's "national union" government brought two

---

[15] Pierre Darlu's page.

years of "cartellist" policy to an end. The situation was difficult for the new Governor right from the outset as, for the previous ten years[16], nothing less than hatred had separated Poincaré and Caillaux. Moreau, who was a friend of the latter and had been appointed by him, would find it hard to be accepted by the former, who was even reluctant to keep him on at the head of the Banque.

I will not go into an explanation or a chronological review of the monetary policy from 1926 to 1928, except to say that the ruling classes, the politicians, the State and the Banque de France were, during this period, divided into two camps: "revaluers" and "stabilisers". The latter were simply realistic proponents of the stabilization at the exchange rate since January 1927. Governor Moreau became more and more in favour of stabilisation – devaluation. Poincaré agreed to it, against his will, at the last moment, when it became absolutely necessary in June 1928, but not before the Governor had put much pressure on him. When, on June 8, 1928, Poincaré made it known to the Governor that he would resign and leave his successor with the task of devaluing the franc, Moreau, unruffled, sent the ball back into his court and wrote in his diary on June 9: "Mr Poincaré is trying to intimidate me or to deceive me ... I have replied that I would regret his resolve, and that I would stabilise the franc with his successor" (Moreau 1926–28: 582). That is "independence" of the Banque.

At any rate, "independence" is the constant concern of the Governor, first of all vis-à-vis the big credit houses to which the bank of issue was linked by a double relationship of collaboration and of competition (the extension of "direct discounting" by the Banque between the two world wars). On October 18, 1926 Moreau said: "The big credit houses claim to be on an equal footing with us. This is yet something else that must be changed." But, above all, vis-à-vis the State, that is to say all governments, and vis-à-vis the *Régents*. To the commission of enquiry that had been set up to look into the Oustric banking scandal in 1930 Moreau declared: "I have always told Ministers: you have but one right, that of firing me; you have no other." Deep down Emile Moreau did not see himself as an ordinary top civil servant. By the very fact of being put at the head of the Banque he espoused its business logic, while at the same time automatically taking on its duties and traditions: in a way he was the official defender of the franc. In the sharing out of monetary power with the State he did not want to give an inch. He saw it as

---

[16] The deep disagreement dates back to the war, because of the "pacifism" of Caillaux, who was arrested in January 1918, when Poincaré was President of the Republic, and found guilty in April 1920 by the *Haute Cour*.

his constant duty, as the imperative of his position. It was to be the same, throughout the 20th century and right up to the present day, for all the Governors (even more so when they had strong personalities), both before and after the period from 1936 to 1945. *This is a permanent situation, regardless of whether the bank of issue is nationalised or not.* This is the great, two centuries old continuity of the position and the "discourse" of the Banque. This is the permanent propensity of the great governors, who can find support against the government, or the Minister of Finance, or certain *Régents*, if necessary, depending on the circumstances. They get this support from top Treasury civil servants, from important employers and employers' organisations, from some members of parliament, from the press, too. Moreau, for example, often secretly paid economics reporters and politicians to write for him, when asked. He even went so far as to provide the outline of the articles[17]. In 1934–35 a very brilliant young lawyer, with a great political career ahead of him, lectured various audiences in defense of the orthodox monetary position of the Banque against the devaluationist theses of Paul Reynaud[18].

As early as the summer of 1926 Moreau tried, in vain, to get Poincaré to guarantee his position for a fixed number of years. It is interesting to note that he did this on the insistant advice of Strong (Federal Reserve Bank of New York) and Norman (Bank of England), with whom he was dealing in July–August 1926, and who went so far as to propose modifications to the statutes of the Banque to support this. We can easily guess their ulterior motives. But, on this point at least, there was a complicity between the heads of the big central banks; it was one of the signs of the developing power and desire for power of the "technocrats".

On November 22, 1926 Moreau wrote about the head of the Treasury, Clément Moret[19]: "The Ministry of Finance must get out of the habit of considering the Banque de France as one of its branches." And on February 22nd 1927: "One of the most important aspects of the role of Governor is to fight against the overt or covert attempts of the State to take over the rights

---

[17] See December 7, 1927 and June 8, 1928 of the *Souvenirs* for some examples. Emile Moreau even received the spontaneous, unsolicited support of Léon Jouhaux (CGT, reformist) in October 1926. He does not mention it in his *Souvenirs,* and the information was provided by Jacques Rueff after 1945.

[18] Information given by Marcel Netter in the typewritten *Histoire de la Banque de France dans l'entre – deux – guerres*. This book, which was written in the 1970s by a former director of the *Services des Etudes* of the Banque, has never been published. The copy in may possession was given to me by the author shortly before he died.

[19] Between the two wars this department was still called the "Mouvement général des fonds".

and prerogatives of the Banque de France." Moreau, in June 1928, did not hesitate to engage in a kind of "trial of strength" with Poincaré. Nor, on July 26, 1926, with the Treasury in an acute state of crisis and the franc collapsing (sterling stood at 243 francs) had he hesitated to push the *"Cartel"* government of Herriot and de Monzie (Minister of Finance) into resigning. On the 20th July he had warned the latter that he would "cut off all credit from the Treasury as soon as their account (with the Banque) were empty, that is to say probably tomorrow evening" (Moreau 1926–28: July 20th 1926), if the Government did not take emergency financial measures. On July 22, the Government resigned. On the 23, Poincaré returned to power. The Governor had therefore played his part in the downfall of the left wing *Cartel,* even though he had been made Governor on June 26 by Joseph Caillaux, Minister of the *Cartel.* In doing so his only objective was to *sound* finance. The powers of the Governor have always been inversely proportional to the political solidity of the government of the day.

Thus, in the 1920s, the Banque was really able to measure its powers of influence, in very different and opposing political contexts: 1920–1924, 1924–1926, 1926–1928. We do not have the time or space here to analyse this any further. But we can just relate one more fact to illustrate our point. In September 1931 the centre right government asked the Banque to prepare a contract similar to that of November 1911, which provided for the granting of an exceptional immediate advance to the Treasury, if war were declared. In December 1931 the Banque refused and the matter stopped there. The Governor of the time was Clément Moret, former head of the Treasury, who had replaced Emile Moreau in September 1930. Why such a snub? According to M. Netter, the Banque wanted first and foremost to "demonstrate its power"[20].

Having seen what happened during the 1920s we can better understand the reform of the Banque de France in July 1936. The causes, form and limitations of the reform are fairly well known[21]. So are the ambiguities. The reform was mainly a political one and so the opportunity was lost, (not to arise againuntil 1945), to consider the relationship between the Banque and the banks, between the Banque and the economy, as a whole. The "credit policy" that was demanded in 1935–1936 by some (reformist) socialists and trade unionists of the banking sector was hardly mentioned. Of course, the government struck while the iron was hot and the reform was introduced

---

[20] Quoted by Marcel Netter (1972).
[21] For a condensed presentation see Bouvier (1973: 178–92).

while the right was temporarily excluded from government. The reform had not been prepared within the Banque but by an informal extra-parliamentary commission working only with the Minister of Finance, Vincent Auriol. It was a question of removing the representatives of big private interests from the Board of the Banque. Hence the abolition of the *Régents* and the new composition of the *"Conseil Général"*, whereby the State apparently had full control of the management of the bank of issue. The shareholders remained, but with even less influence than before, if that is possible, at least as far as the 20th century is concerned[22]. The new Governor, de Labeyrie, who had come from the *Cour des Comptes,* would be despised, throughout the rest of his life, by the right and by a large number of important businessmen, for having agreed to head a Banque that had been mutilated by the Popular Front. Yet in 1936–1937 Vincent Auriol always kept excellent relations with top Treasury civil servants, like Jacques Rueff, kept of the Treasury in the autumn of 1936, or Wilfrid Baumgartner, his predecessor.

4 Change and Continuity from 1936 to the 1980s

4.1 1936–1944

Without doubt it is since 1936 that, *in the eyes of the historian,* the relations between the Banque de France and the State have become less and less clear. The historian is no longer sure of anything, neither of official texts and statements, nor of the work of economists and lawyers concerning the central bank. This is not because of ignorance of details or of events, but because, I must repeat, of the growing lack of investigative tools, so that it is no longer possible to compare published texts and internal documents (of the State and the Banque de France). In part four of this paper, therefore, my analysis is at times somewhat hazy and uncertain.

From September 1940 to June 1941 the argument was not between the Banque de France and the Government of Vichy, but between the Banque and the Chairmen of the big deposit banks, concerning the preparation of the important Bank Act of June 1941, the main provisions of which were to be

---

[22] Alain Plessis shows us that during the Second Empire the Annual General Meeting of the two hundred biggest shareholders could more or less gracefully accept the appointment of such and such new agent. Alphonse de Rothschild was elected with difficulty, because of the latent antisemitism of this most traditionalistic of groups.

preserved after the Liberation. According to Claire Andrieu, who had access to the archives of the Banque (Andrieu 1983), "the government partly took into account" (Andrieu 1983: 17) the observations of the bank of issue. The latter defended "a certain liberalism and a certain economic interventionism, provided it was a semi-state interventionism, not a corporative one."

The two protagonists in the debate were the Banque de France and the *Comité provisoire d'organisation professionnelle des banques* (summer 1940), dominated by the big deposit banks and presided over by Henri Àrdant, "boss" of the *Société Générale,* who was to be president, from June 1941 to September 1944, of the *Comité d'organisation des banques*[23]. Henri Ardant and his group wanted gradually to privatise the public and para-public banking sector (*Crédit Agricole, Crédit National,* etc.) and to hand over to the *Comité d'organisation* alone, i.e. to the "profession" or, in other words, the big credit houses, the control of the commercial banks, to the exclusion of the Banque de France. The *Service des Etudes* of the Banque bitterly opposed this total corporative interventionism and for many months proposed its own brand of "semi-state interventionism" (Claire Andrieu). One of its memoranda, dated October 10, 1940, asserted that if the Ardant project were followed, "it would be difficult to defend the general interests of the nation" and that there was a "risk of giving the banks the means whereby they could continue to do just what they liked and to impose their laws, even more so than in the past, on their less powerful competitors and their customers" (Andrieu 1983). A compromise was reached which saved the main demands of the bank of issue. But the documents available do not allow us to see what the attitude of the Governor of the Banque was, caught between his Minister (Bouthillier) and the Ardant group. At any rate, the episode shows the ability of the Banque to defend itself against and to counter-attack certain big private interests.

4.2 1945–1986

4.2.1 Continuity of Mechanisms, Logic, and Behaviour

a) Testimonies

The continuity is fundamental since it is an integral part of the relations between monetary constraints, the imperatives of economic and social devel-

---

[23] Henry Ardant was imprisoned for one year after the liberation, then later cleared of all suspicion of "collaboration". Do not mix him up with his brother, Gabriel, who was a friend of Pierre Mendès-France.

opment, and political uncertainties. André Chaineau, the economist, made a classical statement in 1974 when he wrote:

> The Banque de France, guardian of the value of the currency, must have its own goals which, of course, must be compatible with those of the Ministry of Finance. So it must have sufficient personality to present them and get them either totally or partially accepted.

The verb "must" is to be taken here both as an imperative and as an expression of a wish. But as we all know, some wishes are mere "pious hopes". During a conference in November 1955 Governor Wilfrid Baumgartner, a man of character, had said in equally classical terms:

> In the same way as the clergyman of history was against sin, so is the Banque de France against inflation. It reacts tirelessly... On the whole the Banque de France is what it has always been... It has to defend itself against the dangers that come from the evolution of the balance of payments, or from private credit, or from the Treasury (Baumgartner 1955: 16).

This is an old attitude of suspicion, of defense, of vigilance on the part of the central bank(s).

In his precious work, *Les institutions monétaires,* published in 1967, Marcel Netter who, as we all know, made his career at the Banque, remarked that since nationalisation of the Banque de France in 1945, "no text" has provided for "any kind of State intervention in the affairs of the Banque" (Netter 1967: 28). But, he went on, "in fact the relations (between the two) are based on tradition... No important decision is taken by one or other of the two parties without prior consultation" (Netter 1967: 29). Hence the comment that "the letter of a text carries little weight. It's all a matter of climate. On this point both sides are naturally discreet" (Netter 1967: 31). In such circumstances how can one do one's job as a historian?

François Bloch-Lainé, director of the Treasury from 1947 to 1953, recognises that

> on the strength of his moral authority, the Governor should have been far more closely associated (by the Minister of Finance) with the taking of major decisions and given the wherewithal to defend the overriding interests of the currency, during the discussions that threatened it (Bloch-Lainé 1976: 114).

But the same author also declared that

> Wilfrid Baumgartner, in the traditional dialogue, embodied the monetary authority, against the economic and financial authorities and he carried, if not the same weight as that of the Minister (which would have shocked), at least sufficient weight to play a real role.

This autonomy appeared to go too far when, on the Minister's side, there was nothing. At such moments the power of the permanent top was nothing. At such moments the power of the permanent top civil servants seemed great. In fact it was excessive and consequently vain (Bloch Lainé 1976: 98).

In the conclusion of Henri Koch's *La Banque de France sous la 4ème République* (1983) the author reminds us of the point of view of the "top civil servants" of the Ministry of Finance, according to whom "the Banque de France cannot possibly have at its disposal all the information necessary to take decisions in matters of credit and money", which would justify the accusations "of censorship, of traditionalism and of ignorance of Keynes" (Koch 1983: 372) made against the Banque. But the author who, let us not forget, made his whole career in the Banque, remarked that under the Fourth Republic, "the Governor often gave his opinion in the most varied of ways... He has obviously had the impression, too often, of having gone unheard" (Koch 1983: 372).

Another witness who also took part in the decision – making process concerning monetary matters, Jean Saint-Geours, first of all a colleague of François Bloch-Lainé at the Treasury, then at the *Crédit Lyonnais*[24], wrote a thought-provoking work (Saint-Geours 1979) in which he made the following distinction: under the Fourth Republic "the position of Governor falls into line with the monetary policy of the government" (Saint-Geours 1979: 107). But "paradoxically his criticism is vigorously exercised against a different source of monetary creation: the covering of the budget deficit". This was the favourite position of Wilfrid Baumgartner, for whom, wrote Jean Saint-Geours, "the budget deficit is the principal sin of a bad government" and who, with his letter to the Minister Edgar Faure in February 1952 "slayed a young, inexperienced government" (Saint-Geours 1979: 107). But there is no paradox here: according to the classical way of looking at things, the budget deficit feeds inflation. Jean Saint-Geours thus analyses the attitude of Wilfrid Baumgartner and the historian sees, intact, the "values" defended, and exalted by the Banque de France in the 19th century:

> The Governor wanted to be the representative of a vague financial community, made up of small savers and businessmen, to whom he would appear as the guarantor of monetary reason and confidence... The action of the Governor well matched the psychological reactions of the less wealthy and wealthier propertied classes alike... Confidence: the Governors, under the Fourth Republic, clamoured the word in unison with the big industrialists and private financiers (Saint-Geours 1979: 108–109)[25].

---

[24] Francois Bloch-Lainé was Chairman of the *Crédit Lyonnais* from 1967 to 1974.
[25] This theme is very well argued in Plessis (1985c: vol. 3).

The situation did not change under the Fifth Republic. But, according to the same observer, since the sixties, with a State that is more "powerful" than before 1958, "the power of the Governor has tended to decline" (Saint-Geours 1979: 109). Jean Saint-Geours pointed out that the great cleaning up programme of the de Gaulle government at the end of 1958, with Antoine Pinay at the Ministry of Finance, had been neither provoked nor set up by the Governor, but by the head of the Treasury (Schweitzer) and Goetze (member of General de Gaulle's cabinet). Still according to the same author, the so-called "stabilisation" plan introduced in the summer of 1963 by the Minister of Finance, Valéry Giscard d'Estaing, was initiated not by Governor Brunet but by the Minister for Foreign Affairs, Couve de Murville and by Olivier Wormser, head of the "Economic and Financial Affairs" Department at the Foreign Office *(Quai d'Orsay)* and future Governor from 1969 to 1974. Both of them had been alarmed by the inflationary tensions. So that, according to Saint-Geours, "the Banque de France has limited itself to a role concerning almost exclusively technical and general matters" (Saint-Geours 1979: 110). He qualified this, however: "the action of the central bank brings into play a compensatory, even a corrective monetary power against the financial power which is political in nature" (Saint-Geours 1979: 114).

We can add here a most pertinent remark made by Jean-Yves Haberer when he was director of the Treasury (from 1982 to 1986 he was at the head of the nationalised *Banque de Paris et des Pays-Bas*). We can read in the course he gave at the *Institut d'Etudes Politiques* in Paris that:

Unlike budgetary policy, monetary policy allows us not to have to confront Parliament, not to have to confront touchy trade unions or socio-professional categories. Monetary policy therefore goes with a fairly strong degree of political and social anesthesia[26].

Monetary policy, which is a sophisticated form of State intervention in the economy, is therefore decided within very limited circles, by few people, who are connaisseurs of well broken-in, immutable arguments. This is the insufficiently well-known territory, at least as far as the historian is concerned, where the relations between the State and the Banque de France develop with the greatest discretion. This discretion is quite understandable but nevertheless remains the greatest hurdle to any kind of realistic research.

For a large number of economists, at any rate, the "monetary power" of the Banque de France in the last twenty years has become more and more

---

[26] Quoted by Francois Renard (1985) in his article on Jean-Yves Harberer.

limited[27] by the banking system (the development of the structure of M1 is ample proof) and by the circuit of the Treasury itself.

> No important decision has been taken for years at the Banque de France without the prior and absolute agreement of the Rue de Rivoli (Ministry of Finance) or under their orders, sometimes even going against the suggestions of the Service des Etudes and the top management of the Banque (Prissert 1976).

And he then went on to say: "The electorate has understood this only too well, by lobbying Mr Fourcade (at the time Minister of Finance) rather than Mr Clappier" (Prissert 1976), Governor of the Banque.

The different testimonies and comments quoted so far confirm that the relations between the State and the Banque have been based, during the Fifth Republic, on a generally more docile Banque, but that the personality of the Governor, during the two Republics, has been an important "variable". Is it possible to take certain episodes as landmarks?

b) Some Episodes

Henri Koch considers that "the task of the Banque was not made any the easier" under the Fourth Republic, because "of the general orientation of the economic and budgetary policies" (Koch 1983: 371). The reform of the Banque (1936) followed by nationalisation (December 1945)

> had been decided and passed in the perspective of a greater subordination of the Banque to the State, although no text had ever given a precise definition of the nature and degree of this subordination.

At the beginning of 1946 the socialist Minister of Finance, André Philip, in the preamble to a Bill on the new statutes of the Banque (which were to replace the statutes of 1936) had had it written that

> in order to reinforce the spirit in which this nationalisation has been decided, and also to avoid the Banque de France being tempted in the future to continue to carry out policies independently of the Government, the *Conseil Général* is to have its powers' limited to the role of the governing board of any nationalised bank (Koch 1983: 371).

The outcry was such that the Bill got no further. The myth of "independence" remained, the Banque's discourse on currency, too, as did the various patterns of relations between the State and the Banque, within a vague ambiguous sharing of the monetary decision-making power. "The delicate

---

[27] An economist Pierre Prissert (1976).

transition" (Koch 1983: 372) from the position of the Banque before 1936 to that which the new statutes of January 1973 attempted to define was a gradual one, with some ups and downs. It is these ups and downs that, for the period from 1945 to 1954, Wilfrid Baumgartner in his conference at the Université des Annales described when he said: "the periods... where a certain antagonism is apparent give the Governors an opportunity to return somewhat ironically to their past" (Baumgartner 1955: 25), that is to say to the period where they themselves were director of the Treasury, as was frequently the case even before 1936 and which meant that an Inspector of Finance could easily, during his career, move from the Treasury to the Banque. To what extent did the crossing of such an institutional frontier guarantee the influence of the Ministry of Finance over the Banque or, on the contrary, lead to a conversion of the former director of the Treasury to the internal logic of the bank of issue? In 1966 Dominique Leca was able to write that: "In certain critical circumstances the relations between the Minister and the Governor, as far as who should supervise who was concerned, were from time to time reversed" (Baumgartner 1966: 16).

Let us now have a look at some of these "circumstances". On April 6th 1945 Pierre Mendès-France gave a press conference to justify his resignation from the Ministry of the Economy. He blamed the "intolerable pressures exercised by the Banque de France" against his drastic monetary policy (partial blockage of the exchange of old banknotes for new tender, also applied to bank accounts), which policy in fact it was not possible to apply. In volume 2 of Pierre Mendès-France (1985: 149–151) there are some passages which are extremely critical of the bank of issue. But the Minister had many other enemies, and the Banque (with Emmanuel Monick as Governor since the Liberation) was in complete agreement with René Pleven, Minister of Finance.

May to December 1945 was a very trying time for the Banque de France. Those in charge, with Governor Monick at their head, were unanimous in their hostility to the nationalisation of the bank of issue, which was to be passed by Parliament on December 2. The Banque prepared its own reform bill, in which it tried to "keep up a façade" in order to avoid, as far as possible, the defavourable psychological reactions of the French" (Koch 1983: 46)[28]. The Banque would be transformed into a mixed economy company, the State holding half the capital plus one share. The Governor and Deputy-Governors would be nominated for a period of five years, which

---

[28] The quotation cames from an "internal study".

came down to applying the desires of Emile Moreau in July 1926. The exclusive right of the Banque to issue notes would be renewed for an unlimited period (Koch 1983: 46–47). Of course, the Governor "had few illusions" (Koch 1983: 48) as to the fate of such a "façade". The Banque's own project was presented to René Pleven, Minister of Finance, on November 9th: in vain, of course. In the political atmosphere of the time, and in accordance with the very "state authoritarian" views of the head of the Government, General de Gaulle, nationalisation was passed three weeks later, having been entirely prepared by the Treasury. Here we have an example of the limits of the influence of the Banque, when the Government and the parliamentary majority, working together, know what they want.

In 1947, in the context of the serious economic difficulties afflicting Western Europe, Governor Monick and his *Conseil Général* were in favour of raising the rate of discount. But François Bloch-Lainé, director of the Treasury since spring was, according to Henri Koch, "more reserved" (Koch 1983: 145); concern not to increase the cost of financing the Treasury was a determining factor in the attitude of the Rue de Rivoli (Ministry of Finance) (Koch 1983: 146). Here is yet another often repeated situation in the history of the Banque. It was resolved, after numerous meetings, by a series of compromises. Henri Koch naturally thinks that "the preoccupations peculiar to the Treasury can lead to denying to the modification of the discount rate its role as an instrument of monetary policy": we are back in the 19th century. Tension was revived in September 1948, in a highly inflationist climate. Monick convened the *Conseil Général* in an extraordinary meeting on September 4 (Koch 1983: 147) and suggested raising all the Banque de France rates by one point. Once again the director of the Treasury "expressed the greatest reservations", "challenged the urgency of the measure" and asked the Banque to "avoid burdening the State". A few weeks later, after difficult discussions, the famous mechanism emerged ("a new monetary policy") that was imposed on commercial banks: they were to hold a compulsory minimum volume of Treasury bonds and an equally compulsory maximum volume if they wished to get a rediscount from the central bank. This was intended to "reduce the risks of the less restrictive system of interest rates" (Koch 1983: 147–148).

But other problems had arisen, first in March 1947 and then from November 1947 to June 1948, when the Government had required the Banque to increase its "advances" in its favour. The Banque had to give way, of course. But not without showing its "anxious vigilance" (Annual Report 1947).

But this "commedia dell'arte" (Jean Saint-Geours) seemed to intensify with the famous *lettre de remontrances* sent by Wilfrid Baumgartner to Edgar Faure, head of Government (published in *Le Monde,* February 29, 1952). Edgar Faure was at this time overthrown by the *Assemblée,* and his successor, Antoine Pinay, implemented an economic policy which seems to have been inspired by the Governor. Here you see how difficult it is to be a historian. For this episode we only have two "sources": the *Journal* of Vincent Auriol, President of the Republic (1952) and the first volume of the *Mémoires* of Edgar Faure (1982). The two works offer two versions of the facts. The notes that Auriol took every day, as things were happening, show Edgar Faure reeling from the shock of the letter from the Governor, quite prepared to think that it was a dirty trick and convinced that it was connected to the fall of his Government. Edgar Faure's account, written thirty years later, is totally different. The event has been stripped of all drama, has been smoothed over, and the former crisis is now described as an incident of minor importance. So, who is to be believed, what is to be said?

François Bloch-Lainé speaks of this period as a "rather equivocal forced system of power sharing between the two parties" (the Banque and the Ministry of Finance) and recognises that "this power sharing was difficult in practice"[29]. In *Profession: fonctionnaire* the same actor-witness underlines the "shadow theatre", the "acting", the "tricks and artifices", the "tragicomedy" that characterised the relations between the two monetary authorities, as the *remontrances* of the Governor never came "in time" and so were useless: the Banque was forced to help the Treasury in times of acute crisis (Bloch Lainé 1976: 114–15). He recognises the influence of certain governors (Wilfrid Baumgartner, in particular), who were able to play "a real part" (Bloch Lainé 1976: 98) alongside the Minister, especially when "the latter was feeble". In any case, the former director of the Treasury (1947–1953) wrote in his memoirs in 1976 that the State should acknowledge that certain top civil servants, starting with the Governor, enjoy an "independence" (Bloch Lainé 1976: 237–38) and an "influence almost equal to that of the Executive from which they come", in order to accomplish "that which they are there for", a kind of technical and moral *"magistrature"*.

4.2.2 The New Statutes of the Banque de France (January 1973)

For a score of years after 1952 the relations between the State and the Banque continued as before with, if anything, an effective reduction in the

---

[29] Courses given at the *Institut d'études politiques* of Paris from 1952–1953. Quoted by Henri Koch (1983: 372).

influence of the Banque on monetary and economic policies. This became visible, as I have already said, at the end of 1958 and again in 1963. The question of the Banque came to the fore in 1972 during the drawing up of its new statutes, a problem that had been pending since nationalisation.

It was no doubt about time. But the delay in drawing up the new charter of the Banque de France, nationalised since 1945, meant that the new roles of the Banque, which had only fully become a "central bank" after the second world war[30], could be recorded. These roles included ever greater intervention on the money and exchange markets, and the handling of the different and increasingly sophisticated instruments of "credit control".

It was at the end of 1971 that the initiative was taken by Governor Olivier Wormser (who died in April 1985). With his strong personality and a highly cultured background in economics he had very successful diplomatic career in the French Foreign Office behind him, although he had never been Inspector of Finance. So he was not part of the financial establishment, a fact which probably consolidated his original position and independent behaviour. He was appointed Governor in April 1969 by the Government of Couve de Murville, an old friend of his[31]. In 1972 Valéry Giscard d'Estaing was Minister of Finance. If the French (and German) press are to be believed, agreement between the two men was no easy matter. The Governor insisted on the independence of the Banque; the Minister stressed the submission of the Banque to the Rue de Rivoli and the Government. I should point out here that the thorny relationship between the two men (that Valéry Giscard d'Estaing has never tried to hide)[32] was also political in nature.

The Governor was a Gaullist of long standing (he had been in London alongside General de Gaulle from 1943 onwards) and, without pushing his political sympathies forward, had played an important role under the Fifth Republic as a formidable negotiator in matters of foreign trade.

According to the German press in 1972 *(Die Welt, Frankfurter Rundschau, Bank Betrieb),* the Minister wanted "the Banque de France to have even less autonomy" (Bank Betrieb 1972 May 5) and "to have merely a consultative role in questions of monetary policy" (Die Welt 1972 March 23). The right-wing French weekly *Valeurs Actuelles* (1972: March 27 to April 2)

---

[30] It was indeed in the 1940s that the Banque, which had been strongly encouraging "direct discounting" since the end of the 19th century, dropped it in favour of "rediscounting".

[31] Obituary notice in *Le Monde,* April 19, 1985.

[32] According to *Le Nouvel Economiste* of December 1979, the Minister of Finance had confided to some union representatives of the Banque the France that he did not get on with Olivier Wormser.

criticised the Minister, accused him of wanting to "shackle" the bank of issue and considered that the "liberalism of Giscard only produced interventionist fruit". According to *Le Monde* of May 12, the Bill presented by the Ministry of Finance had provoked "a great emotion in other countries". A compromise was reached, and on the same day the headline in *Le Monde* read: "Unlike the text prepared a month ago, the newly proposed statutes for the Banque de France will give it a fair amount of autonomy". A few months later the *Journal des Finances* (1972: July 6) came to the same conclusion. The National Assembly started debating the Bill in November 1972. During the discussions it became clear that some centrist and rightwing deputies were afraid the Banque would be too dependent on the State, and the Minister of Finance set out to allay their fears[33].

The fact is that the law of January 3, 1973 (to which was added the decree of January 30th) was deliberately worded in such a way as to wrap up the compromise in the broad vague terms of the new statutes. What was not said was as important as what was contained in certain articles. The aim was to enable the Banque to adapt to changing needs and circumstances and to modify its forms of intervention without having to go through new legislative procedures. Hence the need for a "sufficiently general text", to quote the phrase used by Hubert Morant, Secretary General of the Banque[34].

It was, he went on, a question of "limiting ourselves, in operational terms, to the laying down of broad principles, to the drawing up of a framework within which the Banque can freely adapt its actions to circumstances" (Morant 1973: 26), in order to benefit from "all the flexibility that is required to efficiently implement the different tools of monetary policy" (Morant 1973: 29).

The Banque is thus "henceforth governed by modern texts" (Morant 1973: 30). It was all the more necessary as, according to the Secretary General,

> the prospect of the gradual integration of the different European economic and monetary policies would require that the central banks, which would need to work in close cooperation, enjoy, in their respective fields of activity, the same freedom of action and the same degree of initiative.

---

[33] According to the 1958 Constitution, Article 34, rules concerning the issue of banknotes and the organisation of nationalised companies shall be established by legislation passed by parliament. The decree of January 30 contained provisions that did not depend on the legislative process, such as the level of capital (250 million), the setting up of "commissions of committees" of the *Conseil Général,* the creation of a reserve found, the salary of the Governor, etc.

[34] An article by Morant (1973: 25).

The new statutes, coming after those of 1800, modified in January 1806[35] and in July 1936[36], replaced a long series of provisions that had been accumulated over the years. The 42 articles of the law of January 3, 1973 repealed 22 laws, decrees and edicts (from 1802 to 1967). And the decree of January 30 (18 articles) wiped off the statute books 32 previous decrees or edicts (from June 1834 to June 1972). The new legislation recognised the evolution of the monetary system, and at the same time introduced procedural changes and modified certain legal terms. The new texts were signed by Georges Pompidou (President of the Republic), Pierre Messmer (Prime Minister) and Valéry Giscard d'Estaing (Minister of the Economy and Finance).

Let us have a look at the law of January 3. There is a preamble of six articles to define the "general vocation" (Morant 1973: 26) and "different missions" of the Banque. Section I of the Act deals with the "organisation" of the Banque; section II with the "operations" of the Banque; section III contains miscellaneous provisons.

Some of the articles of the Act had given rise to long discussions between the Banque and the Ministry of Finance and had been drafted several times, but we cannot get any details about this. It is quite remarkable that the preamble does not contain any "information about the juridical nature of the Banque de France" (Morant 1973: 26). Is it a national company, a public undertaking, a public industrial and commercial body? There is not a word about this most delicate matter, as if the lawmakers were afraid of admitting that, when you come down to it, the Banque had been in the hands of the State since 1936 and 1945. In 1972 the question had been the object of long debate. And what do we have? The bank of issue, "a body *sui generis*", which belongs "to absolutely no determined juridical category": a perfect example of legal flexibility. The Banque is thus defined "by what it does rather than what it is".

Let us look now at Article I, which is the decisive one:

The Banque de France is the institution which, *in the framework* of the economic and financial policy of the nation, *receives from the State the mission* of watching over the currency and credit. As such the Banque makes sure the *banking system* is functioning properly. The capital of the Banque belongs to the State.

I have underlined some significant words. The State, we see, delegates a mission to the Banque. Monetary power comes from the State. This is the

---

[35] Creation of the position of Governor and Deputy-Governors.
[36] Reform of the Banque which in effect nationalised it by doing away with the *Conseil de Régence*.

"authority of the state". The Banque has "a statute half way between that of an independent institution and that of a public service dependent on the Ministry of Finance". It has the right to control the whole of the "banking system". This is a greater power than in 1945, since the central bank now "keeps an eye" not only on "registered banks" (commercial banks) but also on banking establishments that have a special legal status (such as the *Crédit Foncier, Crédit Agricole, Crédit National*). This provision heralded (and has allowed) the slow and gradual "uniformisation" of the practices of the different banks in recent years.

Article 4 is important, since "it defines the responsibilities of the Banque in the field of monetary policy" (Morant 1973: 26). It specifies in particular that

the Banque helps to prepare and takes part in the implementation of the monetary policy *that has been decided by the government,* with the assistance of the *Conseil National du Crédit, according to its terms of reference.*

The compromise is obvious. The Banque has its place "before and after the decision is taken" (Morant 1973: 27), but the decision-making power of the Minister is "expressly reserved". Confirmation of the authority of the state. Article 4 also gives the Governor complete latitude to "give his opinion on all matters monetary". Since there are no limits to the form his opinions may take, he has free rein to intervene as he sees fit. The Secretary General of the Banque, in the article he wrote in 1973, allowed himself to remark that even if such opinions "are not always followed", the importance of the role of the Governor is hereby recognised, because of his "moral authority". We will see Olivier Wormser himself fall victim to his own power.

Section II of the Act describes the organisation of the Banque de France. The powers of the Governor and the *Conseil Général* are increased, but so are those of the *Censeur*. The latter, appointed by the Minister, now has real power, "as he can oppose the decisions of the *Conseil Général*". It means that the State has a power of veto. Valéry Giscard d'Estaing, during the debate in Parliament, gave the assurance that "the solemn character of such a procedure was a guarantee that this right would only be used advisedly". Apparently this procedure has not yet been used.

Article 7 increases the influence of the Governor who henceforth is both "manager" and "administrator" of the Banque, whereas in the previous statutes the *Conseil Général* alone was in charge of the administration. As Hubert Morant said, this is a "transfer of responsibilities". This shift is confirmed in Article 15, which provides that the *Conseil Général* "may delegate some of its powers to the Governor, particularly as far as the forms of intervention in the market and the fixing of rates are concerned": in other words, the main activities of the central bank. But in fact this is just acknowledgement of a longstanding state of affairs, which were the result of the need to adapt the Banque's forms of intervention from day to day. The intervention of the Banque now has a juridical basis that cannot be questioned. (Morant 1973: 27).

The composition of the *Conseil Général,* a deliberative assembly, was modified in January 1973 and, in a way, its powers were increased. The former *Conseil* was made up of 17 members, including four members as of right (representing the *Caisse des Dépôts,* the *Crédit Foncier,* the *Crédit National* and the *Caisse Nationale du Crédit Agricole*), and seven members designated by the Minister, to represent economic interests[37]. Henceforth there are no longer any members as of right, nor anyone to represent the economic interests. The nine members appointed by decree "are chosen from among those who are competent in matters monetary, financial or economic" (Morant 1973: 28). In 1972 the Government felt that "the fact of representing certain interests... could lead to the risk of some members having a less global view of the general interest" (Morant 1973: 28). As for the abolition of the membership as of right, it was logical, according to Valéry Giscard d'Estaing's statement in the National Assembly, since the law did not allow commercial banks to be represented on the *Conseil.* Such provisions, said the Minister, guaranteed "the independence of mind of the *Conseillers Généraux*" (Morant 1973: 28). The new *Conseil* found itself with wider powers, as Article 15 gave it the right to decide the "general conditions of operations". But we have already seen that the *Conseil* delegates part of this power to the Governor. It did acquire, however, with the decree of January 30th, the right to create its own "commissions" or "committees", on which outside personalities, among others, could sit: these commissions included a "consultative council" where economic interests could henceforth be represented, albeit indirectly.

It is, of course, essential to know the rules and regulations of the machinery of the Banque de France. It is not, however, sufficient. But the historian has no way of knowing how this new system functioned. In particular whether, when and how much the traditions, old patterns of behaviour and relations between the different cogs of the machine did or did not orientate the actual functioning of the system and the balance of powers. But one thing

---

[37] The other members were the Governor, the two Deputy-Governors, the two *Censeurs* and a representative of the employees of the Banque.

is for certain: the State did not give up one iota of its rights and prerogatives, on the contrary.

Section III deals with the "operations" of the Banque and defines them in a mere twelve articles, as opposed to the fifty or so of the former statutes, in order to allow as much flexibility in the management of the Banque as possible. The operations are classified under three headings: help given to the State by the Banque; gold and foreign currency transactions; and finally, "other operations". The provision of the Constitution of the Fifth Republic (1958) is confirmed by the statutes of January 1973, whereby "recourse to the exceptional mechanism of the creation of money that comes about from advances granted to the State must be submitted to parliament for approval" (Morant 1973: 29). The other two categories of operations, the contents of which may be guessed at, ratify the new activities of the Banque since June 1938 (the open market) and, above all, 1945.

According to the article by the Secretary General of the Banque:

the independence of the Banque de France has not been affected in the slightest, despite the fears that have been expressed on this matter and which were taken up in the economic and financial press during the first few months of 1972 (Morant 1973: 29)[38].

Antoine Coutière, an economist, wrote in 1977 that:

Henceforth the French model of central bank is much closer to that of foreign central banks, though it cannot yet claim to have the same degree of autonomy as that apparently enjoyed by those in charge of the German and American central banks.

Indeed, in May 1974, sixteen months after the enactment of the January 1973 law, Olivier Wormser published an article in *Le Figaro* where he strongly criticised the government's economic policy. Right in the throes of an inflationary period, with the economy trying to keep ahead of the impending recession that was to befall it in the second half of the year, the Governor was asking for greater stringency in business and monetary matters. But the Minister of Finance, who was at the time running for president, did not want an increase in the rate of discount. It was really exceptional for a Governor to intervene in such a way in the press, and moreover in the middle of the presidential elections. Proof, if necessary, that the relations between the Governor and the Minister of Finance had not improved despite (or because of) the compromises of the law of 1973. As soon as he became President,

---

[38] The author points out that, in creating a reserve fund, Article 9 of the decree of January 30, 1973 "is likely to strengthen the financial independence of the bank issue".

Valéry Giscard d'Estaing immediately removed the former Governor from office and put Bernard Clappier in his place: the Governor, if not the Banque, was dependent. There is always a gap between what the law says and what actually happens. Shortly after this decision another similar one was taken by the new President of the Republic. He had his Minister of Finance, J. P. Fourcade, dismiss the person who had been president of the *Crédit Lyonnais* since 1967, François Bloch-Lainé. In the two cases the ulterior political motives behind the dismissals were known.

It is to be noted that De la Genière, who became Governor in 1979, sailed through the change in government in May 1981 without any problems, to relinquish his (unofficial) five-year mandate peacefully in November 1984. And that during the discussion of the new Bank Act in 1983, in the tensely polarised political climate that had prevailed since 1981, the right strongly attacked the left, accusing it of threatening the independence of the Banque.

In the spring of 1986 the new parliamentary majority said it wanted to make the Banque de France "independent". It is certain that the monetary authorities at the Banque applauded this trend. Journalist Paul Fabra, at times more catholic than the pope, encouraged them in this, though he set certain conditions (*Le Monde,* 1986 April 22). The underlying problem, however, remains: can that power which the State has always had over monetary matters really be shared? Is it possible to imagine, institutionally, juridically, a two-headed monetary authority? A law will not suffice to decide the question. Because "matters political" are part of "matters monetary", and vice versa.

References

Andrieu, C. (1981): La loi du 2 décembre 1945, *Fondation Nationale des Sciences Politiques,* symposium papers, December.
Andrieu, C. (1983): Genèse de la loi du 13 juin 1941, premiére loi bancaire française, *Revue Historique.*
Andrieu, C. (1984): Les preparation et l'adoption de la loi du 13 juin 1941, *Revue Historique.*
Banaian, K., L. O. Laney, and D. Willet, (1983): Central Bank Independence, *Economic Impact,* n. 44, 4th quarter, Washington.
Bank Betrieb, (1972) May 5.
Baumgartner, W. (1952): Lettre de remontrances, *Le Monde,* February 29.
Baumgartner, W. (1955): La Banque de France, tradition et progrès, *Université des Annales,* November 3.
Baumgartner, W. (1966): Préface, in D. Leca, *Du Ministre des Finances,* Paris: Plon.

Bloch Lainé, F. (1976): *Profession Fontionnaire,* Paris: Seuil.
Bouvier, J. (1973): *Un siècle de banque francaise,* Paris: Hachette.
Bouvier, J. (1982): The Policy of the Banque de France Between the Two World Wars, mimeo, Cambridge.
Bouvier, J. (1984): The French Banks, Inflation and the Economic Crisis, *The Journal of European Economic History*
Bouvier, J. (1986): Presentazione, in E. Moreau, *Souvenirs,* Cassa di Risparmio delle Province Lombarde: Laterza, Italian Edition.
Braudel, F. and E. Labrousse (series 1976–1982): *Histoire économique et sociale de la France,* vol. 3 and 4, Paris: PUF.
Coutière, A. (1977): Le système monetaire français, *Revue Economique.*
Debeir, J. C. (1980): Inflation et stabilisation en France, *Revue économique,* July.
Die Welt (1972): March 23.
Dow, J. C. R. (1970), *The Management of the British economy 1945–1960,* Cambridge University Press.
Fabra, P. (1986): *Le Monde,* April 22.
Gueslin, A. (1978): *Les origines du Crédit Agricole 1940–1941, Annales de l'Est,* Nancy: Bialec.
Jeanneney, J. N. (1976): *François de Wendel en République, l'argent et le pouvoir, 1914–1940,* Seuil, doctoral thesis.
Jeanneney, J. N. (1977): *Leçon d'histoire pour une gauche au pouvoir; la faillité du Cartel 1924–1926,* Paris: Seuil.
Journal des Finances (1972): July 6.
Journal Officiel (1983): December 8.
Koch, H. (1983): *L'histoire de la Banque de France et de la monnaie sous la IV République,* Paris: Dunod.
Le Monde (1985): Obituary Notice, April 19.
Le Nouvel Economiste (1979): December.
Mèndes-France, P. (1985): *Oeuvres Complètes,* Paris: Gallimard.
Morant, H. (1973): *Bulletin Trimestriel,* Banque de France, May.
Moreau, E. (1926–1928): *Souvenirs d'un gouverneur de la Banque de France: Histoire de la stabilization du franc.* Paris: Guénin.
Netter, M. (1967): *Les institutions monétaires,* Paris: PUF.
Netter, M. (1972): *Histoire de la Banque de France dans l'entre-deux querres,* mimeo.
Plessis, A. (1980): *Résumé de Thèse,* mimeo.
Plessis, A. (1982): *La Banque de France et ses deux cents actionnaires sous le Second Empire,* Geneva: Droz.
Plessis, A. (1983): L'age d'or de la Banque de France, *L'Histoire,* February.
Plessis, A. (1985a): *Régents et gouverneurs de la Banque de France sous le Second Empire,* Geneva: Droz.
Plessis, A. (1985b): Les concours de la Banque de France à l'économie, 1842–1914, *Etats, Fiscalités, Economies,* Paris: Sorbonne.
Plessis, A. (1985c): *La politique de la Banque de France de 1851 à 1870,* Geneva: Droz.
Prissert, P. (1976): Le pouvoir monétaire limité de la Banque de France, *Le Monde,* February 17.
Renard, F. (1985): Jean-Ives Harberer, *Le Monde,* April 28 and 29.
Saint-Geours, J. (1979): *Pouvoir et finance,* Paris: Fayard.

Valeurs Actuelles (1972): March 27 to April 2.
Wormser, O. (1974): *Le Figaro*, May 15.

Chapter 5
Relations between Monetary Authorities and Governmental Institutions: The Case of Germany from the 19th Century to the Present

Carl-Ludwig Holtfrerich

> "The governor was asked: 'Do you feel your bank has the right to defy the government?' 'Oh, yes', he replied, 'we value that very highly – and wouldn't think of exercising it'."
> George L. Bach, "The Federal Reserve and Monetary Policy Formation", *American Economic Review,* Vol. 39, (1949), p. 1183.

1 Introduction

The institutional arrangements between the central monetary authorities of nation states, usually the central banks, on the one hand, and the governments (and parliaments), on the other, can generally be classified into one of the three following categories:[1]

– integration,
– subordination,
– autonomy.

Integration applies to cases, where the central monetary authority forms part of the government, usually as a ministry, and where its head is a regular member of the cabinet. This arrangement is typical of communist states, e.g., in the USSR and in the GDR.

Subordination subsumes cases where the government or one of its members, generally the one in charge of the treasury, has the right to instruct the central bank and thus to control its actions. This has been the case, for example, in post-World-War-II Great Britain, although in practice the Bank of England has enjoyed a considerable degree of independence.

---
[1] Bernauer (1960): 2. The whole range of possible relations between central banks and governmental institutions is discussed by Hahn (1968).

Autonomy exists where central banks are empowered to act on their own, i.e. independently of instructions either by government, parliament, or any other institution. There are cases, where an autonomous central bank is required to coordinate its monetary policy with the overall economic policy of the government, e.g., in the FRG. Furthermore, there are those with no coordination requirement, but with coordination bodies (constant consultation or round table talks with the government in the U.S.A. or basic policy recommendations by a National Credit Council, in which the government and several interest groups and branches of the economy are represented, in France). There are also types of arrangements, where in cases of conflict between an autonomous central bank and the government the law provides for binding arbitration either by the head of state (the Governor General in Canada and Australia) or by parliament (in Sweden and New Zealand).

The question of autonomy is not only one that concerns the independence of central banks from government interference, but also of governments from central banks. A central bank with a high degree of independence, by restricting credit to the government or by a generally restrictive monetary policy, may cause difficult situations for political parties in power. In Germany, there have been historical cases where the central bank contributed to the downfall of governments.

But even where central banks have attained the highest degree of legal autonomy in shaping their monetary policies, the governmental institutions retain a certain degree of influence. Parliaments pass the banking laws that define the status and functions of the central banks and determine the degree of direct access of governments to central bank credit. In the case of an extreme conflict a parliament could be motivated to change the law. Governments usually play the main role in selecting the leading personnel of the central banks.[2] By appointing or by threatening to appoint congenial personalities, they influence the basic policy orientation of a formally autonomous central bank.

On the other hand, formal subordination of a central bank to government control may restrict a central bank's room for manoeuvre much less than subordination to monetary policy rules, e.g., the rules of the gold standard before World War I, or monetary growth rules, if they were enacted at present. For, such rules tie the hands not only of central bankers but of governments at the same time. Therefore, cases where the central bank is subordinated to the government and also subjected to monetary policy rules

---

[2] This limits the influence of their private stock owners, (mainly the big domestic banks), when the central bank is not owned by the state.

have to be judged differently from cases where the bank is subordinated and monetary policy is left to discretion rather than rules. At the same time, the way in which government access to central bank credit is regulated has to be taken into consideration. A subordinated central bank that is not tied to monetary policy rules is most open to government abuse, when no limits for direct credits to the government exist.

2 The Historical Evolution

2.1 From the Foundation of the Reich to the First World War

When the German Reich was founded in 1871 the monetary situation was still in disarray. The specie circulation consisted of numerous coins of different values and metals and of totally different denominations according to the traditions of the German regions. The circulating paper money consisted of (legal tender) treasury notes issued by 20 different states and bank notes issued by 33 note banks ("Zettelbanken") (Borchardt 1976: 3). The creation of the Reich did away with the political obstacles to a more unified German monetary system. The French reparations payments to Germany totalling approximately 5 billion gold francs provided for sufficient gold on which a unified currency could be based. The new German legislative authorities, the "Reichstag" and the "Bundesrat", regulated the issuance of the Reich's gold and silver coins as well as fractional money – all on the Mark basis – by laws of 1871 and 1873. In 1874 a law provided for the substitution of the states' treasury notes by the Reich's treasury notes, the issuance of which was limited to 120 million Marks. On March 14, 1875, a banking law was enacted that stipulated the creation of a central bank in Berlin, the "Reichsbank", defined her functions and regulated her range of activities as well as those of the still existing private note banks. These were permitted to continue to operate, but only under heavy restrictions outside of the territory of the state that had chartered them.[3]

The "Reichsbank" that began to operate on January 1, 1876 was the Prussian Bank in Berlin taken over by the Reich (*Von der Königlichen Bank zur Deutschen Reichsbank* 1940: 29). The Prussian Bank had functioned

---

[3] Reichsgesetzblatt (1875): 177–198. For the complete legislation and its history, see Koch (1926), Lotz (1888), Helfferich (1898). On the coinage laws see Grasser (1971): 11–24, 64–103.

under a Prussian bank charter since 1847 and had in practice served as a German central bank, since it had issued almost two thirds of all bank notes circulating in Germany.[4]

Twelve of the 32 remaining note banks gave up their note issue privileges immediately after 1875. 16 others followed until 1906. Thus at the beginning of the First World War, only 4 note banks (in Baden, Bavaria, Saxony and Württemberg) were still operating besides the Reichsbank (Borchardt 1976: 13–14). Their share in the total issue of bank notes, however, had become insignificant.

2.1.1 The Legal Arrangements

The legal status of the Reichsbank resembled closely that of the Prussian Bank, her immediate forerunner. Both were based predominantly on private share capital, with the state holding only a minor portion in total equity. They were, however, not private stock companies, but "juridical persons under public law" and under formal control of the government, much more so than the central banks in other European states, like France and Great Britain.

§ 1 of the Prussian banking law of October 5, 1846, ennumerated the functions of the Prussian Bank as follows:

- to promote the circulation of money,
- to make capital available,
- to support commerce and manufacture,
- to prevent an excessive increase of the interest rate (Stoepel 1861: 675–687).

The head of the Prussian Bank was appointed by the Prussian King. Traditionally, it was the Prussian Minister for Commerce, Manufacture, and Public Works (Borchardt 1976: 15). This and the latter two functions mentioned above indicate that the Bank was intended to be an instrument of the state to promote productive activities. This is also evidenced by § 6 of the law that stipulated 6 percent as the maximum lombard rate the Bank could charge.

The executive organ of the Prussian Bank, the Bank Directorate and its President, were placed under the command of the head of the Bank, a member of the Prussian government. They were nominated by the head of the Bank and appointed for life-time tenure by the Kaiser (§ 56). In addition,

---

[4] This corresponds to Prussia's share in the total population of the Reich.

the government exercised supervisory functions over the Bank through the "Kuratorium" that consisted of high government officials.

The private owners of the Bank, mainly the big banks, were represented in the Assembly of Equity Holders ("Versammlung der Meistbeteiligten") and in the Central Committee. The Assembly's main function was to receive the annual reports and to elect the Central Committee's 15 members (§ 65), subject, however, to confirmation by the head of the Bank (§ 69). The Central Committee had to be informed by the Directorate in monthly intervals about the current state of the Bank's business and it had advisory functions, especially in credit policy matters and in the appointment of members of the Directorate (§ 78). A group of three delegates of the Central Committee ("Deputierte") was empowered to check the Bank's activities on a daily basis and to participate in all meetings of the Bank's Directorate in an advisory capacity (§§ 82 and 83).

The banking law of 1875 (§ 12) defined the functions of the Reichsbank:

– to regulate the circulation of money within the Reich's territory,
– to facilitate the settlement of payments, i.e. mainly to promote cashless transactions,
– to care for the utilization of available capital (Reichsgesetzblatt 1875: 180).

The additional explicit functions of the Prussian Bank, namely to support commerce and manufacture and to prevent an excessive increase of the interest rate, had been dropped from the list of the Reichsbank's functions. But in practice, the Reichsbank kept this tradition alive, especially until her 1924 reform. For example, private business, not only banks, retained direct access to Reichsbank credit, and especially during Germany's great inflation from 1914 to 1923 low discount rates were justified by the Reichsbank in reference to the needs of commerce and industry.

With the enactment of the 1875 banking law, the Reich's Chancellor became head of the Reichsbank (§ 26). The Directorate with its President remained the executive organ of the Reichsbank. It could decide matters of policy by majority vote, but in cases of conflict with the government, it had to follow the instructions of the Chancellor (§ 26). The personnel of the Reichsbank were given the status of civil servants of the Reich (§ 28).

The members and the President of the Reichsbank's Directorate were nominated by the "Bundesrat", the federal legislative chamber in which the states were represented, and appointed for life-time tenure by the Kaiser (§ 27). The "Kuratorium" was retained as the supervisory body. The Reich's Chancellor was made its chairman, which gave him a second line of influence over the Bank's activities. In addition, the "Kuratorium" consisted of four members, one appointed by the Kaiser, the three others by the "Bundesrat" (§ 25). It was to meet quarterly to examine the report of the Bank on all its operations.

The private shareholders of the Reichsbank were represented in the General Assembly ("Generalversammlung"), with functions similar to the Prussian Bank's Assembly of Equity Holders. Also the Central Committee and its three "Deputierte" retained their roles.

On one issue, the Central Committee, i.e. the representatives of the private owners of the Bank, was given additional powers. Before the Reichsbank engaged in business with the Reich or state treasuries on conditions other than normal, i.e. on a preferential basis, the Central Committee had to be informed, and the deal could proceed only if the Committee approved it by majority vote (§ 35). This veto power of the Bank's private owners reflected the concern that the credit facilities of the government-controlled Reichsbank should not be easy prey for the treasuries.

The strong dependence of the Reichsbank on the Reich's governmental institutions was further accentuated by the fact that the Reich retained the right to terminate the activities of the Reichsbank or to nationalize the Bank by purchasing her capital shares at face value. An agreement between the Kaiser and the "Bundesrat" was necessary before this option could be exercised, and the Reichs's Chancellor was required to notify the Reichsbank Directorate one year prior to the termination or nationalization of her activities. This option could be exercised for the first time on January 1, 1891, 15 years after the Bank's creation, and afterwards every 10 years. The extension of the Reichsbank's activities on those occasions required the consent of the "Reichstag", i.e. the elected representatives of the German voters (§ 41).

The Reichsbank's room for manoeuvre in monetary policy was also restricted by the rules that regulated the issuance of banknotes. Until 1856 the Prussian Bank had been allotted a maximum amount for her issue of banknotes, subject to a one-third coverage in silver (bullion or coins). Thereafter she was free to issue unlimited amounts, as long as one third was covered in silver (Borchardt 1976: 19).

The regulations for the Reichsbank's note issuance were more complicated. Like the Bank of England she was allotted a fiduciary quota for banknote issues beyond the amount of issues against her gold reserves and some other items (§ 9).[5] But the Reichsbank was also empowered to exceed

---

[5] Besides the gold reserves: German silver coins, a limited amount of the Reich's treasury notes, and bank notes of other German note banks. The maximum amount of fiduciary issues was raised several times.

this quota subject to a five percent tax on the banknote amount that surpassed the quota allotment (§ 9). The real limit to the note issue was set by the requirement that the Reichsbank had to cover one third of her note circulation in legal tender German money, i.e. gold and silver coins that had been coined by the mints of the states and the Reich, plus the Reich's treasury notes that were strictly limited in total volume, and gold bullion and foreign gold coins valued at 1,392 Mark per ½ kilogram. The rest had to be covered by qualified commercial bills (§ 17). On demand of the bearer, the Reichsbank had to exchange her notes for legal tender German money, i.e. since 1871 gold coins minted by the Reich and silver coins mainly previously minted under state authority. The money base on which the Reichsbank could create her credit and money (banknotes) was thus dependent on the inflow of gold from abroad, i.e. on Germany's balance of payments and on the production of legal tender German money by the Reich's mints. The smallest denomination permitted for banknotes was 100 Marks until 1906, when it was reduced to 20 Marks in order to draw gold out of circulation and to increase the reserves of the Reichsbank. Until then, money in circulation consisted predominantly of legal tender coins and not of banknotes. In 1906, for example, the circulation of coins amounted to about double the volume of banknotes in circulation (Deutsche Bundesbank 1976: 14). June 1, 1909 marked an important turning point towards modern conditions in that banknotes were also declared legal tender (Reichsgesetzblatt 1909: 507). This strengthened the position of the Reichsbank. It induced some experts to demand the nationalization of the Reichsbank, because it should remain the prerogative of the Reich alone to issue legal tender (Mammel 1955: 14).

2.1.2 The Degree of Dependence in Practice

In spite of the legal subordination of the Reichsbank to the Reich, and especially to the Reich's Chancellor as the head of the Reichsbank, the Reichsbank Directorate in fact enjoyed a considerable degree of autonomy and – with minor exceptions – it was free from government interference in shaping its monetary policies. The Bank's mixed status between private ownership and government control actually helped increase the autonomy of the Bank vis-à-vis private or state interests (Borchardt 1976: 16). In 1871, the Reich had in effect adopted the gold standard, since the mints were producing mainly gold coins and only small amounts of silver coins. The 1909 law explicitly stated that the Reich was on the gold standard.

In practice, the gold standard rules restricted the autonomy of the Reichsbank much more than the legal subordination of the Reichsbank under the

Reich's Chancellor. As has been noted in an earlier study: "The strongest restriction of a central bank's freedom of action in its credit policies exists under a pure gold standard."[6] It is further stated there that only in times of a manipulated monetary standard the independence of the central bank – as the guardian of the value of money ("Hüterin der Währung") – becomes an indispensable precondition for sound money.

2.1.3 Cases of Conflict

The Reich's Chancellor as the head of the Reichsbank rarely interfered with the conduct of the Bank's monetary policy. It is known, however, that Bismarck did so twice. In December 1880 he ordered the Reichsbank to raise the discount rate and to restrict lombard credit. The Bank complied (Sommer 1931: 18). In 1887 Bismarck instructed the Reichsbank to stop lombarding Russian bonds. This was a matter of foreign policy and not a conflict over the conduct of domestic monetary policies.[7]

2.1.4 Debates on the Central Bank's Position vis-à-vis the Government

Each time the Reich was permitted to either nationalize the Reichsbank or terminate or prolong her privileges, heated debates took place in the "Reichstag" in 1889, 1899 and 1909. By the time of the first debate in 1889, the Reichsbank had already demonstrated her useful role in developing the economy to such an extent that her dissolution was out of the question. Instead the debates on all three occasions gathered their momentum from the issue, whether the Bank should be nationalized or whether it should retain its mixed status.

Nationalization was favored by the right-wing political groups and parties that stood for the interests of agriculture and handicraft. These conservatives saw the Reichsbank as serving primarily the interests of big industry, commerce, and the banks. They expected that a nationalized Reichsbank could be made to pursue a credit policy more favorable to the wishes of agriculture and small business.[8] Those who demanded nationalization also argued that

---

[6] My translation from Mammel (1955): 5. See also Kroyer (1955): 35–38, Die Bundesbank (1950): 22.

[7] For more details see Sommer (1931): 91–96, Kumpf-Korfes (1968): 154–158, Müller-Link (1977): 319–338.

[8] For details of the 1889 discussions see Walther Lotz (1897), Sommer (1931): 83–90. Otherwise Borchardt (1976): 16.

the Reich, by granting the note issue privilege to the Bank, gave to her private owners a free gift of several million Marks per year (Helfferich 1899: 53).

Defenders of the Bank's mixed status argued that private ownership and governmental control had passed the test of practical experience. This was also demonstrated by a comparison of the performance of the nationalized central banks in Sweden, Russia and Bulgaria and of central banks with a mixed status, especially the Bank of England and the Banque de France. The fear was expressed that a nationalized central bank could easily become an instrument of the fiscal interests of the government. This might become a necessity under extreme circumstances, especially in cases of war. In such cases, however, central banks with a mixed status, as the Bank of England during the Napoleonic Wars and the Banque de France during and after the Franco-German War (reparations) had subordinated the strict adherence to the banking rules under the demands of the treasuries.[9]

It was also argued that the assets of a central bank in *private* ownership would be relatively safe from confiscation by an enemy in case of war, as the Prussians had spared the assets of the Banque de France in 1870–71 (Borchardt 1976: 16). The main argument for preserving the mixed status of the Reichsbank, however, was that a differentation between the Bank's and the state's assets and credit was beneficial for both sides. This advantage would be lost if the Bank were nationalized. The banknotes' value would then be dependent on the Reich's credit standing. The delegation of the note issue privilege to a separate institution, the assets of which had to guarantee the convertibility of the notes into specie and which was subjected to specified banking rules, was seen as the best safety measure against an inflationary use of banknote emission (Kroyer 1955: 43–44).

These arguments prevailed on all three occasions. The Reichsbank was not nationalized and her note issue privilege was prolonged. What was regularly changed, however, was the division of the profits of the Reichsbank between her private owners and the state in favor of the Reich.

2.2 From the Beginning of the First World War to the End of Germany's Great Inflation 1923

During this period the German government had open access to the Reichsbank's credit, which led to inflation during the War and especially during the

---

[9] Kroyer (1955): 43, Helfferich (1899): 60. The subordination of the Reichsbank to the Reich's Chancellor was not an issue. See Keller (1953): 9–10.

first five years following the War. When the Mark was finally stabilized in November 1923, 1000 billion paper Marks equalled one new Mark (Holtfrerich 1986: 17).

This experience, with its tremendous redistribution of income and wealth, created a trauma among the German population which helps to explain the German public's strong demand for stable monetary conditions up to the present day.

2.2.1 The Legal Arrangements

At the beginning of the War, Germany went off the gold standard in that the Mark was made inconvertible into gold. Several measures were taken to allow for an increase in the Reichsbank's note circulation and to make the Bank's credit accessible to the government. The banknote tax that had been levied on note issues beyond the Reichsbank's quota was abolished. The Bank was allowed to use treasury bills along with commercial bills as coverage for two thirds of its banknote liabilities. The one third coverage requirement, however, was kept. Yet, in addition to gold, the Reichsbank was empowered to use loan bureau notes to meet this requirement. This was a cosmetic measure, because the newly created loan bureaus were subsidiaries of the Reichsbank and issued their notes on collateral (commodities or bonds). Thus, war bonds that were issued by the government as a means of long-term financing of the war effort were increasingly used to draw cash. They were exchanged for loan bureau notes (which also circulated as money) that the Reichsbank gladly exchanged for its own notes. The more loan bureau notes the Reichsbank accumulated in addition to gold, the more money it could issue in exchange for treasury notes. This practice put the Reichsbank's credit machine at the disposal of the Reich, even more so, when, in May 1921, the one-third coverage requirement was dropped altogether.[10]

In this manner the government's and the Reichsbank's previous strict adherence to the rules of the gold standard ended. The concern of the past that the Reich's Treasury would gain unlimited access to central bank credit was now borne out by facts. It was justified, however, by the necessities of the War.

---

[10] Holtfrerich (1986): 115–116, 167. A minor change of the banking law had been enacted in December 1919. See *Reichsgesetzblatt* (1919): 2117–2119. *Die Reichsbank* (1925): 94–98.

An important change in the legal relations between the German government and the Reichsbank came about, when the Reichsbank – on demand of the Allies as a condition for a moratorium on reparations payments – was made "autonomous" by law of 26 May 1922.[11] The Reich's Chancellor ceased to be the head of the Reichsbank and the Reichsbank could decide on monetary policies on her own. Nonetheless, the Reich's supervisory body, the "Kuratorium" with the Reich's Chancellor as its chairman, remained in place. The procedure of appointing the Bank's President and the other members of the Directorate was also changed. From then on, the Bank's President could be nominated by the "Reichsrat" (the second chamber of parliament representing the states) and be appointed by the Reich's President only after the expert opinion of the Central Committee and of the Directorate had been heard. The Directorate members were nominated by the Directorate and – with the consent of the "Reichsrat" – appointed by the Reich's President after the opinion of the Central Committee had been heard (§ 27).

2.2.2 The Degree of Dependence in Practice

By cutting loose from the gold standard at the beginning of the War and by granting the Reich open access to the Reichsbank's credit, the *legal* subordination of the Bank under the Reich's Chancellor until May 1922 also became a *practical* reality. Contemporaries already accused the Reichsbank of never resisting the government's demand for credit until the last stage of the inflation. This is true. Yet, to blame the Reichsbank for the inflationary development that resulted from the deficit financing of the Reich's budget would be unfair. In its confidential annual reports to the government since 1918 the Reichsbank pointed out that the increase in the unfunded debt of the Reich was a cause of the inflation and that balancing the Reich's budget was an "essential precondition" for the recovery of currency conditions. She demanded the Reich to act accordingly. This was as far as the Bank could go until May 1922. Any resistance to the government's demands for credit would have been futile, because the Reich's Chancellor had the authority to give instructions to the Bank at any time. The Bank never went to the brink of a forelorn conflict with the government in this period, since it was then completely dependent on the Reich. As Schacht noted, resistance by the

---

[11] *Reichsgesetzblatt* (1922/II): 135–136. *Die Reichsbank* (1925): 101–102. The independence of central banks from political influences had already been demanded by the participant nations at the International Financial Conference of Brussels in 1920 and again at the Genoa Conference on European Reconstruction in the spring of 1922.

Reichsbank to the government's credit demands would at best have been of moral, but of no practical value.[12]

This changed legally in May 1922. At about the same time some fiscal measures had just been taken by the Reich that actually improved its budget situation. There was a real chance for stabilizing the German currency at that time. But in June 1922 when the bankers' committee of the Reparation Commission under the leadership of J. P. Morgan shattered expectations that Germany would receive foreign loans, the Mark started to fall dramatically on the foreign exchange markets and hyperinflation set in. This again unbalanced the Reich's budget and made short-term financing of the deficit through the Bank necessary. The Bank could have refused it, a hope that had motivated the Allies to press the German government for the autonomy of the Reichsbank. The Bank, however, continued to discount the treasury bills and, in addition, increased the discounting of commercial bills, thus allowing hyperinflation to run its course. As she explained to the government on one occasion, the Bank cooperated, because she gave priority to the "fulfillment of state necessities" over controlling the inflation.[13]

From May 1922 on, the Reichsbank was dependent not on the government, but on the national interest, as the Bank's leaders judged it to be.[14] One of the responsible members of the Bank's Directorate, J. Friedrich, later stated that at the time the situation did not allow full utilization of the Reichsbank's legal autonomy. The question of what would happen if the Bank simply refused her credit to the Reich had been examined and answered to the effect that the denial of credit most probably would have had economic and political consequences much worse than the monetary implications of further credits to the government (Friedrich 1923/24: 342).

2.2.3 Cases of Conflict

In June/July 1922 – some weeks after the Reichsbank had become autonomous from the government – the Mark's value on foreign exchange markets fell dramatically, and the Reich's government urged the Reichsbank to use

---

[12] Schacht (1927b): 116. For the Reichsbank's admonitions to the government see Holtfrerich (1986): 164–167.

[13] Letter of the Reichsbank Directorate to the Finance Minister of August 23, 1923, quoted in Holtfrerich (1986): 168–169.

[14] Schacht (1927b): 117 argues similarly that on account of the unfortunate foreign policy situation of Germany, the Reichsbank lacked the will to restrict the Reich to its own financial means.

her gold reserves to intervene in order to stabilize the Mark exchange rate. The Reichsbank complied only reluctantly and temporarily. She saw no use in sacrificing too much of her gold reserves in such a stabilization action, as long as the causes of the inflation internally and externally (excessive reparations demands) had not been removed. The conflict ended in the weak compromise of a short-breath intervention program (Schacht 1927b: 53).

Schacht also reports that in the following year the President of the Reichsbank Havenstein and the government were "not on very good terms" (Schacht 1955: 180). One reason for these strained relations was that the Reichsbank had defied the government for the first time in its history. In August 1923, she had informed the German government that by the end of the year she would terminate discounting the Reich's treasury bills (Friedrich 1923/24: 342; Schacht 1927b: 117), the means by which the Reich had financed almost all of its expenses during the hyperinflation since the summer of 1922 and which had fueled the inflationary course. The Reich's Chancellor Stresemann and even the Reich's President Ebert had urged Havenstein to resign. The Reichsbank's President, who held a life-time tenure since 1908, resisted. He obviously wished to ensure that his successor would be as conservative as he himself (Schacht 1955: 180, 188).

After several disputes with the government over the details of the stabilization measures, Havenstein died on November 20, 1923, just five days after the Reichsbank had stopped discounting treasury bills and after the new currency, the Rentenmark, had been introduced. It was the very day the government decided to stabilize the Mark exchange rate at 4,200 billion paper marks for one U.S. dollar.

2.2.4 Debates on the Central Bank's Position vis-à-vis the Government

The introduction of the Bank's autonomy in May 1922 was not preceded by major public debates. President Havenstein, however, had discussed the issue with the President of the Bank of England, Lord Norman, during a visit to London in October 1921. It was reported that Havenstein won Norman's support for strengthening the Reichsbank's position vis-à-vis the German government in a new banking law (Sayers 1976: 175–176).

When the autonomy bill had been framed, Karl Helfferich, whom Havenstein favored as his successor, published his views on it. In a judgment typical of conservative and nationalist circles, he pointed out that the change in the Reichsbank's status was not a voluntary action by German legislative authorities, but "the execution of a dictate" by the Allies. He nevertheless approved of the change arguing that in the new republican-parliamentary system the Bank needed protection from interference by partisan and non-expert governments.[15]

2.3 From the End of Hyperinflation to the End of the Weimar Republic

Monetary policy and its legal framework in this period were to a certain degree the outcome of the inflation experience. They were shaped with a view to avoiding a similar disaster.

2.3.1 The Legal Arrangements

The "Rentenbank" that since November 1923 issued Germany's new currency on collateral of debentures on the German industry's and agriculture's real estate was accorded the legal status of a "juridical person under private law", while the Reichsbank had always been a "juridical person under public law". This, as well as the foundation of her note issue on private property and her private management, reflected the public's total loss of confidence in state monetary institutions, including the Reichsbank, at the end of the hyperinflation. The leadership of the Rentenbank was completely independent of the government. It was, however, obliged to cooperate with the Reichsbank that had been assigned the function to transfer the "Rentenmark" issues into circulation (Kroyer 1955: 64). The situation was similar to the organization of the Bank of England with her Issue Department (Rentenbank) and her Banking Department (Reichsbank) (Eynern 1928: 24).

The government's Rentenbank decree limited the Rentenmark issues to 2.4 million. 1.2 million Rentenmarks were issued in favor of the Reich's government to keep it financially afloat. The rest was earmarked for private demand. Aside from these funds, the Reichsbank's paper money – stabilized since November 20 – continued to circulate. It remained the legal tender money, a status denied to the Rentenmark that had to be accepted by all public treasuries. The Reichsbank was free to issue more money as long as this did not endanger the stability of the Mark exchange rate (Holtfrerich 1986: 314–318).

In March 1924, a third note-issuing institution of central banking importance was founded in Germany, the Gold Discount Bank. Half of her capital was provided by the Reichsbank, the other half by private banks. Her main purpose was to mobilize foreign credits to overcome Germany's capital short-

---

[15] Helfferich (1921/22): 215–217. For a different view regarding the autonomy as alien to the German tradition and, therefore, opposing it see Singer (1922): 734–735.

age in this period. Her note issue was to be denominated in Pound Sterling, because the Bank of England had provided credits for the Bank's founding capital. The note issue privileges of the Gold Discount Bank and of the Rentenbank were to fall back to the Reichsbank as soon as the latter's functions would be revived fully in connection with a comprehensive currency reform (Hardach 1976: 42-44; Schötz 1987: 133-135).

Based on the Dawes Plan and the ensuing international commitment of Germany, the Reichstag and Reichsrat passed the new banking law of August 30, 1924, that put the old Reichsbank of 1875 on a new legal footing (Notzke 1924; *Reichsgesetzblatt* 1924/II: 235-252; Spohr 1925). The structure of the new banking law and the new Reichsbank resembled that of 1875. The main difference was that § 1 of the 1924 banking law stated the independence of the Bank vis-à-vis the government. This time, the Bank was granted her note issue privilege for a period of 50 years (§ 2) instead of 15 years (renewable every 10 years), as in 1875. Thus, the formerly recurrent nationalization debates were meant to be avoided for half a century. The Directorate was given the final say in shaping credit policies (§ 6). The Reichsbank was merely obliged to *report* to the government on her credit policies (§ 20) and not to *support* the overall economic policy of the government, as the Bundesbank is obliged to do now. Even in matters of appointing the Directorate and its President, the Reich's authority was much reduced. The Reichsbank President and the ordinary members of the Directorate were to be elected by the newly created "General Council" that consisted of seven German and seven foreign members (§ 14). It succeeded the "Kuratorium" through which the Reich had previously supervised the Bank. The German members of the General Council were elected by the private owners of the Bank, represented in the General Assembly, which had been in existence since 1876. The only influence that the Reich retained was the Reich's President's right to veto the appointment of an elected Reichsbank President twice. The third time around, however, the Reich's President was obliged to carry out the appointment.

The life-time tenure for the members and President of the Directorate was removed. Directorate members were appointed for twelve years, and they had to resign at the age of sixty-five. The President was appointed for four years. Reelection as well as revocation at any time of members or the President of the Directorate by the General Council were possible. The Central Committee, elected by the General Assembly, was retained as an advisory body (§ 13).

A completely new institution was the Commissioner for the note issue that had to be a foreigner (§ 19). He was to ensure that the banknote circulation was managed according to the law (§ 27), in other words that inflation would not be repeated.

With the same purpose in mind, § 25 strictly limited the Reich's access to the Reichsbank's credit to a total of 100 million Marks and to a three-months term at most. At the end of each business year the Reich was not allowed to have an outstanding Reichsbank credit at all.

In this way, the Reichsbank was completely cut loose from the German government. Instead, she was subjected to influence by foreign agents, albeit legally to a lesser degree than during her subordination to the Reich's Chancellor from 1876 to 1922. But the Reichsbank and the foreign agents were operating under the same rules, those of the newly established gold-exchange standard:

– The Reichsbank was obliged to cover her note circulation by 40 percent in gold and foreign exchange instead of the 33.3 percent gold coverage requirement before the First World War.[16] The remaining 60 percent were to be covered by qualified commercial bills and checks.
– The Reichsmark was put at par with gold on the prewar basis: 1,392 Reichsmark per ½ kilogram gold.
– The convertibility of the Reichsmark for foreigners was assured by stabilizing the Mark exchange rate vis-à-vis the U.S. Dollar (4.20 Reichsmark = 1 U.S. Dollar). The Bank was obliged to ensure convertibility of her notes into gold or foreign exchange for domestic citizens also. This requirement was practically met all the time, but legally suspended until both the Directorate and the General Council had decided on its application (§ 52). This happened in connection with the legal changes in the banking law in March 1930 that followed the acceptance of the Young Plan (Bayrhoffer 1941: 93).
– A quota on banknote issues was *not* reintroduced. The Bank was allowed to fall short of the 40 percent coverage requirement. But in this case she had to pay progressive taxes to the government and had to charge a discount rate of at least 5 percent (§ 29).

A revision of the banking law in July 1926 allowed the Bank to discount more treasury bills if they had also been accepted by at least one solvent private debtor. The maximum amount of such credits was then raised to 400 million Reichsmark.[17]

---

[16] The gold coverage alone had to amount to at least 30 percent of the banknote circulation (§ 28).

[17] *Reichsgesetzblatt* (1926/II): 355. This change was motivated by the Reich's acute shortage of funds. See Hertz-Eichenrode (1982): 111.

Another revision of the 1924 banking law that followed the acceptance of the Young Plan in 1930 eliminated the control foreigners had exercised over the Reichsbank. The position of the Commissioner for the note issue was abolished. The General Council consisted of German members only, thus strengthening the influence of the Bank's private owners. At the same time, however, the Reich's President was given the ultimate right to veto the appointment or the revocation of members of the Reichsbank's Directorate and of its President. This strengthening of the powers of the Reich's President, in fact, amounted to a strengthening of the government's role, because his decision had to be countersigned by the Chancellor or the cabinet member in charge. In addition, the Bank was allowed to accept treasury bonds on collateral for lombard credits, thus easing the Reich's access to the Bank's credit.[18]

2.3.2 The Degree of Dependence in Practice

The "miracle" of the German currency stabilization in 1923/24 had come about by isolating the management of the new currency from government interference completely. The importance of this factor was demonstrated by the fact that until August 1924 the new currency, the Rentenmark, and also the old paper Mark were essentially based on *private* paper assets instead of *government* paper assets, as during the inflation. This alone restored confidence in the Mark to such a degree that the Reichsbank could allow a substantial increase in her note issue after November 15, 1923, without the familiar inflationary consequences.

While in May 1922 the Reichsbank had become legally autonomous, the Treasury continued to have access to her printing press. This was not stopped until November 15, 1923. From then on, the Reichsbank was independent not only of government instructions but also of government demand for credit. Before the gold exchange standard with its 40 percent coverage was introduced at the end of August 1924, the Reichsbank was not only legally free of foreign supervision and influence but also of the discipline imposed by a gold standard. Under the strong leadership of her new President Schacht, the Bank forcefully used her instruments, including strict credit rationing in the spring of 1924, to defend the currency's value. What the Reichsbank to

---

[18] *Reichsgesetzblatt* (1930/II): 355–356, Heymann (1930): 42–51, Parchmann (1933): 56. For the countersignature of the government see Kroyer (1955): 73–74. Important changes of the banking law were, however, conditioned on the agreement by the Bank for International Settlements (BIS). Singer (1930): 133–136.

the Allies' disappointment had failed to do after having gained autonomy in May 1922, was now demonstrated by her skillful manipulation of the currency.

While the Bank's independence from the government was strengthened under the law of August 30, 1924, her room for manoeuvre was curtailed by subjecting her to the rules of the gold exchange standard and by establishing foreign supervision to ensure that those rules would be guarded. When foreign supervision was terminated in 1930 after the acceptance of the Young Plan, full convertibility of the German currency was also introduced legally. This strengthened the gold exchange standard's grip on the conduct of German monetary policy. When foreign exchange control was introduced in Germany after the financial crisis in the summer of 1931, after which the Reichsbank also failed to meet the 40 percent coverage requirement, the Bank's dependence on the rules of the gold exchange standard was again softened.

All through this period, Germany's central bank enjoyed a freedom of action vis-à-vis the government that it had never had (or used from May 1922 to November 1923) before and that it would never retrieve.

2.3.3 Cases of Conflict

It is not surprising, therefore, that a number of conflicts occurred. A first test of the non-accessibility of central bank credit to the Reich took place soon after the stabilization of the currency. When the government failed to raise enough tax receipts to cover its expenditures, it asked the Rentenbank in December 1923 for an additional credit beyond the amount the Rentenbank decree had stipulated. The Rentenbank's leading managers stood firm and refused, forcing the government to reduce its expenditure further (Eynern 1928: 89). This time, the autonomy of the Rentenbank worked the way the foreign supporters of the Reichsbank's autonomy had expected in vain during 1922.

A major conflict between the Reichsbank and the government occurred at about the same time over who should succeed Havenstein as the Reichsbank's President. The Reich's Chancellor Stresemann had, at first, strongly favored Hjalmar Schacht, at the time a leading member of the liberal German Democratic Party, to be the Finance Minister in his second cabinet which was formed in October 1923. This failed when the conservative German National People's Party, a potential coalition member, spread rumors as to the personal integrity of Schacht. As a government official in occupied Belgium during the War, he was alleged to have promoted the private business of the Dresdner Bank, in which he had played a leading role before 1914. In addition, he was accused of having attempted to conceal these activities (Müller 1973: 16–17). Stresemann then favored Schacht to succeed Havenstein, whom he urged to resign. He even tried to force the resignation of Havenstein and the Bank's Vice-President – through letters by the Reich's President to Havenstein (of November 6 and 9, 1923) – arguing on the basis of the Decree for the Reduction of Civil Servants (of October 27, 1923) that provided for compulsory retirement of the Reich's civil servants at the age of 65. In Stresemann's view, the conservative Havenstein was too much identified with inflation policy to ensure the success of the stabilization program. Havenstein had only vaguely hinted at his willingness to resign in the course of 1924. In order to make use of Schacht's expertise in the execution of the stabilization program, to raise Schacht's profile, and to show his determination to replace Havenstein by Schacht, Stresemann appointed Schacht as the Reich's "Commissioner for the Currency" at the Reichsbank on November 12, 1923.[19] On November 19, Havenstein defended his position in a letter to the Reich's President on the grounds that the banking law guaranteed the autonomy of the Bank and his life-time tenure. The resignation issue was settled the following day, when Havenstein unexpectedly died of a heart-attack.

The question of succession, however, remained a matter of conflict. The law that had introduced the Reichsbank's autonomy in May 1922 had also altered the procedure for the appointment of the Bank's President. It provided that the President was to be nominated by the "Reichsrat" and appointed by the Reich's President for life-time tenure, but only after the Bank's Directorate and Central Committee had presented their opinion. They both recommended the conservative Karl Helfferich for the Reichsbank's Presidency on December 4, 1923. The new government with Marx as Chancellor and Stresemann as Minister of Foreign Affairs was divided over the issue. Marx and the majority of his cabinet favored Helfferich to please the conservatives and to gain their support. But Stresemann promoted Schacht's candidacy and gained the Social Democrats' support for it. Foreign financial circles strongly favored Schacht and even the British Ambassador in Berlin, D'Abernon, who disapproved of Helfferich because of his role in financing the War with inflationary methods, intervened in favor of Schacht.

It was the Prussian government that formally nominated Schacht in the "Reichsrat" as the Bank's new president on December 12, 1923. On December 16, the Directorate and the Central Committee of the Reichsbank

---

[19] For the range of the Commissioner's authority see Schacht (1927b): 92, 95.

again presented their expert opinion favoring Helfferich. They strongly rejected Schacht and questioned his expertise and his personal integrity, alluding to his war-time activites in Belgium. Stresemann had meanwhile convinced the cabinet of the importance of foreign policy considerations in favoring Schacht over Helfferich. The "Reichsrat" finally put aside the objections of the Reichsbank and nominated Schacht, who was appointed to the Reichsbank's Presidency by the Reich's President on December 22, 1923.[20] This was the only conflict during the Weimar period in which the Reichsbank was flatly defeated by the government.

The autonomy of the Reichsbank – once in 1922 and again in 1924 – had been enacted on a formal demand of the Allies, i.e. as a foreign policy concession to the victors of the War. This explains why from his national point of view Havenstein had been reluctant to use the increased authority of the Reichsbank against his own government. Schacht, on the other hand, turned out to be completely free from such scruples and constantly made use of the Weimar Republic's foreign policy situation to pressure the government into following his ideas. Of all German politicians, Schacht enjoyed the most goodwill abroad. In skillfully playing on it, Schacht strengthened his position vis-à-vis Weimar's relatively unstable governments to such a degree that the Reichsbank under his leadership has been called the "Extra-Government" (Müller 1973: 38–43). Any attempt of the government to influence the Bank's credit policy was strictly blocked, for example, when the cabinet wanted to discuss the wisdom of the Bank's discount policy after Schacht had reported on it on February 26, 1925 (Müller 1973: 40).

Schacht, in turn, successfully imposed his will not only on his colleagues in the Directorate, but often also on the government's conduct of fiscal and foreign policies. Usually, his most important ally in his struggles with the government was Parker Gilbert, the Reparation Agent in Berlin.

The Reichsbank under Schacht from December 1923 to March 7, 1930 disagreed with the government on four main issues:

– the centralization of public funds,
– foreign loans to municipalities,
– reparations policies,
– fiscal policies.

Since 1925, Schacht had complained that the Reich kept public funds, such as those of the railways, the post, the internal revenue, and the social security

---

[20] Details of the story are reported in Schacht (1927b): 121–128, Peterson (1954): 49–52, Müller (1973): 27–37, Hardach (1976): 21–26, Habedank (1981): 98–99.

institutions, not with the Reichsbank but in state banks (Upmeier 1973: 163; *Verwaltungsbericht der Reichsbank für das Jahr 1924:* 4). Schacht wished to bring these funds under the control of the Reichsbank.[21] He also wanted to discipline the states' fiscal policy by drawing funds away from their banks.

Schacht typically argued that the current practice not only affected currency stability but also the transfer of reparations. He managed to mobilize the U.S. Treasury, the Federal Reserve Bank of New York, and Parker Gilbert in his support. While this charge was the stick, he offered the discounting of additional treasury bills as the carrot. Schacht was successful in March 1927, when the Reich's government conceded the partial administration of public funds to the Reichsbank and ordered the protesting states to act accordingly (Müller 1973: 61; Upmeier 1973: 163).

When especially U.S. loans started to flow to Germany in great amounts from 1924 on, Schacht became immediately concerned about their size and their too rapid growth (James 1985: 41–55; McNeil 1986: 52–56; Upmeier 1973: 160; *Verwaltungsbericht der Reichsbank für das Jahr 1924:* 4). He saw the capital inflow as a danger to the Reichsbank's control of credit conditions at home (Schacht 1927a: 27), and in June 1927 he publicly declared that Germany had two Reichsbanks, the one represented by him and the other one consisting of foreign credits (Ausschuss zur Untersuchung 1929: 203).

Schacht's opposition to foreign loans was directed against foreign credits to *public* institutions, i.e. federal, state, and local governments. He argued that the stability of the German currency depended on Germany's balance of trade. Foreign trade equilibrium could only be achieved if governments on all levels balanced their budgets. The Reichsbank, in addition, insisted that foreign credits be put to productive use, especially to increase export earnings so that Germany would be able to service the foreign debts. Therefore, Schacht was little concerned with the industry's and agriculture's use of foreign capital, but regarded the public institutions' use of credit as generally unproductive (McNeil 1986: 55–56). Especially the welfare orientation of the municipalities was seen by the Reichsbank as a great danger to Germany's international competitive position. It should not be supported by foreign credits (Müller 1973: 64; Upmeier 1973: 167–168).

The Reich agreed to create an Advisory Board for Foreign Credits in early 1925. It consisted of five members, representatives of the Reich's Economy and Finance Ministries, the Reichsbank, and the Prussian and Bavarian State Banks. They screened requests for municipal and state loans by majority

---

[21] Nowadays it is customary that central banks determine where public funds have to be kept. It is today an important instrument of monetary policy.

vote, the criterion for approval being its productive use. In the first two years of its existence, the Advisory Board rejected one third of the examined credit requests, mainly those of the municipalities.[22]

In March 1927, Schacht demanded that the position of the Reichsbank on the Board be strengthened after her opposition had been outvoted in 56 cases involving 400 million Marks. When nothing happened, the Reichsbank withdrew from the Board, thus blocking its operations. In this case also Schacht mobilized the support of the Reparation Agent Parker Gilbert, who – with a view to reparations transfers – was as worried about public expenditures and deficits as Schacht. The result of Schacht's initiative was minor. From November 1927 on, even credit requests for productive uses could be rejected "if further borrowing threatened the economy or the stability of the currency" (McNeil 1986: 182; see also Habedank 1981: 149; Upmeier 1973: 162–165).

In reparations politics, Schacht had always voiced his opinion. This is not surprising because the Reichsbank's foreign exchange position played a crucial role in transferring the payments. Also, foreign central bankers like Benjamin Strong in New York, Montagu Norman in London, and Emile Moreau in Paris had done likewise. Schacht had always regarded the Dawes Plan of 1924 as a reasonable settlement, as a victory of economic expertise over politics (Müller 1973: 74). It was clear that the temporary solution of the Dawes Plan would have to be followed by a final settlement. Especially after the Stresemann-Briand politics of conciliation, starting with the treaty of Locarno in October 1925, Schacht nourished the expectation that Germany could receive a substantial reduction of its reparations obligations from a final settlement.

It was Parker Gilbert who, in 1928, took the initiative for a final reparations plan (Hardach 1976: 99–100; McNeil 1986: 221–222). He, B. Strong, and Schacht agreed that the prior credit restrictions of the Federal Reserve Bank of New York (counteracting the stock market and real estate speculation in the U.S.) might well affect the credit flow to Germany and wreck the functioning of the Dawes Plan (Hardach 1976: 99, 101). Schacht expected that the Americans would play into the hands of the Germans because of their huge private investments in Germany. "Private debts first", so he thought, would induce the American experts and government to demand a low amount of reparations. As against the Dawes Plan obligation of 2.5 billion Reichsmark annually, "Schacht hoped to pay as little as 700 million

---

[22] Müller (1973): 65. The working procedure of the Advisory Board is described by Dietrich-Troeltsch (1973): 174–186.

RM a year, a sum considered even by most other Germans to be unrealistically low."[23] Before the opening of negotiations, Parker Gilbert, however, had made it clear to the German government and to Schacht that an unnual figure of around 2 billion RM had to be expected.

The Reich's government, led by the Social Democratic Chancellor Müller, nominated Schacht and the industrialist Vögler in 1928 as the German experts on the Young Committee and conceded that they could negotiate independently of instructions from the government. "Schacht was undoubtedly selected to represent Germany because of his enormous stature in foreign circles, and his determination to reduce or end reparations." (McNeil 1986: 231). Vögler was chosen in order to gain the conservatives' acceptance of the negotiations' outcome, or, in case of failure, to use him as a scapegoat.

During the negotiations from February 9 through June 7, 1929 Schacht used his independence of the government to play far more than his central banker's role. Gilbert had already observed that the Reichsbank's President was "extraordinarily jealous of Herr Stresemann", Germany's Foreign Affairs Minister (McNeil 1986: 224). And, in fact, Schacht not only negotiated German reparations annuities, transfer protection, and elimination of foreign control over Germany's credit and financial policies, but also demanded foreign policy concessions, namely the return of the Polish corridor and of the former colonies to Germany, in exchange for paying 1.65 billion RM annually on reparations account without transfer protection. Schacht's political demands antagonized not only the Allied governments and experts, but also the German government and especially Stresemann. Schacht retorted that he had been stabbed in the back by his own government, an allusion to the ominous legend about the cause of Germany's defeat in the War.[24] The political demands were dropped from the agenda. Owen Young proposed and reached a compromise solution of an average annuity of 2 billion RM starting with 1.675 in the first year, gradually increasing to 2.43 in 1965/66 and then declining until the end of reparations in 1987/88. Foreign supervision and interference with the management of the German economy was ended. A modified transfer protection was retained for two thirds of Germany's annual obligations. And, on Schacht's initiative, the Bank for International Settlements (BIS) was created to coordinate and facilitate the payments (Habedank 1981: 173–174). All this, in contrast to Germany's

---

[23] McNeil (1986): 225. Schacht (1931) reports the story of the Young Plan negotiations as Schacht saw it.
[24] Müller (1973): 84. Documents cited in Habedank (1981): 171–172, rather support Schacht's viewpoint.

Dawes Plan obligations, was objectively quite an advance, as historians have recently asserted (Jacobson 1972: 272–276; Leffler 1979: 211; Link 1970: 469–477). But Schacht's expectation that the American private creditors' interest would prevail in the negotiations and help Germany to reduce its reparations obligations by much more had not materialized. Instead, it was the American taxpayers' and government's insistence on the repayment of the inter-allied debts that shaped the outcome of the Young Plan. While Vögler resigned under pressure from his conservative friends, Schacht signed the Young Plan for fear of the Reichsbank's position and Germany's credit in case of a failure. And – in his own judgment – the payments would soon prove to be economically impossible and lead to new negotiations. Characteristically, however, he shifted the responsibility for the consequences to the German government.[25]

Since Schacht had failed to reach his financial and political objectives in the negotiations but had nevertheless signed the Plan, he was caught in the dilemma of defending and denouncing it. During the first months after signing the Plan, he still defended it with loyalty to the German government. But with the publication of his memorandum on December 6, 1929, he started to distance himself from the Young Plan. He argued that the German government had destroyed the conditions under which the Plan could have functioned. In fact, the experts' report had recommended tax reductions, especially for business. Schacht contended that he had given his signature in exchange for the government's promise to implement a substantial fiscal reform and that now the government procrastinated. In addition, he blamed the government for the so-called Liquidity Agreements of October 1929 with Great Britain and Poland in which Germany abandoned claims to property lost in the First World War (Müller 1973: 88–89).

The government's public answer followed the next day and was clear enough: "The hastiness with which the Reichsbank President has taken position, endangers the unified conduct of the state's affairs".[26] But Schacht's memorandum was applauded by the Nationalists and the National Socialists who had organized a referendum against the Young Plan. The conservative Nationalists, representing mainly agriculture and heavy industry, had launched their very popular attack on the Young Plan chiefly in order to

---

[25] Schacht (1955): 240–247, 243. How Kastl, the RDI's (= Association of German Industries) executive member of the board who replaced Vögler and advocated a more flexible position, managed to get Schacht's signature, is described by Lüke (1958): 176–177.

[26] My translation from a quotation in Müller (1973): 89.

bring down the Great-Coalition government (Social Democrats, Center, and bourgeois parties) in favor of a dictatorial government to be instituted by the Reich's President Hindenburg, a conservative nationalist himself. After the Association of German Industries had published a crushing critique of the government's fiscal and economic policies on December 2, 1929,[27] Schacht's memorandum added fuel to the flames.

When the German and Allied governments met in January for the second Hague Conference to implement the Young Plan, Schacht launched another forceful attack. He threatened that the Reichsbank would not participate in the BIS if the Liquidity Agreements were not revised and if provisions for sanctions against a defaulting Germany were implemented. This declaration stunned the Allied governments and threatened to break up the conference. But the German government reacted with determination to the "mutiny" of the Bank. Within hours, a consortium of banks under the leadership of the Prussian Bank was organized by the government to take up the German shares in the BIS. At the same time, the creditor nations were assured that the Reich would force the Reichsbank by law to play its role in the BIS as planned. This saved the conference, but set the stage for Schacht's resignation. Especially Foreign Affairs Minister Curtius was now determined to stop Schacht's trespassing into the field of foreign policy. The state-within-the-state situation had to be ended. When at the end of February 1930 Schacht sent a telegram to Owen D. Young informing him that the experts' Plan had been so mutilated in the recent process of implementation that he would "decline any responsibility whatsoever" (McNeil 1986: 273), the matter was discussed in the cabinet on March 4, 1930. Three days later and four days before the Young Plan was adopted by the Reichstag, Schacht declared his resignation to the Central Committee on the grounds that the Young Plan endangered the stability of the currency. Worried about the effect of Schacht's move on currency stability, the government insisted that the official minutes of the meeting stated that Schacht was no longer willing to take responsibility for the government's foreign policy (Habedank 1981: 190–193; Hardach 1976: 107; Kroyer 1955: 79–80).

Schacht, as well as Parker Gilbert, had been criticizing the government's fiscal policies for years, especially since 1927.[28] From that year on, the Reich's budget showed deficits that could not be funded by long-term loans

---

[27] *Aufstieg oder Niedergang* (1929). Schacht had always been close to the RDI's position. See Habedank (1981).
[28] Pentzlin (1980): 101, 108, 130. On this and the following points see also James (1985): 95–118.

(Institut für Konjunkturforschung 1933: 174; Lüke 1958: 87–96). Not only the interest payments for government debt, but also the Dawes annuities on reparations account were rising rapidly. Previously, during the economic crisis of 1926, the government had reduced a number of tax rates and started a work creation program to spur the economy and to raise employment. This was sort of a Keynesian anticyclical policy (Blaich 1977: 109; Hertz-Eichenrode 1982: 81–206; Krohn 1974: 195–205; McNeil 1986: 124–129). When the economy had recovered in 1927, the government decided on a pay increase for civil servants that averaged about 25 percent and for some groups even reached 40 percent (Brüning 1970: 127; McNeil 1986: 169–170). This widened the budget deficits even more and set the stage for a desperate fiscal situation in 1929 which Schacht used to exert pressure upon the government in favor of a fiscal reform. It eventually led to the downfall of the last elected government of the Weimar Republic.

Just when the Dawes Plan annuities had reached their maximum, the economy began to falter. Tax yields fell and the government's unemployment outlays rose. At the same time, there was a liquidity squeeze on the German money market due to the fading of capital imports since the Federal Reserve Bank of New York had started its restrictive credit policies in 1928. Germany's big private banks refused a request by Finance Minister Hilferding for providing additional long-term or short-term loans to the government (McNeil 1986: 258–259). At the end of 1929, the Reich was short of cash and desperately needed credit. It had begun, but not yet terminated its fiscal reform program.[29] In spite of assurances given to Parker Gilbert that the Reich would not seek new foreign credits as long as the Young Plan bonds were not placed on the international capital market, the German government, in December 1929, found itself compelled to ask Dillon Read & Co., New York, for a short-term credit of $ 75 million (McNeil 1986: 265–266). But the German intermediaries, the Mendelssohn Bank and the Deutsche Bank, had been forced by Schacht to withdraw from the deal (McNeil 1986: 268–269). Parker Gilbert and the French government had also protested such a tapping of the American credit market. On December 19, Dillon Read refused the credit. The German government then realized that there was no way around Schacht to avoid the government's default. In this situation, Schacht could and did dictate the conditions. He insisted that the Reich oblige itself to establish a sinking fund (out of ordinary revenue and from cuts in expenditures) to redeem its floating debt. This was the content of the "Lex

---

[29] Müller (1973): 95–96. For details of fiscal measures taken in 1929 see Habedank (1981): 183, 187.

Schacht" that the Reichstag passed on December 22, 1929, after the Social Democrat in the Finance Ministry, Hilferding, and his State Secretary Popitz had resigned as a consequence of their defeat by Schacht.[30]

Schacht's move was a time-bomb for the Great-Coalition government. It had to keep raising revenues and cutting expenditures. The question of who should pay overstrained the coalition ranging from left-wing Social Democrats to the industry-oriented bourgeois German People's Party. The government fell on March 27, 1930 over the issue whether the finances of the unemployment insurance should be put on a sounder basis by cutting the doles or by raising the fees (Maurer 1973: 129–139). Heinrich Brüning took the Chancellor's office on March 30, 1930. Henceforth, Germany was more and more governed by emergency decrees, a suitable preparation for Hitler's totalitarian state from 1933 on.

As much as Schacht's personal aversion against the Social Democrats, Chancellor Müller, and Finance Minister Hilferding, had contributed to his bitter conflicts with the government in 1929/30, the high esteem of the conservative Luther (Schacht's successor at the head of the Reichsbank) for Brüning served to bring about a rather good cooperation between the Reichsbank and the government in the following years.[31] Luther also reports that after the experience with Schacht's behavior vis-à-vis the Müller government he took pains to reintroduce a clear division of functions between the Reichsbank and the government and to leave political matters exclusively with the government (Luther 1964: 128–129). Luther's style differed completely from Schacht's. He never criticized or fought government proposals in public. Instead, in public he loyally identified with the Government (Luther 1964: 133). Cooperation was all the more easy, as Luther shared Brüning's basic policy aims, especially in reparations and deflation politics (Luther 1964: 137, 157, 245). Without being required to do so by legal arrangements, he sought prior consent from the government for his credit policies, especially for discount changes.[32]

Nevertheless, several issues led to conflicts:

- the financing of work creation programs,
- credit creation during the banking crisis and after,

---

[30] Müller (1973): 97–98, Pentzlin (1980): 131, Habedank (1981): 188–189. By the end of 1930, the sinking fund actually reached the amount of 450 million RM.
[31] Luther (1964): 129–130. Brüning, however, remained critical of Luther's abilities. See Brüning (1970): 376.
[32] Examples are mentioned in Brüning (1970): 286, 323, 343, 479.

– the reduction of the discount rate in connection with the fourth emergency decree in December 1931.

In July 1930, the Brüning government proposed an employment creation program. It provided for investments in infrastructure and was to be financed by funds of the Reich's railway and postal companies and by a 300-million-RM foreign loan to the Reich. For the loan operation the government needed the support of the Reichsbank. Luther refused and thus killed the project (Habedank 1981: 200). Again in Mai 1932, when Brüning prepared a work creation program, for which he needed an 800-million-RM credit from the Reichsbank, Luther resisted (Brüning 1970: 572). "Luther opposed all these plans each time" (Brüning 1970: 575). This, however, was in line with his basic conviction that the financing of such programs had to wait until the end of reparations, which came about in Lausanne in June/July 1932 (Luther 1964: 240, 250, 256). The subsequent employment programs of the Papen and Schleicher governments were supported by the Reichsbank.

Although basically in line with Brüning's deflationary course, the Reichsbank also turned out to be more restrictive in her credit policy during and after the banking crisis of July 1931 than Brüning or other members of the cabinet wished. Luther had no contingency plans for such a credit crisis (Brüning 1970: 299, 309), and he was evidently unaware of the Bagehot principle, i.e. to satisfy the private demand for banknotes in case of a domestic run on the banks. Brüning mobilized two reputed foreign financial experts, the Swedish banker M. Wallenberg and the Harvard professor O. Sprague, to talk Luther into a less restrictive credit policy. Obviously, it was very hard work to convince him that the Reichsbank's immediate help for endangered banks and savings institutions was absolutely imperative and not inflationary (Brüning 1970: 346–349). When the depression deepened further, even politicians close to Brüning began to develop ideas about how to stimulate the economy (Holtfrerich 1982). Warmbold, Brüning's Minister for the Economy since October 1931 and a member of the board of IG Farben, fought a bitter dispute with Luther over the Reichsbank's too restrictive credit policy. Both had threatened to resign over the issue, but Brüning was eager to reconcile the two and to keep them both on his crisis management team. Brüning's own view was that Warmbold had the right recipe, but that it was the wrong moment to prescribe it (Brüning 1970: 503–504).

The greatest conflict between Luther and Brüning came about in preparation of the fourth emergency decree for the protection of the economy and the finances (promulgated on December 8, 1931). It further reduced German prices, rents, salaries, wages, and interest rates in response to the devaluation of the British and other currencies since September. Luther, since the summer under pressure from the Americans and British to keep interest rates high in Germany, resisted Brüning's demands for a lower discount rate (Brüning 1970: 413, 419, 474).

> Between Luther and me matters came to a dramatic clash on the evening of the 7th (Dec.) and during the night. Everything was at stake at the last minute. Finally, Luther agreed to a discount rate reduction of (only) 1 percent, which made the (planned) compulsory conversion of interest rates by 3 percent impossible (Brüning 1970: 478).

Luther had obviously threatened to resign if Brüning insisted on a larger reduction (Brüning 1970: 479). His resistance was due to the realistic fear that a cut of the discount rate might antagonize the Allies and endanger the goodwill and the work of the Wiggins Committee at the BIS in Basel (Brüning 1970: 489). The cut of the discount rate by only 1 percent was, however, tolerated by the Allied bankers.

2.4 The Nazi Period (1933–1945)

During this period the Reichsbank was gradually subjected to total control by the Reich. For, the principle of divison of power is alien to a totalitarian state. Furthermore, the Nazi government needed complete subordination of the central bank in support of its war efforts.

2.4.1 The Legal Arrangements

By the law of October 27, 1933, the banking law of 1924 was again revised (*Reichsgesetzblatt* 1933/II: 827–828). The General Council, through which the private owners of the Bank had exercised an important degree of control over the Reichsbank, was abolished. The Bank's President was to be appointed by the Reich's President, after hearing the opinion of the Bank's Directorate. The Directorate members were to be nominated by the Bank's President, but appointed by the Reich's President. In addition, the right to revoke Directorate members or the Bank's President was transferred from the General Council to the Reich's President alone.

The Reichsbank was empowered to trade on the open market in treasury and regular bonds without any limitation. This not only meant the introduction of a new instrument of monetary policy, the open market policy, but also easier access to the Bank's credit for the Reich. The Reichsbank was authorized to fall short of the 40 percent coverage requirement, subject to majority decisions by the Directorate and the Central Committee. The provision for taxes in this case was abolished.

The next legal change came about on January 30, 1937, this time by a simple declaration of the "Führer" in the Reichstag that the Reich had resumed unlimited sovereignty over the Reichsbank. It is probably not a coincidence that it took place on the fourth anniversary of the Nazi's seizure of power. This declaration was the final breach of Germany's international obligations from the Treaty of Versailles, in particular those that concerned the Reichsbank and still provided for a participation of the BIS in changes of the German central banking law (Bayrhoffer 1941: 94; Puhl 1941: 49–50). The Reich's government, not the Reichstag, passed a law accordingly on February 10, 1937 (*Reichsgesetzblatt* 1937/II. 47–48). It stipulated – similar to the law of 1875 – that the Reichsbank Directorate administered the Bank, but that it was subordinated to the "Führer" and Reich's Chancellor.

The final reform came about when shortly before World War II the Reich's government passed the banking law of June 15, 1939 (*Reichsgesetzblatt* 1939/I: 1015–1020; Speyerer 1940: 45–58). The Bank was now totally subordinated to the Nazis' policy aims and to the "Führer". The introduction to the law stated that the Bank was subjected to the Reich's unlimited sovereignty and that she was obliged to support the realization of aims set by the Nazi leadership within her field of functions, "the safeguarding of the value of the German currency" being mentioned as the Bank's prime duty. Further functions were mentioned in § 2:

– to regulate the circulation of money and the clearing of payments domestically and with foreign countries,
– to care for the utilization of the monetary funds available in the German economy, but this on a non-profit basis ("gemeinnützig") and in a way expedient to the national economy ("in volkswirtschaftlich zweckmäßiger Weise").

The Bank's Directorate was subjected to instruction and supervision by the "Führer" and Reich's Chancellor. The Directorate merely administered the Bank. Its decisions were no longer taken by majority vote, but by the Bank's President alone (§ 3). The "Führer" was given the exclusive right to appoint and revoke the Bank's President and the members of the Directorate. The Bank's private owners retained their "General Assembly", but were left powerless. The Central Committee was abolished and substituted by an advisory council with members chosen by the Bank's President alone.

In addition to bonds the Bank was from now on allowed to trade in treasury bills, the total amount of which was left to a decision by the "Führer" (§ 13). Gold was valued at the old parity. The Bank was obliged to buy gold at this price, but the selling was left subject to her discretion (§ 4).

All minimum coverage requirements for the Reichsbank's note issue were dropped. Gold and foreign exchange reserves should only suffice to clear accounts in international transactions and to safeguard the external value of the German currency. Whatever portion of the note issue was not covered by gold or foreign exchange, could be covered by commercial bills and checks, the Reich's treasury bills, bonds and lombard credits on daily notice.

Thus, the "Führer" had attained total control of the Reichsbank and an unlimited access to her credit.

2.4.2 The Degree of Dependence in Practice

In this period of a manipulated currency standard – as against the gold exchange standard from 1924 on and the gold standard before the First World War – the Reichsbank's relations to the government were again the primary factor limiting her freedom of action. From 1933 to the beginning of 1937, the Bank was still formally autonomous vis-à-vis the government, although in October 1933 the Reich's President had assumed control over appointing the Bank's President and Directorate. Schacht, who had helped to pave the Nazis' way to power, was appointed the Bank's President on March 17, 1933, after the General Council had unanimously voted in favor of him. He was dismissed in January 1939. In addition, he was the Minister for the Economy and thus an ordinary member of the Reich's cabinet from August 1934 to November 1937 (thereafter, as a Minister without Portfolio), and the government's General Commissioner for the War Economy from May 1935 to November 1937.[33]

Until 1936, when full employment was reached and conflicts arose between financing the government's armament programs and stabilizing the value of the currency, Schacht cooperated willingly with the Nazi government in skillfully using the Reichsbank's credit to finance the government's employment (and later on armament) programs. In practice, however, the Bank had lost her independence already during this period. Formal independence from the government in her decision making was tolerated by the Nazi leadership only as long as an economic policy consensus between the government and the Bank existed, in other words, as long as Schacht's policy of stabilizing the German economy and currency did not conflict with the Nazi government's policy of war preparation. The total subordination of the Bank to the command of the Führer in early 1937 and in June 1939 the

---

[33] Hansmeyer/Caesar (1976): 375. For details of Schacht's activities in his government functions see Boelcke (1983): 77–177.

abolition of all minimum coverage requirements, the opening of the Bank to the unlimited discounting of treasury bills and her obligation to support the realization of aims set by the Nazi leadership were only the final steps to declare formally what the Bank had already lost in practice, namely her independence of the government and of Nazi policy aims.

It is a historical irony that the Bank's President Schacht, skillful, ambitious and conceited as he was, overestimated his influence with the Nazi government to such a degree that he did not realize the erosion of the Bank's independence for a long time. He even invented, demanded or supported measures that – as it turned out later – undermined the Reichsbank's freedom of action. For example, on August 28, 1934 he agreed with Hitler explicitly on behalf of the Reichsbank that for a transition period the Bank would open her credit to finance part of the armament's program (Grotkopp 1954: 286). The Reichsbank also supported the "Führer's" declaration of January 30, 1937 that the Reich had assumed unlimited sovereignty over the Reichsbank and the ensuing law of February 10, 1937 that terminated the Bank's legal independence of instructions by the "Führer" and Reich's Chancellor (Schacht 1937: 137–139; *Verwaltungsbericht der Reichsbank für das Jahr 1936*: 8).

Before Schacht was appointed to the Reichsbank's Presidency, the Nazi government had his and the Reichsbank's promise that the Bank would finance a major employment program (Schacht 1949: 37). On the basis of prior ideas and actions by others Schacht himself invented the ingenious device (the "Mefo" bills) by which several employment programs as well as almost half of the Reich's military expenditures from 1933 to 1937 were financed (Hansmeyer/Caesar 1976: 392). This very issue of "Mefo" bills finally led to the conflict between the Reichsbank and the government that terminated Schacht's Presidency.

Schacht had obviously misjudged his position of power, perhaps because he had inappropriately transferred his experience with Reichsbank-government relations in the pluralistic Weimar Republic to the totalitarian environment in the Nazi period. As one scholar put it:

He felt that he would become the real ruler because it had been his experience that financial difficulties of the State made the government dependent on the wishes of those who controlled the capital market. Schacht intended to use Hitler and the National Socialists to implement his own ideas rather than to assist in establishing the Hitler platform. Some writers even believed that Schacht intended ultimately to lead the new Germany himself with Hitler as a mere puppet (Simpson 1969: 84).

As it turned out, Schacht was used and let himself be used by the Nazi government. Hitler resisted Schacht's resignation as Minister for the Economy for months (Boelcke 1983: 175) and was determined to keep Schacht as the Reichsbank's President when his four-year term in that office ended in early 1937 (Hansmeyer/Caesar 1976: 378). Even after Hitler had dismissed him from the Bank's Presidency, he kept Schacht in the cabinet as Minister without Portfolio until January 1943 (Pentzlin 1980: 254–256). Schacht's public reputation was still too valuable to Hitler to drop him completely. The battle between the Reichsbank, especially Schacht, and the Nazi government over who could use who was clearly won by the government.

2.4.3 Cases of Conflict

When in August 1936, Hitler had initiated a secret four-year plan to mobilize the German economy for a future war and in October 1936 had appointed Hermann Göring as the Commissioner for this plan, Schacht's erosion of power began. Schacht's and the Reichsbank's primary aim had been to reflate the German economy up to the point of full employment, but to reduce credit creation short of inflation. The Nazi government's primary aim, on the other hand, was to prepare Germany for a war irrespective of the economic costs. As long as the Reichsbank's credit creation served the two purposes at the same time, there was no conflict. When, by 1936, the economy had gathered momentum to such a degree that skilled labor became scarce, that prices showed an upward movement, and that foreign exchange for the payment of imports was in short supply, Schacht urged the government to reduce the speed of rearmament in order to avoid its inflationary consequences (Petzina 1968: 19, 50; Schacht 1949: 62).

The main vehicle to put the Reichsbank's credit at the disposal of the Nazi government had been the "Mefo" bills. This invention of Schacht allowed the government to pay private firms for armament deliveries with Reichsbank credits. It was designed to circumvent the clauses of the banking law – itself a part of international treaties – that restricted the Reichsbank in discounting treasury bills. The mechanism functioned as follows. For the payment of deliveries to the government private firms drew bills accepted and signed by the "Metallurgische Forschungsgesellschaft" ("Mefo"), a private firm with no other purpose. The Reich's government, however, guaranteed the "Mefo's" obligations. The Reichsbank, in turn, discounted these bills. The bills formally had a three-month currency term, but were designed to be renewed for a total term of five years (Hansmeyer/Caesar 1976: 392). In fact, they were, first, not short-term but medium- to long-term paper, secondly, not commercial but financial bills, and thirdly, not really obligations of a private firm but of the government. This was a three-fold circumvention of the banking law.

From 1936 on, Schacht urged the government to stop the issuing of "Mefo" bills and to start repaying the outstanding ones. When his four-year term as the Reichsbank's President was up for renewal in early 1937, he insisted on a one-year extension only, which Hitler conceded. This meant that the next reappointment would coincide with approximately the time when – after five years, as agreed – the first "Mefo" bills had to be redeemed by the Reich. During 1937, Schacht, who enjoyed the confidence of the German industrialists and, therefore, was still a key to the Nazis' good relations with private industry, threatened not to remain in his position at the Reichsbank if the issuance of "Mefo" bills continued. He also insisted on the redemption of these bills, which indeed took place on a small scale in 1937 with funds of the Armed Forces and the proceeds of bond sales (Hansmeyer/ Caesar 1976: 393). The government finally conceded to terminate the issuance of "Mefo" bills by March 31, 1938. Schacht, reassured that this would slow down the speed of rearmament, consented to another four-year term as President of the Reichsbank from 1938 on (Schacht 1949: 71–72). But Schacht who had hoped he could force the government to redeem the "Mefo" bills five years after their first issuance, by legal action if necessary, had to concede their prolongation once more.

From 1937 on, he had also quarreled with the government over who should control the capital market after the Finance Ministry had started to bypass the Reichsbank when raising funds there. The Reichsbank protested and argued that she had agreed to help finance the government's armament expenditures only on the condition that the government's use of the capital market would remain dependent on the Bank's consent (Hansmeyer/Caesar 1976: 378). Such protests remained fruitless but contributed to the further straining of relations between the Bank and the government. While the government's armament expenditures and credit needs remained high in 1938, the money and capital markets tightened. The Reichsbank refused the government's demand for a special credit. Instead, credit was supplied by private banks that unloaded more and more of their "Mefo" bills from their portfolio onto the Reichsbank. This development triggered Schacht's famous confidential letter of January 7, 1939, to Hitler, also signed by all other members of the Reichsbank Directorate. It accused the government of inflationary finance and of ruining, at the same time, the credit of the Reichsbank, in other words, of ruining the value of the currency.[34] Hitler reacted immediately and dismissed Schacht and three of his colleagues from office

---

[34] Hansmeyer/Caesar (1976): 380–384, where parts of the letter are reprinted. See also Beck (1955): 135–137.

and appointed the Minister for the Economy, Walther Funk, already Schacht's successor in that office, to the Presidency of the Reichsbank. Funk headed the Bank as a colorless administrator, even more so than the banking law of June 1939 demanded. There were no more conflicts with the government except over details such as the settlement of handling charges for the "Mefo" bills and the amount of pensions (Hansmeyer/Caesar 1976: 388).

2.5 From 1945 to the Present

At the end of the War, when Germany was divided into four zones, the Reichsbank ceased to exist as a central bank for all of Germany. The victorious Allies preferred to reorganize Germany as a decentralized, federal state with a federal central banking structure (Geisler 1953: 83–84; Wandel 1980: 59–62). In the three Western occupational zones, State Central Banks ("Landeszentralbanken") were organized for each state. The British insisted on one coordinating central bank. This resulted in the foundation of the "Bank deutscher Länder" (Bank of the German States) on March 1, 1948 in Frankfurt (Geisler 1953: 86–87; Wandel 1980: 65–68).

The federal two-tier structure of the West German central banking system was similar to the Federal Reserve System in the USA, but compared to the Reichsbank's traditional structure it was an innovation in Germany. After long discussions among the experts, the federal two-tier structure was only rudimentarily preserved when the "Deutsche Bundesbank" was created in July 1957 (Becker 1982: 61–77).

The division of functions between the State Central Banks, on the one hand, and the "Bank deutscher Länder" or later the "Bundesbank", on the other, can be summarized as follows. The "Landeszentralbanken" have no right to issue banknotes. They serve as the lender of last resort for the banks in their state, but the terms on which they do so are decided on by the federal central bank. The latter one possesses a monopoly on the issuance of banknotes, and on shaping monetary and credit policies. The basic difference from the centralized Reichsbank system is that the majority in the decision making body of the Bundesbank (and of its forerunner) consists of the Presidents of the State Central Banks. The structure of decision making, therefore, is different, more federal (Geisler 1953: 95).

This difference to the Reichsbank's structure is an important, but not the main issue to be discussed in this paper. It is rather the degree of dependence or independence of the central banking system's policy vis-à-vis the government.

2.5.1 The Legal Arrangements

In shaping the legal framework of West Germany's central banking structure, Allied political aims and the German experiences with prior central banking organizations played a role. The political aim of the Allies was to decentralize former power centers of the German economy in general and of the banking system in particular (Wandel 1980: 48–65). The German experience with central banking had been: twice a great inflation, when the Reichsbank had been subordinated to complete control by the government, and bitter conflicts between the Reichsbank and the government during the second half of the 1920s, when the Bank could legally work against the government's overall economic policies.

Before the Federal Republic was founded in May 1949, the Allies had organized the decentralized system of "Landeszentralbanken" and the "Bank deutscher Länder".[35] The "Bank deutscher Länder" was founded as a juridical person under public law. Her capital was provided by the State Central Banks. Her functions were defined in the following way:

> to promote in the common interest the best use of the financial resources of the area served by the member State Central Banks, to strengthen the currency and credit system and to coordinate the activities of the said Central Banks (Introduction).

She was obliged to "effect the entire settlement of bank balances resulting from transfers between the Länder" (Article 3). It was explicitly stated that "the Bank shall not be subject to the instructions of any political body or public non-judicial agency" (Article 1). At first, however, the Allies retained some control over the Bank: "In determining the policies of the Bank, the Board of Directors (Central Bank Council) shall be subject to such directions as may be issued by the Allied Bank Commission" (Article 2). The Bank had the exclusive right of note issue and was obliged to "promote the solvency and liquidity of the member State Central Banks". She was to assure "the maximum uniformity in banking policies within the several Länder" (Article 3). For this purpose she was empowered to issue directions as to discount rates, open market operations and minimum reserve requirements. She was established as the "fiscal agent" of the government, but her short-term credit to the government was limited to a fixed maximum. She was empowered to trade in treasury bonds on the open market, the extent of which, however, remained at her discretion.

---

[35] British Military Government Ordinance No. 129. The same law was promulgated in the U.S. (Law No. 60) and French Zones (Ord. No. 155a). Wussow (1955): 22–23.

The policy of the Bank was determined by the Central Bank Council (by majority vote) and executed by the Directorate (Article 4). The Central Bank Council consisted of the Presidents of the State Central Banks (who were appointed by the states), the Chairman of the Directorate, and the President of the Central Bank Council, the latter being elected by the President of the State Central Banks. The Central Bank Council was empowered to elect or recall the members of the Directorate and its President, and to determine their term of office.

In August 1951, the West German parliament enacted a significant change of Article 2 of the Allied law (Bundesgesetzblatt 1951: 509). The Allied Bank Commission and thus its factual veto power over the Bank's decisions were abolished. The Bank, instead, was obliged to support the general economic policy line of the government "within the framework of her functions". To integrate further the government's economic and the Bank's credit policies, the Finance Minister and the Minister for the Economy were entitled to participate in the meetings of the Central Bank Council, or even to call for such a meeting. They had no voting rights, but were empowered to forward a motion. If one of them found that a decision of the Central Bank Council ran counter to the general economic policy line of the government, he had the right to suspend the decision for eight days. The by-laws of the Bank could be changed by the Central Bank Council only, but – instead of the Allied Bank Commission – the West German government had to consent, this being a rudimentary form of government supervision.

The West German constitution of 1949 had already provided for the establishment of a Bundesbank (Art. 88). This happened on July 26, 1957,[36] when the "Bank deutscher Länder" became the Bundesbank. The decentralization of the central banking system was largely reversed. The "Landeszentralbanken" retained their name but were merged with the Bundesbank and became her main offices in each state.

Henceforth, the Presidents of the State Central Banks were formally nominated by the federal chamber of parliament, the Bundesrat, after the opinions of the State's government and the Central Bank Council had been heard. They were then appointed by the Bund's President (§ 8), but this, in fact, was only a formality (Caesar 1981: 186; Kaiser 1980: 36–37). The Bank's capital now belonged to the Bund.

The functions of the Bundesbank were defined as follows: to regulate the circulation of money and the provision of credit for the economy in order to

---

[36] *Bundesgesetzblatt* (1957 I): 745–755. For the standard interpretation of the law see Spindler/Becker/Starke (1973).

secure the value of the currency, and to take care of the clearing of payments between banks domestically and internationally (§ 3). The Bundesbank was obliged to advise the government in important matters concerning the currency (§ 13), for instance, on decisions on the Mark's parity. The Central Bank Council was retained as the policy-making body, while the Directorate of the Bundesbank and the Managing Boards of the State Central Banks were now the executive organs.

The Central Bank Council again consisted of the Presidents of the ten State Central Banks and, from then on, of (up to ten members of) the Bundesbank's Directorate. The President of the Directorate was the President of the Central Bank Council at the same time. The usual term of office was fixed to be eight years. Revocation was possible only in case of an egregious neglect of duty or of incompetence.

The President, Vice-President and the members of the Directorate were no longer elected by the Central Bank Council, but were nominated by the federal government and formally appointed by the Bund's President. Before the nomination, however, the government was obliged to hear the opinion of the Central Bank Council.

The Bank's relation to the government was regulated as in 1951. It was explicitly stated that the Bank was independent of instructions from the government, but that she was obliged to support the government's overall economic policy line "within the framework of her functions" (§ 12), i.e. only insofar as her measures did not conflict with securing currency stability. Decisions of the Central Bank Council could be suspended by the government for two weeks (§ 13). The law, however, contained no further provision to regulate a conflict between the Bank and the government, for instance, by arbitration. The maximum amount of short-term credit to the government was again strictly limited (§ 20). It remains to be mentioned that the Bundesbank can be dissolved only by a federal law, but this at any time (§ 44).

2.5.2 The Degree of Dependence in Practice

Until the change of the banking law abolished the Allied Bank Commission in August 1951, the "Bank deutscher Länder" was completely independent of the German federal government. The states appointed their State Central Bank's Presidents. Thus, in principle, political changes within the states could lead to a different composition of the Central Bank Council. Yet, they could not occur at the same time, since the election dates varied and policital trends in the states were not synchronous.

Until August 1951, however, the Allied Bank Commission was in a similar legal position vis-à-vis the Bank as the Reich's Chancellor had been vis-à-vis the Reichsbank until May 1922. In both periods the Bank could be subjected to instructions. The Allied Bank Commission never used this power, since the Directorate's first Chairman, Wilhelm Vocke, closely coordinated the Bank's policies with the Allied Bank Commission (Wandel 1980: 81).

After the Allied supervision of the Bank's activities had been removed in August 1951, the Bank enjoyed an almost complete independence of the federal government for the reasons given above. As from 1876 to 1914, and again, from 1924 to 1933, her short-term credit to the government was strictly limited. Thus, the Bank's credit could not be "exploited" by the government. In contrast to the earlier periods, the Bank was no longer subjected to any note coverage requirements, a fact enhancing her degree of independence. She was, however, required to defend the parity of the Mark in the fixed exchange rate system that imposed a sort of gold standard discipline. The main restriction to the Bank's freedom of action from August 1951 to July 1957 was her obligation to support the government's overall economic policy.

The law that created the Bundesbank in July 1957 somewhat restricted the Bank's independence from the Bund's legislative and executive institutions (Wandel 1980: 80–81). The Bund's government now nominated the Directorate members and the Bank's President, while, formally the "Bundesrat", and in fact, the state governments nominated the Presidents of the State Central Banks. In both cases, the Bund's President made their appointment in only a formal sense. In order to minimize the danger of political appointments, however, the Bundesbank law provided for a usual term of office of eight years, twice the interval of federal and state elections. The appointments were to take place at such intervals that during one legislative period only a portion of the seats in the Central Bank Council could be refilled.

While the appointment of the Bank's President and the Directorate members has never been controversial from the viewpoint of required competence (the Central Bank Council never gave a negative opinion), this was different for the State Central Bank Presidents in the 1960s and especially in the 1970s. The Central Bank Council forwarded a number of negative opinions on the nominees of the state governments, but never succeeded in stopping an appointment. Thus, political appointments have been made, but this, apparently, never had any effect on the "impartiality" of the Bundesbank (Caesar 1981: 187). Thus, the Bundesbank's decision to date have been relatively free from party politics, all the more so, as her guaranteed freedom from government instructions is often regarded as almost of constitutional rank, even though it could be changed by a simple law.[37]

Thus, the Bundesbank appears to be a fourth constitutional power besides the legislative, executive, and judicial branches of government.[38] This is due to the Bank's unquestionable success in preserving the stability of the Mark, particularly, since Germany underwent disastrous inflations twice in periods when the Reichsbank was not independent of the German government (Caesar 1981: 202–205).

In practice, however, the Bundesbank's room for manoeuvre was somewhat restricted by international capital flows as long as the Mark was tied into an international system of fixed exchange rates, especially after the full convertibility of the Mark had been established in 1958 and until the floating exchange rate system was introduced in 1973. It remained the government's and not the Bank's responsibility to decide on the Mark's parity. Thus, the position of the Bundesbank was strengthened when floating exchange rates were introduced.

In international comparison, it has been observed that "in Europe the central bank with the greatest degree of autonomy is undoubtedly the Deutsche Bundesbank" (Bosman 1979: 255).

2.5.3 Cases of Conflict

The first President of the Bank's Directorate, Wilhelm Vocke (from 1948 to 1958), and the first Chancellor of the Federal Republic, Konrad Adenauer (from 1949 to 1963), were known to have been rather critical of each other (Wandel 1980: 76–77). When in 1950 the Korea boom and Germany's incipient economic miracle led to inflationary pressures, the Bundesbank raised

---

[37] Huppertz (1977): 80. Uhlenbruck (1967): 53–54, even holds the opinion that the independent status of the Bank could not be changed by a simple law, but – like a change of the constitution – only by a two-thirds majority in both chambers of parliament. Federal courts, however, have taken a different position. The *Bundesverwaltungsgericht,* e.g., ruled on January 29, 1973: "The independence of the Bundesbank is neither founded nor excluded by article 88 of the Basic Law [i.e. the Federal Republic's constitution]. Its regulation in the Bundesbank Law is compatible with the Basic Law, especially with its article 20, paragraph 1." *Entscheidungen des Bundesverwaltungsgerichts* (1973): 334. See also Robert (1978): 40–41, Schmidt (1973): 655–680, Schmidt (1981): 63–64, Bonin (1979): 159–190.

[38] Robert 1978: 35. This view was taken once even by a federal court. The *Bundesverfassungsgericht* in a decision of November 3, 1982 described the Bundesbank's position as being "constitutionally independent". *Entscheidungen des Bundesverfassungsgerichts* 1983: 183. But this has not become the dominant view.

her discount rate to 6 percent in October 1950. This was considered an unusually high rate at the time. This measure met the explicit disapproval of Adenauer (Emminger 1976: 489; Vocke 1973: 150–151). He also sharply attacked the Bank's policy in public after she had raised her discount rate in several steps from 3 percent in August 1955 to finally 5.5 percent in May 1956 (Dörge/Mairose 1969: 110–111; Emminger 1976: 492; Hahn 1968: 80–81). The Bund's government generally wished a less restrictive monetary policy of the Bank in order to facilitate West Germany's economic reconstruction. Vocke refused with the stereotyped argument "currency stability first". Adenauer regarded Vocke as a typical bureaucrat (Wandel 1980: 79). At first, he even resisted Vocke's reappointment in 1956. Although the federal government played no direct role in the selection of the Bank's President prior to the Bundesbank law of 1957, a public conflict between the government and the Bank over this issue could have hurt the prestige of both and was avoided. Adenauer favored Karl Blessing, but he was not immediately available. For this reason, Adenauer consented to Vocke's reappointment but only for two more years (Wandel 1980: 76).

After the appointment (in 1958) of Blessing, who had been Adenauer's favorite candidate, conflicts between the Bank and the government continued. The Bank was concerned about inflation during the boom of 1959 and, after futile admonitions to the government, tried to mobilize public opinion against the government's expansionary fiscal policies, again without success (Dörge/Mairose 1969: 217–219). The Bank's own restrictive monetary policy since the fall of 1959 failed due to interest-rate-induced capital imports (Emminger 1976: 500–503; Stucken 1964: 273–281). Consequently, the Bank gave up her restrictive policy in November 1960. She had shifted her priority from stabilizing price developments to stabilizing the exchange rate. The government, in turn, was also concerned about inflation, but – as a remedy – preferred a revaluation of the mark to fiscal restrictions. But the Bank, which the government was obliged to consult in matters of exchange rate parity, resisted revaluation. This policy met with the support of large parts of Germany's (export) industry. Blessing is said to even have threatened (in 1960) to resign in case of a revaluation. The government used a lot of pressure on the Bundesbank (including the threat to use its suspending veto right against a decision by the Bank on credit policy) in order finally to win her consent to a rather modest revaluation of 5 percent in March 1961 without, of course, Blessing's resignation.[39]

---

[39] Hahn (1968): 81, Caesar (1981): 188–189. Emminger (1976): 508, reports that the Central Bank Council had not been asked about the rate of revaluation. It was deter-

Another major conflicts arose in connection with the Bank's restrictive monetary policy in 1965/66. In order to win the federal elections of September 1965, the government under Ludwig Erhard, the famous former Minister for the Economy and Adenauer's successor since October 1963, had excessively increased social expenditures. To counteract their inflationary impact, the Bundesbank tightened her credit in 1965, and, although the growth in demand had already slackened, again in 1966, when West Germany's first major recession set in. The government had in vain pressured the Bundesbank to lift her restrictions. Some weeks before the downfall of Chancellor Erhard in October 1966, the government *publicly* demanded that the Bundesbank should give up her restrictive course. The Bank still refused, thus deepening the recession that brought about Erhard's downfall and the formation of the Federal Republic's first and still only Great-Coalition government in November 1966.[40] The new government under Kiesinger (in his inaugural address to parliament on December 13, 1966) again demanded a quick easing of credit restrictions. In its following meeting in December 1966, the Central Bank Council still refused to change its policy. It was not until January 1967 when the Bank started to reduce her discount rate in small steps until May 1967, a period, in which the government had in fact taken fiscal measures to balance the budget. In April 1967, the new Minister for the Economy, Karl Schiller, publicly criticized the Bundesbank's slow easing of credit, a strong indication of how much the new government's economic policy course had been restricted by the independent Bank's behavior.[41]

The next major conflict soon followed. Huge pressures on the Mark's foreign valuation had developed in 1968 from enormous current account surpluses, and, finally, from speculative capital imports. An inflation was imminent. In this situation, German industry and the conservative Christian parties' wing in the government coalition, especially Finance Minister Strauss, opposed a full revaluation of the Mark. Instead, in November 1968 the government decided on a temporary (until March 1970) tax relief for

---

mined as a compromise agreement between the Bank's President Blessing, Chancellor Adenauer (opponents of revaluation), Finance Minister Etzel, and the Minister for the Economy Erhard (revaluation advocates, see p. 495).

[40] Robert (1978): 18–19. Caesar (1981): 189. It was rumored at the time that Chancellor Erhard was overthrown by the Bank's President Blessing. See Wildenmann (1969): 14. Shortly before his death in 1971 Blessing admitted in a interview that in 1966 he "had tried with some brute force [sic] to put things in order." The rich interview is published in Brawand (1971): 50–68. The quotation is from p. 56.

[41] Robert (1978): 17–21, Caesar (1981): 189–190, Kaiser (1980): 547–59. Schiller also resisted Blessing's reappointment in 1967, but without success. Huppertz (1977): 81.

imports and taxes on exports, in effect, the equivalent of a 4 percent revaluation of the German currency, but for international merchandise trade only. The Bundesbank had opposed this measure as not being sufficient and had pleaded for a real revaluation. This became known in public.[42] Foreign governments and central banks sided with the Bundesbank's position and put additional pressure on the German government to revalue the Mark in the normal fashion. Bonn, however, resisted. Instead, the Bundesbank's behavior stimulated Bonn's political circles to reflect on possibilities for reducing the Bank's independence of the government. Public opinion, however, had rather applauded the Bank in this dispute and contributed to keeping the politicians' hands off the independent status of the Bank (Caesar 1981: 190; Roeper 1978: 161–162; Schöninger 1972: 158–161).

In 1969, massive imports of speculative capital continued. The Bundesbank again pleaded for a real revaluation of the Mark. The Bonn cabinet again refused on May 9, 1969, but was split over this issue exactly along party lines (the Christian parties against, the Social Democrats in favor). This dispute became the major economic issue in the campaign for federal elections in September 1969. The result was a government led by the Social Democrats and, therefore, a revaluation of the Mark by 9.3 percent in October 1969 (Baring 1982: 139–147; Emminger 1976: 518–519; Schöninger 1972: 158–161).

Again in 1972, pressures on the German currency from speculative capital imports triggered a conflict between the Bundesbank under its new President Karl Klasen and parts of the government, especially its Minister for the Economy and Finance Karl Schiller. Both agreed that measures against the influx of capital had to be taken. The Bundesbank favored a license system for the buying of German bonds by foreigners, i.e. the application of § 23 of the existing "Außenwirtschaftsgesetz". Schiller opposed this on the grounds that this measure would be a deviation from the *market* economy and favored instead raising the "Bardepot", the percentage out of foreign credits that Germans had to desposit interest free with the Bundesbank. The Bundesbank had opposed the introduction of a Bardepot, but had given up her resistance and applied the new instrument with a 40-percent-rate since March 1, 1972. This actually stemmed the tide of capital imports for a while.[43] In

---

[42] Emminger (1976): 518, Dörge/Mairose (1969): 92–94. The Bank had decided on this basic line of policy already in September 1968. See Emminger (1976): 517.
[43] Emminger (1976): 529. In the application of the "Bardepot" instrument the Bundesbank is *not* autonomous. The government decides on when to apply it and the Bank decides on the percentage of the "Bardepot". It is a "two-key" instrument. It fell out of use in 1974, but could be reacitvated any time, if need be.

June 1972, however, a crisis of the Pound Sterling set in and again triggered speculative capital imports. The Bank's President Klasen could convince the whole cabinet but Schiller that the license system always favored by him had to be applied now. Schiller was outvoted and resigned. Thus, the independent Bundesbank, by law obliged to advise the government in currency matters, had contributed to the downfall of the cabinet's strongest member, the "Super"-Minister for the Economy and Finance.[44]

After some years of relative harmony between the Bundesbank and the government a new spectacular conflict occurred in April 1981, when Chancellor Helmut Schmidt was "furious" about the Bank's restrictive monetary policy in a situation of alarmingly high and rising unemployment. Schmidt even mustered the support of his friend, the French Prime Minister Giscard d'Estaing, in criticizing the Bundesbank. The two governments raised a loan of 6.3 billion for expansionary fiscal measures in order to counteract the effect of the Bundesbank's restrictions on employment and growth (Issing 1982: 49; Kannengießer 1981: 1; Seuss 1981: 13).

2.5.4 Debates on the Central Bank's Position vis-à-vis the Government

The far-reaching autonomy of West Germany's central bank was overwhelmingly applauded since its inception. Only a few politicians and academic economists argued in favor of restricting the Bank's autonomy in the first two years after the foundation of the Federal Republic (*Die Bundesbank* 1950). By 1951, the independence of the Bank was almost universally accepted (Caesar 1981: 202; Gaugenrieder 1960: 4).

In the following years, when the Bundesbank law was discussed and shaped, controversy concentrated on the issue of a federal decentralized versus a centralized central banking system. This debate also touched upon the issue of the Bank's independence from the federal government, but mainly concerned other questions.[45]

The Great-Coalition government in 1967 introduced a new concept of

---

[44] Robert (1978): 22–23, Kaiser (1980): 60–61, Roeper (1978): 198–199, Herlt (1972): 21, Baring (1982): 670–676. These developments motivated the Bundesbank to publish her interpretations of the Bundesbank law, especially as to her autonomy and her relations to the government. See Bundesregierung und Bundesbank (1972): 15–17.

[45] Geisler (1953): 155–188, Keller (1953): 61–94, Braun (1969): 1–6. The discussions of the autonomy issue in preparation of the Bundesbank law are summarized in Bethusy-Huc (1962): 82–107. Opposition to the Bank's autonomy had become an exception in academic circles, as, for example, by Eynern (1957). Eynern's view is discussed by Pfleiderer (1967): 563–575.

economic policy, the "Globalsteuerung der Wirtschaft" (= global steering of the economy), a sort of Keynesian fine-tuning policy based on the "Stabilitätsgesetz" (Act for the Promotion of Stability and Growth of the Economy) of May 1967. This concept necessitated a stronger coordination of the government's economic policies with the Bank's monetary and credit policies and led to new discussions of the Bank's autonomy into the 1970s. Some politicians, labor unions, and academic economists demanded changes in the Bundesbank Law. Politicians (like Ehrenberg) of the Social Democratic Party – the party that had insisted on the new economic policy concept in the Great Coalition – pleaded for a change in the Bank's status. But they were never able to convince a majority in their own party, let alone the cabinet.[46]

In the early 1970s, however, an extension of the Bundesbank's monetary instruments was planned and reached the stage of a parliamentary bill and extensive discussions. It was proposed to introduce minimum reserve requirements on the banks' assets in addition to those on the banks' obligations and to empower the Bank to stipulate maxima for the extension of bank credit. It was planned, however, to require the agreement of the government for using these instruments. This sort of two-key provision was demanded by the Social Democratic Party as the price for the extension of the Bundesbank's instruments. Neither the SPD's coalition partner, the Free Democrats, nor the Bundesbank were willing to pay the price, which would have meant an inroad into the Bank's autonomy. Therefore, the bill was finally dropped.[47]

On a more general level of public discussions it was demanded that the Bank's policy should be subjected to the same set of economic policy goals the government is obliged to pursue (the "magic" quadrangle: price stability, full employment, fair growth, external balance) explicitly since the "Stabilitätsgesetz" of 1967, and/or that it should be subjected to the government's instructions under certain conditions. The Bank's obligation primarily to secure currency stability could otherwise easily lead to policy clashes with the government, it was argued. One had to differentiate between the formulation of policy priorities and the realization of policy goals. The Bank's independence – it was proposed – should pertain to the realization of goals only, while the choice of policy priorities should be the sole responsibility of

---

[46] Caesar (1981): 199–200, Robert (1978): 37. For Ehrenberg's position see Ehrenberg (1973): 33–34, 197–200. Public opinion strongly resisted any change in the Bank's autonomy then and later. See Huppertz (1977): 79–80.

[47] Robert (1978): 105–155, covers this issue extensively.

the government (Duwendag 1973: 13–52; Kaiser 1980: 64–79; Robert 1978: 36–77).

In 1975, on the other hand, von Schelling, formerly a State Central Bank's President and thus a member of the Bundesbank's Central Bank Council, proposed a change of the Bundesbank Law in the opposite direction. The Bundesbank should be obliged to pursue price stability as her only policy goal. To attain this alone was difficult enough for monetary policy. To charge the Bank with further functions would overstrain the capabilities of her limited set of policy tools (Schelling 1975). None of these proposals met with serious interest in parliament. Discussions of the issue have subsided in the 1980s.

3 Conclusion: The Prime Motives for the Legal Changes in Relations between Germany's Central Bank and Government and a Summary of Arguments Pro and Con the Bank's Autonomy

The Reichsbank was formally subjected to the government's instructions from its foundation in 1876 onward. At the same time, however, she was obliged to adhere to the rules of the gold standard, a fact that counterbalanced her formal subordination to the government. In addition, central bank credit to the government was strictly limited. The legal measures that suspended the gold standard and removed the limitations of the Reichsbank's credits to the government at the beginning of World War I led to a material change of the Bank's relation to the Government. With the Bank subordinated to the government, Germany had adopted a manipulated currency standard and the government had open access to the Bank's credit. This was the most dangerous of all possible constellations in view of currency stability. Actually, the financing of war and postwar expenditures through Reichsbank credits led to extraordinary inflationary developments which the Allies saw as a threat to the fulfillment of their reparations demands.

There were essentially three options to improve the chances for more currency stability in Germany by a change in the banking law:
– the introduction of the Bank's autonomy from the government,
– the reintroduction of the gold standard rules,
– the limitation of Reichsbank credit to the government.

In 1922 the Allies demanded the Bank's autonomy from the government.

The choice of this option was based on the hope that an autonomous Reichsbank would put an end to the government's inflationary finances. But the hope was shattered. The other two options, especially in combination, would have been much more powerful in coping with the inflationary problem, as they would have directly restricted the Bank's credits to the government and changed the conduct of monetary policy.

After the Bank's autonomy alone had failed to bring about the expected results, the Allies also demanded that the second and third options be incorporated into the German banking legislation in connection with the Dawes Plan in 1924. This served the purpose of avoiding inflation well into the 1930s. Until the summer of 1931, the Bank's autonomy, previously unknown to the German tradition, was probably superfluous for securing the Mark's stability. Instead, the conflicts between Schacht and the Weimar governments rather weakened the shaky foundations of the young Republic.

But when foreign exchange control was introduced and the rules of the gold exchange standard were softened in practice under the impact of the credit crisis in July 1931, Germany turned again to a manipulated currency standard. In contrast to the situation at the beginning of World War I, however, government access to Reichsbank credits still remained legally limited. Furthermore, the Bank was autonomous – by modern standards a situation suited to secure currency stability.

With the Nazis' accession to power, a change of the banking law allowed the Reichsbank to trade government bonds on the open market, thus opening a possibility for the Reich to draw on the central bank for credits indirectly. At the same time, with the invention of the "Mefo" bills, the Reich circumvented the still existing legal limits for short-term Reichsbank credits to the government.

After the Bank had started to resist granting further credits to the government in 1936, her autonomy was abolishd by the "Führer" on January 30, 1937. In public, this was officially presented as a revision of the Versailles Treaty obligations, but it served a different purpose: financial preparation for war. In June 1939, the new banking law finally removed all limits for Reichsbank credits to the government. Thus, shortly before the start of World War II, the situation was the same as in August 1914. With Germany being on a manipulated currency standard, the Bank had been subordinated to the government, which had obtained open access to the Bank's credit. This was again the most dangerous of all possible situations regarding currency stability.

After World War II, the central bank's independence of the government was reintroduced for West Germany by the victorious Western Allies. The

Bank's monetary policy success met with the wide-spread approval of the West German society that had been disillusioned by the experience of a second disastrous inflation allowed by a central bank under the government's control. The Bundesbank Law of 1957 that came into being under complete German sovereignty, therefore, preserved the autonomy of the Bank that meanwhile, after Germany's relative success in keeping the Mark stable over a long period, seems to be so well entrenched in the Federal Republic's system of institutions that calls for a change never posed any real threat to the Bank's autonomous status.

The main arguments used to challenge the Bundesbank's independence, particularly during the last two decades, have been the following:

1. Overall economic policies can be executed more effectively, if monetary policy is integrated into the government's economic policy concepts. It has been argued that at least the Bank's independence in her choice of policy *goals* (if not her choice of policy instruments) should be ended. The Bank's primary obligation to secure currency stability would otherwise provoke recurrent clashes with the economic policies of the government, which at times might be forced above all to pursue goals other than price stability, as, for instance, full employment.
2. With monetary policy in the hands of the independent Bundesbank an important segment of overall economic policies is withdrawn from parliamentary, and thus, democratic control. This is all the more debatable, as monetary policy affects not only the value of the currency, but also the economic lot of millions of citizens in as much as it affects employment and economic growth.
3. The theory of bureaucracy has been used recently to interpret the Bundesbank's behavior. It implies that the Bank, like all bureaucracies, might not primarily promote the general welfare, i.e. not pursue the policy goal she has been assigned, but her own goal of securing prestige and status. But it is still in doubt whether this charge is true, and whether the case would be different if the Bank were not autonomous.[48]

The Bundesbank's independence of the government has been defended mainly with the following arguments:

---

[48] That the leading personnel of the Bank is not recruited from within and that the financing of the Bank's budget is not restricted from without does not fit the usual models of the theory of bureaucracy. For the current state of discussions in Germany on this issue see Issing (1982): 55–59, Hartwig (1983/84): 315–321. For a survey of the other arguments pro and con see Bernauer (1960): 54–68, Issing (1982): 50–55, Rittig (1983): 293–294, Caesar (1980): 347–377.

1. Governments and parliaments are prevented from financing budget deficits through the printing press that has twice ruined the German currency in this century and has made the German people particularly sensitive to inflation.
2. The role of the German parliament has changed in the last century. In the constitutional monarchy until the end of World War I, parliament controlled and checked the fiscal behavior of the government and usually had a restraining influence on the government's expenditures. In parliamentary republics, like the Germany of Weimar or Bonn, parliaments tend to be prodigal, especially before and with regard to elections. An autonomous central bank in a parliamentary republic is therefore as useful for checking the growth of fiscal expenditures as a parliament was in a monarchy (Nolting-Hauff 1967: 120; Schöninger 1972: 143).
3. In times of a manipulated currency, monetary policy is better placed into the hands of independent experts than into those of politicians. The latter are subject to all kinds of pressures by political parties and pressure groups. They tend to be pro-inflation as elections approach. As opposed to that, an independent Bank is able to take unpopular measures necessary to secure price stability even in those times and can decide on monetary policy action with much less delay than politicians.
4. An independent Bank conforms to a political system of checks and balances and guarantees continuous care for the stability of money values over electoral cycles and political trends.

As yet, there is no arbitration provision for cases of conflict between the Bundesbank and the government as does exist in some other countries. It has been suggested to institutionalize a parliamentary committee for this purpose and thus, establish some democratic control of monetary policy. Opponents, however, have argued on the basis of the above mentioned four points and, in addition, on the grounds that such a procedure would be too time-consuming in situations where immediate decisions were necessary.

The Bundesbank's independence is best defended by the Bank's prestige in public opinion, which in turn is a function of the Bank's policy success in guarding price stability. It seems to be no coincidence that attacks on the Bundesbank's independent status increased in the 1970s, when the inflation rate reached unprecedented levels in the Federal Republic. In addition, Social Democrats, then in control of the government, had always favored a stronger role of the government in controlling the economy than the more conservative Christian Democrats. The latter tend to favor a division of economic policy powers in order to curtail the degree of state intervention in the economy and to better secure a solid monetary standard as a prerequisite for sound decision making in the private economy.

Meanwhile, with price stability and, thus, the prestige of the Bundesbank firmly reestablished in the Federal Republic, and with the Christian Democrats back in power since 1982, the Bundesbank's independent status seems to be unshakeable at present.

References

Aufstieg oder Niedergang? Deutsche Wirtschafts- und Finanzreform 1929. Eine Denkschrift des Präsidiums des Reichsverbandes der Deutschen Industrie (1929): Veröffentlichungen des RDI, Nr. 49, Berlin: RDI.
Ausschuss zur Untersuchung der Erzeugungs- und Absatzbedingungen der deutschen Wirtschaft (Ed.) (1929): *Die Reichsbank,* Berlin: Mittler.
Baring, Arnulf (1982): *Machtwechsel: Die Ära Brandt-Scheel,* Stuttgart: Deutsche Verlags-Anstalt.
Bayrhoffer, Walther (1941): Die alte und die neue Reichsbank, *Deutsche Geldpolitik,* Schriften der Akademie für Deutsches Recht, Gruppe Wirtschaftswissenschaft, Nr. 4, Berlin: Duncker & Humblot, pp. 87–102.
Beck, Earl R. (1955): *Verdict on Schacht: A Study in the Problem of Political "Guilt",* Tallahassee: Florida State University.
Becker, Wolf-Dieter (1982): Diskussion über ein Bundesbankgesetz im Wissenschaftlichen Beirat beim Bundeswirtschaftsministerium, *Geld- und Währungspolitik in der Bundesrepublik Deutschland,* Ehrlicher, Werner/Simmert, Diethard B. (Eds.), Berlin: Duncker & Humblot, pp. 61–77.
Bernauer, Engelbert (1960): *Staat und Notenbank: Autonomie und Koordination,* Freiburg i.B.: Dissertation.
Bethusy-Huc, Viola Gräfin von (1962): *Demokratie und Interessenpolitik,* Wiesbaden: Steiner.
Blaich, Fritz (1977): *Die Wirtschaftskrise 1925/26 und die Reichsregierung: Von der Erwerbslosenfürsorge zur Konjunkturpolitik,* Kallmünz: Lassleben.
Böhret, Carl, and Dieter Grosser (1967): *Interdependenzen von Politik und Wirtschaft: Beiträge zur Politischen Wirtschaftslehre. Festgabe für Gert von Eynern,* Berlin: Duncker & Humblot.
Boelcke, Willi A. (1983): *Die deutsche Wirtschaft 1930–1945: Interna des Reichswirtschaftsministeriums,* Düsseldorf: Droste.
Bonin, Konrad von (1979): *Zentralbanken zwischen funktioneller Unabhängigkeit und politischer Autonomie: Dargestellt an der Bank von England, der Bank von Frankreich und der deutschen Bundesbank,* Baden-Baden: Nomos.
Borchardt, Knut (1976): Währung und Wirtschaft, *Währung und Wirtschaft in Deutschland 1876–1975,* Deutsche Bundesbank (Ed.), Frankfurt/M.: Knapp, pp. 3–55.
Bosman, H. W. J. (1979): Monetary Policy in the Framework of Economic Policy: Central Banks' Autonomy, *New Approaches in Monetary Policy,* Wadsworth, John E./de Juvigny, Francois L. (Eds.), Alphen a.d.R.: Sijthoff & Nordhoff.

Braun, Karlpeter (1969): *Die Stellung der Notenbank als währungspolitische Instanz: Das Verhältnis zwischen Regierung und Notenbank in der Bundesrepublik Deutschland und in den Vereinigten Staaten von Amerika,* Tübingen: Dissertation.
Brawand, Leo (1971): *Wohin steuert die deutsche Wirtschaft?* München: Desch.
Brüning, Heinrich (1970): *Memoiren 1918–1934,* Stuttgart: Deutsche Verlagsanstalt.
Die Bundesbank. Aufbau und Aufgaben: Bericht über eine Aussprache führender Sachverständiger (1950): Frankfurt/M.: Knapp.
Bundesgesetzblatt. Various years.
Bundesregierung und Bundesbank (1972), *Monatsberichte der Deutschen Bundesbank,* 24. Jg., No. 8 (August 1972): pp. 15–17.
Caesar, Rolf (1980): Die Unabhängigkeit der Notenbank im demokratischen Staat: Argumente und Gegenargumente, *Zeitschrift für Politik,* Vol. 25: pp. 347–377.
Caesar, Rolf (1981): *Der Handlungsspielraum von Notenbanken: Theoretische Analyse und internationaler Vergleich,* Baden-Baden: Nomos.
Deutsche Bundesbank (Ed.) (1976): *Deutsches Geld- und Bankwesen in Zahlen 1876–1975,* Frankfurt/M.: Knapp.
Dietrich-Troeltsch, Hermann (1973): Die Errichtung der Beratungsstelle für Auslandskredite und ihre Funktionsweise, *Kommunale Finanzpolitik in der Weimarer Republik,* Hansmeyer, Karl-Heinrich (Ed.), Stuttgart: Kohlhammer.
Dörge, Friedrich-Wilhelm, and Ralf Mairose (1969): Die Bundesbank – eine Nebenregierung? *Gegenwartskunde,* 18. Jg.: pp. 91–122, 211–251.
Duwendag, Dieter (Ed.) (1973): *Macht und Ohnmacht der Bundesbank,* Frankfurt/M.: Athenäum.
Ehrenberg, Herbert (1973): *Zwischen Marx und Markt: Konturen einer infrastrukturorientierten und verteilungswirksamen Wirtschaftspolitik,* Frankfurt/M.: Societätsverlag.
Emminger, Otmar (1976): Deutsche Geld- und Währungspolitik im Spannungsfeld zwischen innerem und äußerem Gleichgewicht 1848–1975, *Währung und Wirtschaft in Deutschland 1876–1975,* Deutsche Bundesbank (Ed.), Frankfurt/M.: Knapp, pp. 485–554.
Entscheidungen des Bundesverfassungsgerichts (1983), Bd. 62, Tübingen: Mohr.
Entscheidungen des Bundesverwaltungsgerichts (1973), Bd. 41, Berlin: Heymanns.
Eynern, Gert von (1928): *Die Reichsbank: Probleme des deutschen Zentralnoteninstituts in geschichtlicher Darstellung,* Jena: G. Fischer.
Eynern, Gert von (1957): *Die Unabhängigkeit der Notenbank,* Berlin: Colloquium.
Friedrich, Karl (1923/24): Vom alten zum neuen Bankgesetz, *Bank-Archiv,* 23. Jg.: pp. 341–344.
Gaugenrieder, Carl A. (1960): *Die rechtliche Stellung der deutschen Zentralnotenbank im Staatsgefüge in Geschichte und Gegenwart,* Würzburg: Dissertation.
Geisler, Rolf P. (1953): *Notenbankverfassung und Notenbankentwicklung in den USA und Westdeutschland,* Berlin: Duncker & Humblot.
Grasser, Walter (1971): *Deutsche Münzgesetze 1871–1971,* München: Battenberg.
Grotkopp, Wilhelm (1954): *Die grosse Krise: Lehren aus der Überwindung der Wirtschaftskrise 1929/32,* Düsseldorf: Econ.
Habedank, Heinz (1981): *Die Reichsbank in der Weimarer Republik: Die Rolle der Zentralbank in der Politik des deutschen Imperialismus 1919–1933,* Berlin: Akademie-Verlag.
Hahn, Oswald (1968): *Die Währungsbanken der Welt,* Vol. II: Die Abhängigkeiten der Zentralbankleitung, Stuttgart: Poeschel.

Hansmeyer, Karl-Heinrich, and Rolf Caesar (1976): Kriegswirtschaft und Inflation (1936–1948), *Währung und Wirtschaft in Deutschland 1876–1975*, Deutsche Bundesbank (Ed.), Frankfurt/M.: Knapp, pp. 367–429.

Hardach, Gerd (1976): *Weltmarktorientierung und relative Stagflation: Währungspolitik in Deutschland 1924–1931*, Berlin: Duncker & Humblot.

Hartwig, Karl-Hans (1983/84): Bundesbankautonomie und Inflationsbekämpfung: Politische Ökonomie des Notenbankverhaltens, *List Forum*, Vol. 12: pp. 315–321.

Helfferich, Karl (1898): *Die Reform des deutschen Geldwesens nach der Gründung des Reiches*, 2 Vols., Leipzig: Duncker & Humblot.

Helfferich, Karl (1899): *Zur Erneuerung des Deutschen Bankgesetzes*, Leipzig: Duncker & Humblot, pp. 215–217.

Helfferich, Karl (1921/22): Die Autonomie der Reichsbank, *Bank-Archiv*, 21. Jg.: pp. 215–217.

Herlt, Rudolf (1972): Scheidung nach § 23, *Die Zeit*, 27. Jg., Nr. 27: p. 21.

Hertz-Eichenrode, Dieter (1982): *Wirtschaftskrise und Arbeitsbeschaffung: Konjunkturpolitik 1925/26 und die Grundlagen der Krisenpolitik Brünings*, Frankfurt–New York: Campus.

Heymann, Rudolf (1930): *Die Reichsbankgesetze vom 14. März 1875, vom 30. August 1924 und 13. März 1930*, Erlangen: Dissertation.

Holtfrerich, Carl-Ludwig (1982): *Alternativen zu Brünings Wirtschaftspolitik in der Weltwirtschaftskrise*, Wiesbaden: Steiner. Also in: *Historische Zeitschrift*, Bd. 235 (1982): pp. 605–631.

Holtfrerich, Carl-Ludwig (1986): *The German Inflation 1914–1923: Causes and Effects in International Perspective*, Berlin–New York: de Gruyter.

Huppertz, Paul-Helmut (1977): *Gewaltenteilung und antizyklische Finanzpolitik: Ein Beitrag zur Theorie institutioneller Bedingungen der Stabilisierungspolitik in der Bundesrepublik Deutschland*, Baden-Baden: Nomos.

Institut für Konjunkturforschung (Ed.) (1933): *Konjunkturstatistisches Handbuch 1933*, Berlin: Hobbing.

Issing, Otmar (1982): Die Unabhängigkeit der Bundesbank: Theoretisch umstritten – praktisch bewährt, *Geld- und Währungspolitik in der Bundesrepublik Deutschland*, Ehrlicher, Werner/Simmert, Diethart B. (Eds.); Berlin: Duncker & Humblot.

Jacobson, Jon (1972): *Locarno Diplomacy: Germany and the West 1925–1929*, Princeton: Princeton UP.

James, Harold (1985): *The Reichsbank and Public Finance in Germany 1924–1933*, Frankfurt/M.: Knapp.

Kaiser, Rolf H. (1980): *Bundesbankautonomie – Möglichkeiten und Grenzen einer unabhängigen Politik*, Frankfurt: R. G. Fischer.

Kannengiesser, Walter (1981): Der Kanzler und die Bundesbank, *Frankfurter Allgemeine Zeitung*, 24. April 1981: p. 1.

Keller, Dieter (1953): *Staat und Notenbank in Deutschland*, Freiburg i. B.: Dissertation.

Koch, Richard (1926): *Die Reichsgesetzgebung über Münz- und Notenbankwesen*, 7. Aufl. bearb. von Hjalmar Schacht, Berlin: de Gruyter.

Krohn, Claus-Dieter (1974): *Stabilisierung und ökonomische Interessen: Die Finanzpolitik des Deutschen Reiches 1923–1927*, Düsseldorf: Bertelsmann.

Kroyer, Helmut (1955): *Die Stellung der deutschen Zentralnotenbank zum Staat seit 1875*, München: Dissertation.

Kumpf-Korfes, Sigrid (1968): *Bismarcks 'Draht nach Rußland'*, Berlin: Akademie.

Leffler, Melvyn (1979): *The Elusive Quest: America's Pursuit of European Stability and French Security: 1919–1933*, Chapel Hill: Univ. of North Carolina Press.
Link, Werner (1970): *Die amerikanische Stabilisierungspolitik in Deutschland 1921–1932*, Düsseldorf: Droste.
Lotz, Walther (1888): *Geschichte und Kritik des deutschen Bankgesetzes vom 14. März 1875*, Leipzig: Duncker & Humblot.
Lotz, Walther (1897): *Der Streit um die Verstaatlichung der Reichsbank*, München: G. Hirth.
Lüke, Rolf (1958): *Von der Stabilisierung zur Krise*, Zürich: Polygraphischer Verlag.
Luther, Hans (1964): *Vor dem Abgrund 1930–1933: Reichsbankpräsident in Krisenzeiten*, Berlin: Propyläen.
Mammel, Hans Rolf (1955): *Die Einordnung der Zentralbank in das Gefüge eines demokratischen Regierungsapparates: Von der Notenbankautonomie zur Zentralbank als Lenkungsmittel der Volkswirtschaft*, Tübingen: Dissertation.
Maurer, Ilse (1973): *Reichsfinanzen und große Koalition: Zur Geschichte des Reichskabinetts Müller (1928–1930)*, Bern: Lang.
McNeil, William C. (1986): *American Money and the Weimar Republic: Economics and Politics on the Eve of the Great Depression*, New York: Columbia UP.
Müller, Helmut (1973): *Die Zentralbank – eine Nebenregierung: Reichsbankpräsident Hjalmar Schacht als Politiker der Weimarer Republik*, Opladen: Westdeutscher Verlag.
Müller-Link, Horst (1977): *Industrialisierung und Außenpolitik: Preussen-Deutschland und das Zarenreich von 1860 bis 1890*, Göttingen: Vandenhoeck & Ruprecht.
Nolting-Hauff, Wilhelm (1967): Die Souveränität der Bundesbank – ein staatspolitisches Erfordernis, *Die Aussprache*, 17. Jg., Mai/Juni 1967: pp. 114–122.
Notzke, Johann (1924): *Das Bankgesetz von 1924*, Berlin: Jürgens.
Parchmann, A. (1933): *Die Reichsbank*, Berlin: Widder.
Pentzlin, Heinz (1980): *Hjalmar Schacht: Leben und Wirken einer umstrittenen Persönlichkeit*, Berlin: Ullstein.
Peterson, Edward Norman (1954): *Hjalmar Schacht For and Against Hitler: A Political-Economic Study of Germany 1923–1945*, Boston: Christopher Publishing House.
Petzina, Dieter (1968): *Autarkiepolitik im Dritten Reich: Der nationalsozialistische Vierjahresplan*, Stuttgart: Deutsche Verlagsanstalt.
Pfleiderer, Otto (1967): Die Notenbank im Spannungsfeld von Wirtschafts- und Finanzpolitik, *Interdependenzen von Politik und Wirtschaft: Beiträge zur Politischen Wirtschaftslehre: Festgabe für Gert von Eynern*, Böhret, Carl/Grosser, Dieter (Eds.), Berlin: Duncker & Humblot, pp. 563–575.
Puhl, Emil (1941): Die Wiederherstellung der deutschen Währungshoheit, *Deutsche Geldpolitik*, Schriften der Akademie für Deutsches Recht, Gruppe Wirtschaftswissenschaft, Bd. 4, Berlin: Duncker & Humblot, pp. 35–50.
Die Reichsbank 1901–1925 (1925): Berlin: Reichsbank.
Reichsgesetzblatt. Various years.
Rittig, Gisbert (1983): Die 'öffentliche Bindung' der Bundesbank, *Öffentliche Bindung von Unternehmen: Beiträge zur Regulierungsdebatte, Gert von Eynern zum 80. Geburtstag gewidmet*, Thiemeyer, Theo, et al. (Eds.), Baden-Baden: Nomos, pp. 291–308.
Robert, Rüdiger (1978): *Die Unabhängigkeit der Bundesbank: Analyse und Materialien*, Kronberg/Ts.: Athenäum.

Roeper, Hans (1978): *Vom Besatzungskind zum Weltstar: Eine deutsche Wirtschaftsgeschichte der Gegenwart,* Frankfurt/M.: Societäts-Verlag.
Sayers, Richard S. (1976): *The Bank of England 1891–1944,* Vol. 1, Cambridge: Cambridge UP.
Schacht, Hjalmar (1927a): *Eigene oder geborgte Währung?* Berlin: Quelle & Meyer.
Schacht, Hjalmar (1927b): *The Stabilization of the Mark,* London: Allen & Unwin.
Schacht, Hjalmar (1931): *The End of Reparations,* New York: J. Cape & H. Smith.
Schacht, Hjalmar (1937): Die Wiederherstellung der deutschen Währungshoheit, *Zeitschrift der Akademie für deutsches Recht,* 4. Jg.: pp. 137–139.
Schacht, Hjalmar (1949): *Abrechnung mit Hitler,* Berlin: Michaelis.
Schacht, Hjalmar (1955): *My First Seventy-Six Years,* London: Allan Wingate.
Schelling, Friedrich von (1975): *Die Bundesbank in der Inflation: Plädoyer für eine neue Geldverfassung,* Frankfurt/M.: Knapp.
Schmidt, Reiner (1973): Grundlagen und Grenzen der Unabhängigkeit der Deutschen Bundesbank, *Xenion: Festschrift für Pan. J. Zepos,* Bd. 2. E. von Caemmerer et al. (Eds.), Athen: Katsikalis, pp. 665–680.
Schmidt, Reiner (1981): Die Zentralbank im Verfassungsgefüge der Bundesrepublik Deutschland, *Instrumente der sozialen Sicherung und der Währungssicherung in der Bundesrepublik Deutschland und in Italien,* Grawert, Rolf (Ed.), Berlin: Duncker & Humblot, pp. 61–80.
Schöninger, Karl-Eugen (1972): *Konjunkturstabilisierung als Koordinationsproblem zwischen den Trägern der Wirtschaftspolitik. Untersuchung über politische Probleme der Globalsteuerung in der Bundesrepublik Deutschland in den Jahren 1966–1970/71,* Meisenheim am Glan: Hain.
Schötz, Hans Otto (1987): *Der Kampf um die Mark 1923/24. Die deutsche Währungsstabilisierung unter dem Einfluß der nationalen Interessen Frankreichs, Grossbritanniens und der USA,* Berlin–New York: de Gruyter.
Seuss, Wilhelm (1981): Der Zorn des Kanzlers, *Frankfurter Allgemeine Zeitung,* 15. April 1981: p. 13.
Simpson, Amos E. (1969): *Hjalmar Schacht in Perspective,* The Hague: Mouton.
Singer, Kurt (1922): Die Autonomie der Reichsbank, *Wirtschaftsdienst,* 7. Jg.: pp. 734–735.
Singer, Kurt (1930): Reichsbank und Reich, *Wirtschaftsdienst,* 15. Jg.: pp. 133–136.
Sommer, Albrecht (1931): *Die Reichsbank unter Hermann von Dechend (1865–1890),* Berlin: Heymanns.
Speyerer, Siegmund (1940): *Die Reichsbankverfassung unter dem Bankgesetz vom 30. August 1924 und unter dem Gesetz über die Deutsche Reichsbank vom 15. Juni 1939,* Erlangen: Dissertation.
Spindler, Joachim von, Willy Becker, and O.-Ernst Starke (1973): *Die Deutsche Bundesbank. Grundzüge des Notenbankwesens und Kommentar zum Gesetz über die Deutsche Bundesbank,* 4. Auflage, Stuttgart: Kohlhammer.
Spohr, Werner (1925): *Die Neugestaltung der Deutschen Reichsbank,* Stuttgart: Enke.
Stoepel, Paul (Ed.) (1861): *Preussischer Gesetz-Codex,* Vol. 2 (1835–1848), Frankfurt/Oder: Trowitsch.
Stucken, Rudolf (1964): *Deutsche Geld- und Kreditpolitik 1914–1963,* 3. Aufl., Tübingen: J. C. B. Mohr (Paul Siebeck).
Uhlenbruck, Dirk (1967): *Die verfassungsmäßige Unabhängigkeit der Deutschen Bundesbank und ihre Grenzen,* Köln: Dissertation.

Upmeier, Gisela (1973): Schachts Kampf gegen die kommunalen Auslandsanleihen, *Kommunale Finanzpolitik in der Weimarer Republik,* Hansmeyer, Karl-Heinrich (Ed.), Stuttgart: Kohlhammer.
Verwaltungsbericht der Reichsbank für das Jahr... (various years): Berlin: Deutsche Reichsbank.
Vocke, Wilhelm (1973): *Memoiren,* Stuttgart: Deutsche Verlagsanstalt.
Von der Königlichen Bank zur Deutschen Reichsbank: 175 Jahre deutscher Notenbankgeschichte 20. Juli 1765–20. Juli 1940 (1940): Berlin: Reichsdruckerei.
Wandel, Eckard (1980): *Die Entstehung der Bank deutscher Länder und die deutsche Währungsreform 1948,* Frankfurt M.: Knapp.
Wildenmann, Rudolf (1969): *Die Rolle des Bundesverfassungsgerichts und der Deutschen Bundesbank in der politischen Willensbildung: Ein Beitrag zur Demokratietheorie,* Stuttgart: Kohlhammer.
Wussow, Hansjoachim (1955): *Die Zentralbanken, ihre Aufgaben und ihr rechtliches Verhältnis zu Staat und Publikum: Eine Studie zum Zentralbankwesen in Deutschland von 1875 bis in die Gegenwart,* Frankfurt/M.: Dissertation.

Chapter 6
A Central Bank Between the Government and the Credit System: The Bank of Italy after World War II

Giangiacomo Nardozzi

Introduction*

Central banks cannot be studied independently of their relations with the banking or, more generally, the financial system, and in Italy's case these relations are probably more important than usual. The issue, currently under review in several countries, of the policy to be adopted towards the financial sytsem to ensure its stability and efficiency (or, in other words, of the aims of structural supervision) has always tended to be more important in Italy than the relationships between the central bank and the Treasury. Consequently, analysis of the Bank of Italy's attitude to the structural problems of the financial system throws more light on its behaviour in matters involving economic policy and the political sphere than study of major monetary policy developments. The basic cause of this situation is to be found in Italian banking law, which was rooted in the 1931 banking crisis. The first part of this work describes and interprets the 1936 Banking Law, which, with subsequent amendments, is still in force.

The Bank's strategy towards the Government and the political authorities and the way in which it sought to maintain its autonomy are discussed in the second section. This analysis allows monetary policy to be brought properly into focus and its key features are analyzed in the third section.

---

* My thanks go to Paolo Baffi and Guido Carli for reading and discussing an earlier version of this study. I also owe much to illuminating discussions with Federico Caffè, Pierluigi Ciocca, Marcello De Cecco, Marco Onado, Tommaso Padoa-Schioppa, Sergio Ristuccia, and Gianni Toniolo. I naturally remain responsible for what is actually written here. Financial support by the Ministry of Education (FI.SI.MO Project) is acknowledged.

A number of general conclusions are drawn on the basis of Italian experience about the relationship between the history and theory of central banks. This clearly reveals the limits of much contemporary literature on the independence of central banks – a result that is not so much due to any peculiarity of the Italian system as to the intrinsic weakness of the theory underlying this literature.

1 Credit Legislation and the Bank of Italy

The banking law in force in Italy is still largely that enacted in 1936, which rounded off a series of coordinated measures introduced to cope with the serious banking crisis of 1931[1]. The most important of these measures were the setting up of IMI (Istituto Mobiliare Italiano) in 1931 and of IRI (Istituto per la Ricostruzione Indentriale) in 1933.[2] The creation of these institutions brought to an end Italy's experience with the mixed bank formula, which, even before the final crisis in 1930, had engendered misallocation of resources and financial instability.

The Banking Law laid down two general principles:

1) separation of banking and industry; and
2) need of structural regulation and supervision of the credit system.

The first of these principles did not rigidly restrict banks to the supply of commercial credit since the Law did not distinguish between the various categories of credit institutions (deposit banks, medium and long-term credit banks and merchant banks), as did the French legislation of 1941–45, nor did it prevent commercial banks from acquiring corporate securities, as in the United States. Rather, it established a form of specialization (between banks and special credit institutions) based on deposit maturities and required every acquisition of equity to be authorized by the supervisory authorities.[3]

---

[1] See Ciocca and Toniolo (1984) as well as Banco di Roma (1981).
[2] In 1931 the Ministry of Finance and the Bank of Italy required the two major ailing mixed banks (Banca Commerciale Italiana and Credito Italiano) to restrict their activity to ordinary, short-term, credit. IMI was created with public capital to replace the mixed banks in the granting of medium and long-term credit and served as the model for the subsequent special credit institutions. IRI, which formed the basis of the present system of state shareholdings, took over the three leading mixed banks together with their interests in industrial companies. See the references of note (1).
[3] Saraceno argues that the Banking Law can be most effectively interpreted by focusing

This results in the second principle coming to play a major role. In the light of Italy's experience the need for regulation has been seen as a corollary of the assumption that financial systems do not automatically reach efficient or stable positions and that no optimum structure exists to serve as a model. Rather, the structure of the financial system has to be regulated and adapted to the development of the economy.[4] This explains the broad legislative powers delegated to the monetary authorities for the purpose of guiding the development of the financial system according to the needs and problems of the day.

This delegation of powers can be understood better by remembering that the growth of capitalism in Italy had not led, in either the real or the financial sector, to the full development of markets. Economic activity had polarized around two major blocs. The state and the bank-industry combine. "Leave it to the market" would therefore have been hypocritical call for the continuance of a relationship between banks and firms unfavourable to the emergence of competitive forces and for the state bearing the losses while leaving profits to the private sector. The only way to improve market efficiency and to ensure a proper relationship between the private and the public sector was to provide for structural supervision. Beyond this, there was nothing certain enough to be embodied in legislation or, in other words, there were not sufficiently valid reasons for imposing a clearly-defined model of the financial system. Therefore the administrative powers granted to the Italian monetary authorities to shape the financial system were not the expression of an antimarket philosophy. Rather, they reflected awareness of the historical tendency of the bank-industry combine to prevent competition and thus weaken the development of the economy. This awareness is constantly discernible in Italian credit legislation and was the point of convergence of the thinking and action of such distinguished protagonists as Alberto Beneduce, Donato Menichella, Raffaele Mattioli and Luigi Einaudi.[5]

---

less on the distinction between deposit (or commercial) banks and mixed banks than on the division between "ordinary credit" banks and "holding" banks, with the former not excluded from granting medium and long-term credit or acquiring equity interests. See Saraceno (1981 a and b) and Nardozzi (1983).

[4] For an analysis of the theoretical and historical justification for this view, see Ciocca (1982).

[5] *Alberto Beneduce (1877–1944)* began his career as a statistician and soon became a collaborator of Francesco Saverio Nitti (Prime Minister from 1919 to 1920). Though not a fascist, he was Chairman of various public financial bodies and advised Mussolini on numerous domestic and international financial questions. It was he who conceived the idea of IRI and was its first Chairman.

The principle of structural regulation of the financial system was clearly reaffirmed in Article 47 of the Constitution of the Italian Republic.[6] A decree issued in 1947 modified the Banking Law by entrusting supervisory authority to the Bank of Italy and set up the Interministerial Committee for Credit and Savings.[7] As a result of this decree, the central bank acquired full control over the policy of structural regulation.[8]

Taken together, the Banking Law and Article 47 of the Constitution thus reveal the special care taken by Italian lawmakers to set the financial system within a public (but not collectivist) legal framework and accordingly to protect savings. The aspect of the relationship between central banks and Government on which the literature focuses today – the management of the money supply – played a relatively minor role in the development of Italian legislation.

Donato Menichella (1896–1984) joined the Bank of Italy in 1921 and shortly afterwards was appointed to look after the liquidation of Banca Italiana di Sconto. Subsequently, he was called by Beneduce to manage IRI, and he made an important contribution to the drafting of the 1936 Banking Law. In 1946 he became General Director of the Bank of Italy under Einaudi and was appointed Governor in 1948.

Raffaele Mattioli (1895–1973) was recruited by Banca Commerciale Italiana in the mid-twenties after a short period teaching economics at Bocconi University. He collaborated with Giuseppe Toeplitz, the then Managing Director, and was actively involved in designing measures for the solution of the 1931 banking crisis. He then became the head of the bank and kept the position without interruption until 1972. A close friend of Piero Sraffa and many other intellectuals, he promoted the arts and the sciences through a series of initiatives.

Luigi Einaudi (1874–1961) was an internationally famous economist, Governor of the Bank of Italy from 1945 to 1948, a Minister and then President of the Republic. A passionate liberalist, his thinking and actions were aimed at transforming Italy's traditional capitalism (opposed to market forces) into an "ideal" capitalism based on competition. For the Convergence of his thinking with that of Mattioli and Menichella, see Vicarelli (1981).

[6] Article 47 (I comma) states that "The Republic shall encourage and protect saving in every form; it shall discipline, coordinate and control the granting of credit". In the end the Constituent Assembly preferred this wording to others in which explicit reference was made to protecting the stability of the currency. A "monetarist" curb to the discretion of the monetary authorities was thus deliberately excluded.

[7] This Committee is headed by the Minister of the Treasury and comprises the Ministers of Public Works, Agriculture, Industry, Foreign Trade, the Budget and State Shareholdings. It is not difficult to see how the Governor of the Bank of Italy, who prepares the subjects to be discussed, can play a much more important role than is formally attributed to him.

[8] The legislation governing the Bank of Italy's relations with the Government and the financial system comprises not only the Banking Law and Decree 601/1947 but also the

2 The Bank of Italy's Structural Supervision and the Evolution of the Financial System

2.1 Alternative Views on the Financial Structure

The disappearance of the mixed bank left a gap in the Italian financial system that the monetary authorities could have filled in several ways within the framework of the 1936 Banking Law.

The writings of Alberto Beneduce and Raffaele Mattioli, both protagonists of the events leading up to the introduction of the Banking Law,[9] exemplify the two alternatives underlying the compromise upon which the postwar development of the financial system was based.

Beneduce's approach was more radical and less favourable to banks. He believed that "... savings in the form of bank deposits cannot be turned into investment in plant, whereas this is possible for those in the form of shares and bonds."[10] This view inevitably implied a financial system with a low level of banking intermediation, since banks would have been restricted to short-term intermediation. All direct bank intervention in the financing of investment would have been excluded and the principle of specialization applied in its most radical form.

When Beneduce turned to the institutions that would finance fixed investment, however, he recognized the need for a solution better suited to an industrializing country. He believed that the state should intervene in the process of capital accumulation to a much greater extent than budget resources would permit or, in other words, as a financial intermediary. The institutional formula Beneduce advocated, and which he had already implemented in the institutions set up to finance public works (CREDIOP) and firms of public utility (ICIPU), was the special credit institution – publicly owned but free to raise funds in the capital markets like a private borrower.

This setting of the financial system left undetermined the relationship between public and private in the capital markets. How big was the role of special credit institutions to be? Was the private sector to rely on these

---

Bank's Statute (approved by Decree Law 1067/1936 and subsequent amendments in 1948) and Decree Law 544/1948, which fixed the overdraft limit on the Treasury's current account with the Bank of Italy at 14% of the budget expenditure approved by Parliament.

[9] For a discussion of the role played by Mattioli in the debate, see *Rivista di Storia Economica*, 1986/1/2/3.

[10] See Bonelli (1984).

intermediaries or develop its own institutions and channels of investment finance?

While Beneduce (an eminent government official) took savings as the starting point of his analysis and focused on the relationship between the state and the economy, Mattioli (a leading banker) started from credit and focused on the relationship between banks and the economy. His principal argument – a marriage of the banker's outlook with the Keynesian views on finance – was that it was impossible to distinguish between credit providing working capital and that financing fixed investment.[11] Indeed, whether credit is of a short or long-term nature can be only known *after* if has been granted.

Bank credit is thus always potentially long term and the importance of banks in intermediation will necessarily reflect bankers' ability to "... mediate in two complementary ways: between deposits and loans and between saving and investment" (Rodano 1983: 306–8), while ensuring that their loans do not become locked in.

In Mattioli's view the crisis of the mixed banks had been caused by locked-in rather than long-term lending.[12] Accordingly, he argued that banks could still play an important role in the financing of investment, both by providing bank credit in amounts that were small in relation to the size of firms and through industrial credit institutions under their control (the idea that led to the creation of Mediobanca in 1947).

Mattioli considered such operations to be not only possible but also desirable. Firstly, because the relationship between banks and industry called for knowledge and skills that newly-created and publicly-owned special credit institutions would have to build up but which major banks already possessed, secondly, because financing investment through public institutions involved the risk of confusing credit management with the administration of government subsidies and incentives.

Comparison of these two approaches higlights a series of issues that are still highly relevant: the boundary between bank intermediation and financial markets; the efficiency and stability of banks; and the form of public intervention in credit. Issues that the Banking Law did not resolve once and for all but rather left to the discretion of the central bank and hence to dialogue with other vested interests. In what follows I shall examine how the three predecessors of the present Governor exercised this discretion and assess the nature and limits of the Bank of Italy's autonomy.

---

[11] See Mattioli (1962) and Rodano (1983) passim.
[12] R. Mattioli, letter to the Governor of the Bank of Italy, Azzolini, 1937 (reproduced in Rodano 1983).

2.2 The Development of the Structure of the Credit System under Menichella

Donato Menichella, one of the protagonists of the bank salvages of the 1930s and of the drafting of the Banking Law, replaced Luigi Einaudi as Governor of the Bank of Italy in 1948.

Between the late forties and the late fifties the Italian financial system developed a hybrid structure including aspects of both the approaches described above:

1. bank intermediation played a much larger role than Beneduce had envisaged; in line with Mattioli's conception, bank loans also financed fixed investment and made a far from negligible contribution to the industrialization of Italy;
2. the growth of the IRI banks, i.e. those with the greatest experience of corporate lending, was curbed to the advantage of savings and other local banks;
3. special credit institutions were set up, mainly under public ownership, to promote the development of certain categories of firm.

It has been argued that the preference given to smaller banks resulted in a banking system with a low allocative and operational efficiency. Granting smaller banks a monopoly of deposit-taking outside the large metropolitan and older industrial areas channeled saving "... to intermediaries ill-equipped to manage its use and away from those accustomed to invest it" (De Cecco 1968: 74). This reduced the stimulus provided by the banking system to the development of the backwards areas of the country. Moreover the dualism between small banks with excess deposits and large banks with excess demand for credit swelled the interbank market and raised intermediation costs.[13] Another drawback was that the savings banks grew at the expense of PO deposits. This dried up the flow of funds to local authorities via the Deposits and Loans Fund,[14] and resulted in a direct channel of finance being replaced by bank intermediation.

Many of the problems with which the central bank was subsequently faced (and in some instances is still faced) have their roots in this period: the politicization of the banking system owing to the growth of the savings banks

---

[13] De Cecco (1968). The "concentric circles" structure of the banking system has been well described by Carli (1962a).

[14] As in France, the Deposits and Loans Fund is part of the Treasury Ministry. It raises funds in the form of PO deposits and lends primilary long term to finance public works undertaken by local authorities.

with their government appointed organs;[15] the intertwining of long-term credit and government subsidies; and the takeover of a part of the resources of the Deposits and Loans Fund. It is thus tempting to conclude that the central bank conceded a great deal – and perhaps too much – to the political sphere in this period.

2.3 The Rationale of the Bank of Italy's Choices with Regard to the Structure of the Credit System in the Period 1948–59

Though suggestive in view of later events, this conclusion does not stand up to examination of the structural policy the Bank of Italy pursued under Menichella.[16]

In the first place it is worth noting that the wartime devaluation resulted in the savings banks' deposits falling from 38% of the banking system total in 1938 to just over 21% in 1948. The preference subsequently given to these banks in the authorization of new branches increased their share of all bank branches from 26% in 1938 to 31% in 1960, but only raised their share of deposits to 24.5% (Carli 1962a). Turning to the relative growth in savings bank and PO deposits, the former doubled between 1927 and 1943 while the latter (and the deposits of the ordinary banks) increasely roughly sixfold. Moreover, in the immediate post-war period (1947–52) the saving banks lost further ground to the Post Office (Menichella 1986).

In the light of these figures, the Bank of Italy's policy appears to have penalized the large banks less than it is believed. Two basic questions nonetheless remain; first, whether it was desirable, in terms of promoting the development of Italy and its backward regions, to allow larger and larger shares of saving to flow to the Government in the form of PO deposits; and second whether it was advisable to permit the IRI banks to increase their influence.

The Bank of Italy had several valid reasons for taking a negative line on both these issues. In the first place, if the trend growth of PO deposits had continued, there would have been an excessive centralization of the alloca-

---

[15] The appointments to the governing organs of savings banks are made by the Government and have become increasingly contentious (indeed, the terms of office of many appointees expired long ago) as result of the difficulty of reaching agreement both between and within parties.

[16] A valuable contribution to the study of Menichella's Governorship was provided by the "Giornata Menichella" held at the Bank of Italy on 23 January 1986. The numerous recollections offered on that occasion confirm the picture of Menichella outlined here. See Banca d'Italia (1986).

tion of resources in the Deposits and Loans Fund. In the Bank's view, the development of the less advanced parts of the country would be served better by local banks seeking local outlets for their deposits than by the public system concentrating resources in the Fund and subsequently redistributing them. Menichella firmly believed that it was necessary to build up banking services in the backward regions and not simply provide public support for development.[17] Furthermore, it was felt desirable that the budget constraint on current expenditure should not be eased by an excessive volume of PO deposits.[18]

While the Bank of Italy favoured the expansion of savings banks and other local banks as a key factor in the buildup of banking services, it clearly indicated what the monetary authorities expected of these banks in return. They were to lend to local businesses and ensure that the extra government securities issued to make good the shortfall in PO deposits were taken up, primaril by placing them with the public.[19]

Compared with this solution, allowing the IRI banks to expand their role might have increased the operational efficiency of the banking system but was unlikely to have enhanced its allocative efficiency. These banks undeniably had more experience in the management of resources but their traditional links with established firms in the developed areas of the country would probably have led them to use their branches in the backward areas merely as a funnel. This transfer of resources would probably have been larger than that produced by the lending of local banks in the interbank market. The elimination of a phase of intermediation might have improved operational efficiency (or perhaps profits), but not allocative efficiency, as required by a decentralized model of development.

There were probably other grounds, however, for the central bank not wanting a strengthening of the three IRI banks. In the first place in the absence of restrictions on their branching these banks might have crowded out the small local banks and caused the banking system to become excessively concentrated. This concentration would actually have given IRI too much power. The central bank must have thought it preferable to follow a divide-and-rule policy towards the public sector banks (the IRI banks, savings banks and public-law banks).

---

[17] See his criticism of the French system in Menichella (1986).

[18] See Menichella's address to the Conference on Agricultural Credit held in Sassari, 20–23 October 1953 (Menichella 1986). See also "The Governor's Concluding Remarks for 1954", Banca d'Italia (n.d.a: 292–3).

[19] See the Sassari and the Perugia Conferences as well as the ACRI meeting of 5/18/1954 in Menichella (1986).

As for long-term finance, why did the Bank of Italy give its blessing to the system of special credit institutions to replace the mixed banks and not promote the development of a capital market?

The answer probably lies in the nature of Italian postwar development: the policy of "protectionist liberalism" pursued to gradually open the Italian economy to foreign competition required large private firms to become internationally competitive, the IRI companies to provide support and stimulus (by supplying low cost inputs and infrastructures), and the Government to maintain social peace by promoting employment and assisting the poorer parts of the population, especially in the South.[20]

Consequently, most of the demand for long-term finance came from the public sector and large private firms. A structure comprising publicly-owned credit institutions, a small capital market serving large private firms and IRI companies was well placed to meet this demand. The neglected component, that of the mushrooming smaller firms, was not yet on a scale requiring private financial institutions to act as promoters. Mediobanca, created by Mattioli and owned by the three IRI banks, is a case in point. Mattioli was not enthusiastic about the "big business" strategy adopted by this bank and would have preferred to see it pay more attention to the development of small and medium-sized firms, leading to stock exchange listings and to a consequent broadening of the capital market.[21] It is possible, however, that there was not enough "small business" of this kind to justify the existence of an organization outside the channel of subsidized credit and that the gap left by the disappearance of the mixed banks was primarily in the "big business" sector.

Mattioli may have been slightly envious of the merchant bank he had promoted, or perhaps he simply anticipated the times. The problem of long-term credit for smaller firms was to emerge when the new firms had grown bigger in the early sixties. In the fifties these firms were able to meet their investment financing needs through bank credit and the specially-created Mediocrediti Regionali.

The central bank nonetheless had to tackle problems that either directly or indirectly resulted in its being at odds with the leading party in the Government.

The underlying cause of the friction in the Bank's relations with that party was to prevent political infiltration in the growing system of the saving banks. Menichella was well aware of this risk, as can be seen from the frequency

---

[20] See Amato (1972).
[21] See Rodano (1983: 168–69).

with which he called the saving banks to order, and, by the end of his career, perhaps somewhat pessimistic about the outcome. In his last address to the congress of the savings banks in 1959 he once more stressed the public interest inherent in their activities and reiterated, citing Einaudi, that the best control over the credit system is exercised when directors are chosen.[22]

Another problem was to prevent subsidized credit and long-term credit from becoming synonymous and involving the credit system (together with the central bank) in decisions on the allocation of resources taken at the political level. In a country with pronounced territorial and sectoral imbalances, coupled with credit legislation heavily biased towards public intervention, this is an ever-present threat to the autonomy of the central bank, as will be shown hereafter. Menichella supported the creation of the Southern Italy Development Fund with the aim of setting the choices regarding the financing of Southern Italy's development outside the banking system.[23]

2.4 The Early Sixties and the Start of Carli's Governorship

The problems associated with the organization of the financial system took on greater importance at the turn of the sixties, when Guido Carli replaced Donato Menichella as Governor of the Bank of Italy. After a decade of healthy industrial expansion, growth proceeded at an exceptional pace from 1959 on and rapidly accentuated the need to develop non-public forms of long-term credit and supplement it with a broader and less speculative stock market. By contrast, the prospect of a Centre-Left Government pointed to a considerable increase in public intervention likely.

At the outset Carli appeared to set on fashioning the structure of the Italian financial system in an Anglo-American mould, with greater reliance on the money and financial markets than on intermediaries[24]. Confirmation of Carli's stance is to be found both in the proposals advanced in his first two Annual Reports and in the 1962 regulations concerning Treasury bill issues and the interbank market[25].

---

[22] Perugia Congress of 10/11/1959. See Menichella (1986).
[23] This point, which Governor Ciampi stressed in his recent commemoration of Menichella, was brought to my attention by P. Ciocca.
[24] See De Cecco as well as Marconi in Vicarelli (1979).
[25] The method of issuing Treasury bills was changed in November 1962. Previously there had been no connection between the amounts issued and the Treasury's cash requirements, Treasury bills were issued at fixed rates. For the most part they were taken up by banks to meet their compulsory reserve obligations and to invest their liquid balances. The reform maintained the system of tap issues for compulsory reserves but gave the

De Cecco among others was highly sceptical about the chances of the new Governor's "commendable objectives" actually being achieved[26].

This scepticism was confirmed by the "corporativistic evolution of the Governor's economic thinking" apparent in a speech he gave at the beginning of 1966 (Carli 1966). Carli appeared to have "come full circle" in just a few years and to have adapted "to a situation that showed no intention of adapting to him" (De Cecco 1968: 88).

Carli's "Concluding Remarks" and public speeches through 1975 show that he continued to swing between corporativistic and free market positions, producing an extraordinary series of widely differing and sometimes contradictory ideas and proposals for the organization of the financial system.

Since soft thinking can be excluded also in view of the considerable prestige the Bank of Italy acquired both in Italy and abroad during this period, the reason for such swings is to be sought in the political sphere, i.e. in the relationship between the Bank of Italy and the Government. During Carli's long Governorship the central bank's structural policy for the financial system was linked much more closely than ever before to its approach to the problem of autonomy vis-à-vis the Government.

2.5 Carli and the Structure of the Financial System

Can it be claimed that Carli's ideal objective was a market-oriented financial system? And was he satisfied with the allocative and operational efficiency that actually developed while he was Governor?

Carli's published writings suggest that the answer to both questions should be no. Had the Bank of Italy wished to promote markets in competition with banking intermediation, it could have made the 1962 reform of the money market much more radical. The method introduced for the issue of Treasury bills differed from the English and American system in the important respect

---

Treasury discretion in fixing any additional amounts, which were to be sold by auction. The reasons given for the reform were the need to improve the allocation efficiency of the banking system (at times of abundant liquidity the earlier system tended "to reduce the incentive for banks to look for productive investments") and increase the effectiveness of the central bank's interventions (Carli 1962a). Similar motives underlay the regulation of the interbank market. See Sarcinelli (1965) and Marconi (1981).

[26] De Cecco criticized Carli for failing to appreciate "the peculiar differences between the financial development that took place in Italy, and more generally on the continent, and the English and American model". He also accused Carli of overlooking the fact that the Italian credit system had tended in both its history and its institutions towards a "corporativistic planning" of credit. Finally, De Cecco believed that Carli underrated the ability of the banking system to oppose radical reforms.

that the public was excluded. Medium and long-term rates were linked to short-term rates by way of banks' investment (or disinvestment) in bonds rather than operations by the public. Treasury bill rates, which should have played the leading role in monetary control, were left out of the cast.[27]

The rationale underlying the 1962 changes in the money market (which was only to develop its full potential after the much more radical changes made in 1975) was thus not the desire to mould the Italian financial system on the Anglo-American model. Rather, it was designed to enhance the responsiveness of the banking system to central bank stimuli (transmitted primarily via refinancing) and to increase the effect on real variables by connecting long-term interest rates to liquidity conditions. This could be done without curbing bank intermediation provided the link between bank liquidity and the bond market was strengthened as it was in 1962 by closing the outlets[28]. Support for this view is to be found in the banks deposit rate cartel the management of which failed to prevent bank deposits from competing with the capital market.

In the financial markets the aim of the Bank of Italy was the develop the bond market. However, this aim was not coupled with the prospect of a reduction in bank intermediation. Indeed, Carli authorized double intermediation, whereby banks took up huge quantities of bonds. The growth of the bond market was thus accompanied by hand with the maintenance of a large proportion of the public's financial wealth in the form of bank deposits.[29]

While Carli did not advocate a more market-oriented and less bank-dependent financial system, his writings show he realized that the configuration taking form was far from ideal. He quickly and lucidly denounced the disortions produced by the double intermediation the Bank of Italy had helped to stimulate – the encouragement it gave banks to raise deposit rates and, at

---

[27] See Sarcinelli (1965: 1118).

[28] It is interesting to note that the reasons given in 1970 for developing the money market moved in the opposite direction. The aim then was to protect the capital market from short-term fluctuations in liquidity. See Banca d'Italia (n.d.b: 410–411) and Andreatta (1973: 130 and 137).

[29] The development of the financial markets was mainly achieved through the absorption by banks of very large quantities of government securities and bonds issued by the special credit institutions, which served primarily as instruments of government intervention. Double intermediation, which thus transferred a sizable proportion of bank's lending decisions to the state, was favourable assessed by Carli in his "Concluding Remarks for 1965". Starting in October 1965, banks were allowed to use bonds to meet part of their compulsory reserve obligations, and shortly afterwards the Bank of Italy embarked on the policy of stabilizing bond yields (see Fazio 1969).

least in part, to abdicate their basic function in the allocation of credit[30]. He even went so far as to envisage a tax to discourage banks from competing with the direct placement of securities with the public[31].

Carli was also aware of the shortcomings in terms of allocative efficiency associated with banks delegating a part of their lending activity to the special credit institutions, whose own discretion was being curtailed by the growth in subsidized credit. The expansion of the bond market thus served to finance state-aided capitalism:

> Entrepreneurial and productive capitalism, of which Italy could boast some excellent examples, rapidly gave way to state-aided capitalism. Bond issues – the typical means of financing state-aided capitalism – replaced share capital. This is one of the most telling episodes of economic decadence in Italy's history (Carli 1977:84)[32].

Carli was therefore aware from the beginning of the dangers inherent in a financial system tailored for the administrative management of credit operating in an increasingly pervasive political environment. As time passed, Carli's denouncement of the degradation caused by the political appropriation of the economy became increasingly explicit.

2.6 The Structure of the Financial System and the Relationship with the Government

> Setting aside the warnings you gave in your Concluding Remarks, in many instances you were the inventor, or at least the protagonist in the implementation of the structural projects that transformed the financial market in the way you have just described. There was a sort of schizophrenia in this behaviour, a clearly discernible dissociation. You appeared to be talking like a Dr. Jekyll but acting like a Mr. Hyde – on the one hand, you deprecated what was happening; on the other, you sought to make it happen as painlessly as possible (Carli 1977:85).

The schizophrenic attitude of the Bank of Italy towards the financial system during Carli's Governorship owes nothing to the unresigned submission of the Bank of England described by Montagu Norman. Firstly, there is no evidence that the various Governments that succeeded each other in this period had a plan for the financial system to impose on the central bank. The

---

[30] "The Governor's Concluding Remarks for 1966" (Banca d'Italia n.d.b: 364) and those for 1971 (Banca d'Italia n.d.b: 379–80).

[31] See "The Governor's Concluding Remarks for 1966" and Carli (1968). The scheme foresaw a tax rate varying with the differential between the yields on deposits and bonds. The proposal was never implemented. See also Marconi (1981).

[32] Questioned by Scalfari in Carli (1977: 84).

configuration that emerged was very much the handiwork of the Governor, who, by contrast, had a clear idea of the requirements and tendencies of the political class. Secondly, from the beginning Carli was a respected participant in Government policy-making on economic matters and hence in a position to influence its course.[33]

These features make the analysis of Carli's Governorship of considerable interest for the theory of central banking since the Bank of Italy's position in this period did not correspond to any of the traditional classifications. It was neither counterbalancing (à la Bundesbank), nor cooperative (à la Bank of England), nor executive (à la Banque de France).

The Bank of Italy's policy for the financial system was not imposed by the Government, but rather a part of Carli's strategy vis-à-vis the political authorities.

In order to understand this strategy, it needs to be remembered that Carli was appointed Governor on the eve of farreaching changes in the political scene. The nascent Centre-Left coalition did not only involve the prospect of a series of economic reforms but also marked a political turning point, both for the Christian Democrats, who distanced themselves from the economic establishment they had previously relied on for support and gave free vein to their interventionist instincts, and for the Socialists, who got their hands on the levers of government with the declared intention of strengthening the role of the state in the economy. In these conditions, there was clearly a likelihood of greater government interference in credit matters, especially in connection with the needs of the planning process that was being inaugurated. Carli clearly recognized this change in the environment of the relations between the Bank of Italy and the Government and publicly addressed the issue of economic planning on several occasions in the early sixties.[34]

Carli's attitude towards the banks in this period can be seen as reflecting his desire to strengthen the position of the central bank vis-à-vis the banking system and hence the Government. Menichella had relied principally on moral suasion for the implementation of monetary policy, but both Carli's personality and the changes under way in the banking system led him to abandon this instrument. The strength of moral suasion derives from "the

---

[33] Carli (1977: 36–37). Indeed according to a bon mot that circulated in the international banking community during the sixties, central banks had the problem of maintaining their autonomy everywhere – except in Italy – where it was the Government's autonomy that was at risk.

[34] See Banca d'Italia "The Governor's Concluding Remarks for 1961" and Carli (1962 b and c).

precarious equilibrium of the consensus among the parties involved".[35] The chances of reaching agreement depend on the central bank's power of persuasion and on the number of interlocutors. The latter was tending to rise as a result of the development of local banks and trend towards despecialization[36]. Moreover, moral suasion requires the central bank to make its opinions and plans known on each occasion.

There were thus valid grounds for the rapid switch Carli made from moral suasion to other monetary policy instruments more effective in controlling banks.

The major risk was that of interference by the Government in the management of credit. The approach Carli adopted at the very beginning of his Governorship was that of an institution sharing the aims of the development policy of the Centre-Left coalition and alone able and willing to organize the financial markets so that the necessary resources would be available. In short, in Carli's view it was indispensable to convince the Government that the implementation of its economic development plans did not require interference with the Bank's management of financial flows. The policy Carli pursued in his early years as Governor of using monetary instruments that were less dependent on consensus not only did not conflict with the planning of credit he advocated subsequently, but was a necessary prerequisite.

2.7 Monetary Versus "Real" Policy Making

The measures Carli took in the early years of his Governorship were designed more to bring the financial system into line with the policies adopted by the Bank of Italy than to modify its structure with the aim of improving its allocative and operational efficiency.

This "dirigiste" attitude was to be one of the hallmarks of Carli's Governorship.[37] It provided the linchpin for the Bank of Italy in its relations with the Government on the one hand, and with the banking system on the other.

Vis-à-vis the Government, "dirigisme" gave the central bank excellent credentials for planning the financial flows needed to implement public expenditure plans. Vis-à-vis the banking system, it resulted in the banks de-

---

[35] See De Cecco (1968).
[36] For a discussion of the structural changes in the banking system and despecialization, see Carli (1962c).
[37] The administrative constraints on credit and bank lending introduced in 1973 were only the institutionalisation, made necessary by the changed environment, of the administrative concept of credit implicit in Carli's approach. See Nardozzi (1983).

legating the major choices regarding the allocation of credit to the central bank or to the special credit institutions. In exchange, it was understood that banks would receive desirable intermediation business and protective treatment in the event of crises[38].

Such relationships with the Government and the banking system certainly minimized conflict, but they exposed the central bank, together with the financial system as a whole, to the risk of excessive compliance with the Government's wishes or, in other words, of a damaging loss of autonomy. Carli can be seen to have buttressed that of the central bank by participating in Government decision-making over the whole range of economic policy and not just its short-term and monetary aspects. This is the key to the Bank of Italy's strategy towards the political authorities during Carli's Governorship.

This participation in Government decisions required the cooperative and understanding attitude towards political needs that De Cecco labeled as "Carli's corporativistic philosophy". The shortcomings of this approach were nonetheless offset to some extent by the authority the Bank of Italy enjoyed. Its enormously strengthened Research Department and the recognition it received abroad gave the Governor an unquestionable "technical" superiority.

The autonomy of the central bank was thus shifted from its natural focus, the government of money and the credit system, to the real aspects of the economy. Ground was ceded on the first front with the aim of getting more power on the second[39]. The Bank joined forces with the Prince to act as a counterweight at a higher level of policy making.

One field in which the Bank's involvement in economic policy-making stood out clearly and fomented considerable discussion was the distribution

---

[38] Carli himself recognized the sedative effect on banking entrepreneurship of the easy conditions of intermediation business (e.g. "The Governor's Concluding Remarks for 1970" p. 384). It has also been argued that banks were allowed to shift from productive customers entailing risk to borrowers guaranteed at the end of the line by the state, thereby diverting them from their primary function (Savona 1978).
For a discussion of the inhibiting effects on banking entrepreneurship and innovation, see Nardozzi(1983).
On the failure to use the supervisory function to stimulate the operational efficiency of banks, see Onado (1983).
On the indulgent protection of banks in difficulties, see Carli (1968) and Onado (1983).

[39] This explains Carli's remark that the Bank of Italy had considerable power but consequently sometimes lacked "the autonomy monetary policy requires" (Carli 1977: 36–37).

of income[40]. Though it has always been recognized that monetary policy is not neutral vis-à-vis the distribution of income, the interest of economists was aroused by the peculiarity of a central bank seeking less to achieve the traditional objectives of internal and external stability than to foster the formation of profits, seen as underlying the accumulation of capital. The debate focused primarily on the implicit reference-model of the Governor on the relationships between monetary policy, income distribution and capital accumulation. Interestingly, the analysis showed that the Bank of Italy had interpreted the 1962–63 cyclical difficulties as a structural problem related to the fall in profit margins and *consequently* in investment and considered that the shift in the distribution of income could be tackled with monetary instruments. This led in the early seventies to an interpretation of the Bank of Italy's policy that linked three key developments (the 1962–63 monetary policy, the squeeze imposed at the beginning of 1969 in anticipation of the effects of the Hot Autumn wage increases and the February 1973 decision to allow the lira to float) and saw them as part of the same design: to protect profits.[41] The need to safeguard profits and hence corporate self-financing was a constant concern of Governor Carli's. On at least two occasions in 1962 and 1973, he gave this objective priority over that of maintaining price stability.

This interpretation of the Bank of Italy's policy throws light on its strategy vis-à-vis the Government. By acting to protect profitability, the central bank reduced the need for firms to have recourse to a financial system tailored to the requirements of the public sector. In this way it curbed the spread of the "state-aided capitalism" that the changes in the financial structure promoted by the central bank itself had encouraged. The protection of profits balanced the concessions made to the public sector under the policy of cooperation with the Government. In addition, it helped to minimize the negative effects of the credit system's declining allocative efficiency. Indirect support for this view is to be found in the fact that Carli considered resigning at the end of 1969 when it appeared that monetary policy had been spiked as a means of countering wage claims.[42] This strategy preformed its function as long as the distribution of income and the budget deficit remained under control. When both these conditions ceased to hold in the first half of the seventies, the only pillar of Carli's strategy to remain standing was the compliance of the central

---

[40] This was initiated by an article written jointly by Modigliani and La Malfa. For a survey of all the contributions, see Nardozzi (1979 and 1981).

[41] See Graziani and Meloni (1973) and Nardozzi (1980).

[42] Cf. Carli (1977: 53–56).

bank towards the political sphere. To restore its autonomy, a radical change in attitude towards both the Government and the credit system was necessary, and was made under Governor Baffi.

2.8 The Change in Strategy During the Seventies

The strategy described in Section 2.7 was formulated in the light of conditions in the labour market, public finances and the world economy that changed radically between 1969 and 1973. These changes made the problems of monetary control the decisive factor in the central bank's attitude to the Government and the credit system. Whereas from 1947 to the turn of the seventies the Bank of Italy sought to preserve its autonomy by participating in the guidance of the country's economic development, subsequently, and especially after 1975, it focused its efforts on maintaining its autonomy in the more specific field of monetary policy.

The new conditions in Italy and abroad clearly revealed the restrictions that financial compliance towards the public sector imposed on the central bank's freedom of action and which had initially been offset by the influence in the management of the real economy.

The crucial point is that this compliance, designed to facilitate the financing of huge *public investments*, had come to involve the Bank in the financing of a rapidly expanding *budget deficit on current account* in precisely the conditions – inflation and floating exchange rates – that made such action dangerous. The budget deficit was financed directly by the central bank and by the banks, through both purchases of Treasury bills and lending to central and local government bodies. In his Concluding Remarks for 1973 Carli stated that to have blocked the monetary financing of the government through the Treasury of the refinancing of banks "would be a seditious act in the form of monetary policy; and would be followed by a paralysis of the public administration" (Banca d'Italia n.d.b.:426).

Since the control of credit via the monetary base was consequently not feasible, the dirigiste approach that was already implicit in the choices made in the sixties was accentuated with the introduction of selective credit ceilings and portfolio constraints for banks.

These administrative controls, coupled with the benign neglect shown towards the efficiency of banks, virtually annulled bankers' entrepreneurial function. In a protected market like Italy's this inevitably imposed costs on the collectivity that were later to become clearly visible.

The limits of such a "financial engineering" had been reached and further recourse to it was unadvisable from the point of view of both its effectiveness and the autonomy of the central bank[43]. If control over the monetary and credit aggregates was to be restored, the Bank of Italy would have to adopt a new position towards both the Government and the financial system. This meant undoing the double bind whereby the Bank was unable to intervene to improve the efficiency of the credit system because the latter's inefficiency was largely a consequence of the way the Bank participated in the management of the country's economic policy.

Governor Baffi abandoned the role Carli had developed of fulcrum for the political mediation of macro and microeconomic interests to promote a monetary policy focusing on the traditional cyclical and structural objectives of a central bank. The shift to this new strategy was also undoubtedly in response to the foreign exchange crisis of January 1976 (see below) and was made, especially as regards the structural aspects, in gradual steps. The foundations had nonetheless been laid by the change in the method of issuing Treasury bills that Carli introduced in the last few months of his Governorship with the aim of promoting an efficient money market (open the public as well as banks). The development of this market was the linchpin of the central bank's new strategy vis-à-vis both the Government and the banking system. We do not know how Carli managed to overcome the resistance of the banking system, which had caused a similar plan to be shelved in 1968, but the issue was clearly much more important for the central bank's autonomy on this occasion.

The reform, which the Treasury followed up with curbs on bank lending to the public sector (local authorities were forbidden to borrow from banks and their outstanding debts were funded by the Treasury, while public bodies' bank balances were transferred to a centralized Treasury account), was subsequently crowned in 1981 by the so-called divorce, the termination of the agreement whereby the Bank of Italy undertook to take up any Treasury bills unsold.

The new relationship between the central banks and the Government took time to become established, as can be seen from the five years that separated the activation of the money market from the "divorce". By contrast, the

---

[43] In his first concluding remarks Baffi paid homage to Carli's creativeness in the field of financial ingeneering but also noted that "There is something profoundly unsatisfying in having to direct central bank action in such a way that it suffocates a system that possesses its own valid parameters and mechanisms, ... Unsatisfying not only from the point of view of logic but also because the effects tend to the ephemeral" (Banca d'Italia n.d.b: VII–VIII).

change in the Bank of Italy's attitude towards the banking system quickly made itself felt in a new "style" of supervision.[44]

While previously supervision was cast in a residual role with respect to the central bank's main objectives in its relations with the Government[45], Baffi made it into one of the cornerstones of the central bank's strategy. The abandonment of the privileged Treasury-bank channel for public finances undermined the protected market in which banks had operated and called on them to behave more efficiently. Supervision, including inspections, was directed to increase efficiency and its effectiveness was considerably enhanced.

Two other factors contributed to supervision being given a new and more important role: first, the long period of restrictive monetary policy that started after the 1976 foreign exchange crisis inevitably put banks under pressure and explicitly revealed the social cost of inefficient intermediation and second, the increase in financial fragility associated with the crises of whole branches of industry and the scope for speculation provided by international monetary disorder and inflation.

The new approach of the Bank of Italy in its supervisory activity thus did not only reflect a desire to moralize the banking system but was also in response to changing conditions[46].

This, however, did not prevent the leadership of the Bank of Italy from being subjected to a vicious smear campaign in the press during the early months of 1979, culminating in the arrest of one of the Deputy Directors General, Mario Sarcinelli, and the bringing of charges against the Governor. Both were accused, and subsequently acquitted, of embezzlement in connection with loans granted by IMI (of which they were Directors) to a major chemical company (SIR).

This frontal attack on the autonomy of the central bank did not culminate in the political appointment of a new Directorate. When he resigned later in the same year, Baffi was able to indicate his successor, Carlo Azeglio Ciampi, from within the Bank.

The central bank thus succeeded in fending off political interference in a country where the occupation of the institutions by political parties is very

---

[44] See Onado (1983).
[45] Indirect support for this view is to be found in the contributions of the Research and Banking Supervision Departments to the Bank's Annual Report. Under Carli, the predominance of the former was almost absolute; under Baffi, though he himself came from the Research Department, the balance shifted considerably in favour of the latter.
[46] See Onado (1979).

extensive. This may appear strange in the light of developments of other countries as England (the Leigh – Pemberton case) or U.S. (the recent Greenspan case). The explaination lies however in the relative weakness of Italian coalition governments, which is in part due to the large number of political parties.

In countries where system of government is based on alternation, the head of the executive is identified with an economic program approved by the electorate. In Italy such a link between the electorate, parties programs and the Government is virtually non existing. The political stability deriving from the absence of any real alternation on Government is coupled with a set of institutions designed to guide the economy on the light of long term guidelines. When these are lacking the exercise of political power degenerates into outright appropriation of economic strong points. However such appropriation is weakened by the disappearance of the unifying force provided by a common program and serves fragmented special interests.

This explains the continuation under Governor Ciampi, notwithstanding the hiatus in 1979, of the strategy pursued by Baffi in the Bank's relations with the Government and the credit system.

3 The Major Monetary Policy Choices

Conflicts between the central bank and the Treasury are exceptions rather than the rule in Italy. The Bank of Italy has in fact enjoyed considerable freedom in the formulation of monetary policy and in the choice of instruments even if in a way which is different during each of the three periods here considered.

3.1 Monetary Policy Between 1947 and 1960

In the period immediately following the Second World War, the Bank of Italy found itself in a position whereby friction in its relations with the Government was limited by three different factors:

1. The Governor was Luigi Einaudi and, as Paolo Baffi noted,

> five of the six Ministers of the Treasury in this period (1945–48) were linked to Einaudi by ties dating far into the past ... Einaudi undoubtedly exercised a powerful influence on their actions (Baffi 1965:178).

2. The substantial reductions, following the end of the war and the high inflation rate in four major items of the budget: the public debt, defence, the colonies, and wages and salaries (Baffi 1965:184).
3. The Bank of Italy was without doubt the best qualified center of economic analysis, which gave in an edge over the Government and made it the natural interlocutor for the Allies and international institutions[47]. It was to maintain this edge without interruption up to now.

These factors explain the relative ease with which the Bank imposed the objective of internal and external stability with sharply deflationary measures in the summer of 1947, when the international climate was more in favour of expansion[48]. The adoption of these measures was facilitated by the composition of the new Government (Christian Democrat, with Einaudi Deputy Prime Minister and "guardian" of economic policy also in his role of Minister of the Budget). It probably also benefited from the fact that inflation was due more to the expansion in bank credit that banks' holdings of liquidity with the central bank permitted than to deficit financing. Consequently, it was possible to implement the monetary squeeze simply by arranging for the newly-created Interministerial Committee for Credit and Savings to approve the introduction of compulsory reserves. This set the precedent for the powerful technical influence that the bank was to exercise over this Committee, institutionally entrusted with the formulation of monetary policy.

The 1947 deflationary policy was the result of Einaudi's idealistic rightwing fight against inflation, but it was also consistent with the less idealistic view of Italian capitalism of the drafters of the 1936 Banking Law.

In their view, to break with the protected capitalism of the past – dominated by large monopolistic industrial groups with a propensity to rely on state support – the economy would have to be opened to international competition. This, however, required a preliminary building up of the reserves and an improvement in the balance of payments. Donato Menichella, who had been one of the protagonists of the 1936 Banking Law, succeeded Einaudi as Governor in 1948 after implementing the 1947 stabilization plan as his substitute. His thinking envisaged large multiyear investments in infrastructures and basic industries, which were not to be interrupted if a drain

---

[47] For a masterly reconstruction of the Bank's role as a reference point for foreign observers, see Baffi (1985).
[48] See the criticism of the Einaudi-Menichella line in the ECA Country Study published in 1949. Cf. Also De Cecco (1968) and Baffi (1985).

on the reserves made it necessary to impose restrictions to correct unsustainable external imbalances.[49]

The monetary policy pursued after the 1947 stabilization up to the end of 1949 was designed to replenish the reserves. The caution shown in this period was criticized abroad but was not a cause of friction with the Government. The business cycle associated with the Korean War was weathered without serious difficulties thanks to the reserves that had been accumulated. From then until the end of the fifties the monetary authorities sought not to offset the changes in liquidity due to the balance of payments and the budget deficit. Between 1953 and 1957 the latter decreased and the foreign sector also contributed to a reduction in liquidity. Starting in September 1957, both these channels contributed to an exceptional increase in the monetary base[50]. This swing into substantial external current account surplus, this "new development" as Menichella called it, was accompanied by a recessionary phase in the domestic economy and led him to advise the banks to channel the public's surplus liquidity to the capital market and the Government to increase public investment[51].

Since the budget deficit remained small throughout the period, the monetary authorities concentrated their attention on the balance of payments. This does not imply, however, that the Bank of Italy followed a succession of short-term monetary policies in the fifties[52]. Rather the external accounts served as an indicator of the scope for increasing the openness of the economy as part of long-term strategy of promoting growth and the competition.

Consequently, as Menichella himself observed, his phase of monetary policy came to an end with the declaration of the convertibility of the lira at the end of 1958, and indeed shortly afterwards Guido Carli succeeded him at the head of the Bank[53].

3.2 From 1964 to 1973

Between 1959 and 1962 the current account of the balance of payments was constantly in surplus, notwithstanding the exceptional expansion in economic

---

[49] This point is stressed in many of Menichella's Annual Reports. See for exemple Banca d'Italia (n.d.a: 106–269–271–279–545–547).

[50] See "Stabilità monetaria e sviluppo economico in Italia: 1946–60", in Baffi (1965) and Baffi and Occhiuto (1960).

[51] "The Governor's Concluding Remarks for 1958" and those for 1959, in Banca d'Italia (n.d.a).

[52] See Marconi in Vicarelli (1979).

[53] "The Governor's Concluding Remarks for 1959" in Banca d'Italia (n.d.a).

activity. In 1961–62 the improvement in the external accounts was almost entirely attributable to that in the trade balance – a confirmation that the objective of combining structural external equilibrium with high growth rates had been achieved.

This opened a new phase for monetary policy in two important respects. In the short term it was now possible to aim at keeping the economy on its potential growth path through fine tuning. Together with the factors discussed in Section 2.6, this helps to explain Carli's adoption of direct instruments in place of moral suasion up to then adopted. As for the long-term, it was necessary to revise the strategy to which Menichella had referred in formulating monetary policy.

The Bank of Italy pursued an expansionary monetary policy, culminating in the reduction of the compulsory reserve ratio in January 1962. For its part, the Treasury did not apply any pressure since government expenditure did not contribute to the growth in the monetary base[54]. The rationale of this monetary policy has some points in common with the philosophy of the previous Governor, insofar as it was designed to prevent any interruption of the investment needed the country's growth. However, the way in which Carli defended it from the criticisms leveled after the monetary restrictions imposed in the autumn of 1963 indicates that the Bank had developed the new long-term strategy for its relations with the first Centre-Left Government, described in the previous section.

The analysis of all the events in this period is beyond the scope of this study[55]. It is sufficient to note that the about-face in monetary policy was made in the autumn of 1963 – at a time of alarm, not only in Italy but also abroad, about the future of the Italian economy, hit by inflation, a balance-of-payments deficit and heavy capital outflows – without objections by the Minister of the Treasury, Emilio Colombo (who maintained this post in several subsequent Governments and enjoyed a relationship with the central bank that became known as the "Colombo-Carli axis").

The 1963 restrictive measures rapidly produced substantial effects. As early as the second quarter of 1964 the external current account had started to improve and the economy, under the impact of a series of fiscal decrees, had entered a sharp recession.

Once the critical phase of this adjustment had been overcome, the posi-

---

[54] On the development of the budget deficit, see Sarcinelli (1965). Carli took full responsibility for the expansionary policy adopted in his "Concluding Remarks for 1962" and 1963 (Banca d'Italia, n.d. b: 476–77 and 479). See also Nardozzi (1981).

[55] For a thorough chronicle of these events, see Forte (1966).

tion of the Bank of Italy vis-à-vis the Government was strengthened by the demonstration both of the need for political initiatives to respect "economic compatibilities" and of its ability to restore the international good standing of the Italian economy.

The events of 1964 reinforced Carli's strategy of sharing political power with the Government and building up the central bank's influence on economic policy. The contribution the Bank of Italy made to the formulation and implementation of economic policy in this period filled a vacuum created by the inability of the coalition parties to agree on a programme, but was nonetheless to become a feature of the Italian scene.

Between 1965 und 1969 monetary policy was based on the total credit required by the Government's planning guidelines and the forecast growth of the economy[56]. This choice was supplemented by the policy of pegging bond yields with the aim of expanding the volume of securities to meet the needs of the public and private sectors with only limited growth in the monetary base[57].

Thus monetary policy achieved both "financial compliance" vis-à-vis the Treasury, since the budget deficit was mostly financed with long-term securities, and the aforementioned dirigistic management of financial flows, through the authorization of bond issues and subsidized credit.

There is no evidence in the subsequent period – which saw the ending of the stabilization that preceded the 1969 "hot autumn" and the measures to cope with the latter's consequences up to the switch to free floating in February 1973 – of the central bank's autonomy being curbed except, as will be discussed in the next section, as a result of the role it had elected to play in the government of the economy and in its relationship with the Government.

3.3 From 1973 to the Present

Not only did the relationship established with the Government in the sixties break down in the seventies, but so did the policy of monetary fine tuning (a development common to several other countries besides Italy). The last attempt to maintain the approach of the sixties was probably the 1973 devaluation of the lira, which was intended both to restore corporate profit margins – eroded by wage increases and industrial conflict – and to ease the external constraint and thereby allow the recovery under way to continue. The oil

---

[56] "The Governor's Concluding Remarks for 1965" (Banca d'Italia, n.d.b) as well as Caranza and Fazio (1983).

[57] See OECD (1976), Introduction by Savona.

shock hit Italy when it was already suffering from inflationary pressures and largely thwarted this design. The flare up of inflation and the huge deterioration in the external accounts forced the Bank to adopt a restrictive monetary policy at the beginning of 1974.

The events in 1975 and the early part of 1976 accentuated the need for the Bank of Italy to modify its relationship with the Government by revealing the perverseness of the "go" phase of fine tuning in the new conditions. The recession into which the Italian economy had plunged at the beginning of 1975 (along with the rest of the industrial countries), together with the improvement in the external accounts and the slowdown in inflation, persuaded the monetary authorities to reverse their stance and pursue an expansionary policy for the rest of the year. In march the import deposit scheme introduced in May 1974 was abolished and the non-renewal of the ceiling on credit expansion was announced. Subsequently, the discount rate was lowered twice, the restrictions on banks' net foreign positions were lifted, and measures introduced to facilitate the short-term financing of export credits. Further, there was a sudden sharp rise in the government's financing needs, met through the creation of monetary base[58]. The outcome demonstrated that an expansionary monetary policy tends to finance speculation rather than investment when operators' expectations are strongly inflationary. In January 1976, with a Government crisis under way and virtually no foreign currency reserves left, the Bank of Italy was forced to close the official exchange market for forty days.

These events, which seriously undermined the standing of the Italian economy abroad, convinced the central bank of the need to give top priority to the replenishment of the country's reserves and were decisive in the Bank of Italy's adoption of a less ambitious and more separatist attitude towards Government policy.

The further large devaluation of the lira that was required when the exchange marked was reopened was accompanied by severe restrictive measures that produced a current account surplus at the end of 1977. Since this was doubled in the following year, the Governor was able to announce in May 1979 that the level of the reserves made it possible to reconsider the country's economic policy objectives and envisage "greater use of the exchange rate for the purpose of countering imported inflation" (Banca d'Italia

---

[58] This caused some friction between the Bank of Italy, of which Paolo Baffi had been appointed Governor a few months previously, and the Directorate General of the Treasury, headed by Ferdinando Ventriglia, who some had seen as a possible successor to Guido Carli.

n.d.c.:374). In the event, no such action was taken either by the Government – to whom the message was directed with the aim of underlining the Bank's respect of the new division of roles – or by the Bank, even though the Government's inertia would have justified its invoking the urgent need to combat inflation. Towards the end of 1979 monetary policy was given a new restrictive turn in conjunction with the new increase in oil prices and monetary policy has maintained this rigorous stance ever since.

Since 1974 the intermediate objective of monetary policy has been total domestic credit. During the 1976–77 restriction the principal instrument used to control this aggregate was the ceiling on bank lending. Its effectiveness declined, however, as time passed, owing to the increase in the budget deficit and the growth of uncontrolled forms of intermediation designed to circumvent the limits on lending to the private sector. Consequently, the maintenance of a given degree of monetary restriction required increasingly extensive administrative constraints, which produced harmful side effects on banks' efficiency.

It was in this phase that the desirability of central bank autonomy with respect to the financing of the Treasury emerged, as discussed in Section 2.8. Basically this reflected the need to transmit monetary policy via money market interest rates and led to contractual (market) relationships replacing those of a respectively consensual and administrative nature with the Treasury and the banking system.

The switch to a market-based approach was made gradually: the "divorce" between the Bank of Italy and the Treasury in 1981; the new compulsory reserve system in 1982; and the application for the first time of the 1948 decree establishing the limit of the Treasury's overdraft with the Bank of Italy. Since this limit was being exceeded, the central bank called on Parliament in 1983 to approve an extraordinary advance, in accordance with the provisions of the decree. This step, to which public opinion did not give the attention it deserved, marked the Bank's desire to make the Government responsible to Parliament for its financial decisions. Later in the same year the ceiling on bank lending was abolished. Monetary control has thus come to rely increasingly on interest rate impulses, though a safety net of moral suasion vis-à-vis the major banks has also been put in place.

4 From (Italian) History to (General) Theory

This account of Italian experience can serve as the basis for some general considerations regarding the theory of central banking.

A superficial examination of Italy's laws defining the position and role of the central bank would suggest that it has very limited power vis-à-vis the Interministerial Committee for Credit and Savings and the Treasury – a conclusion that is belied by the experience of the last forty years as outlined by our historical sketch.

It is history that reveals the conditions under which the markets for goods, labour and money actually work as well as their interrelations with which macroeconomic models are concerned. However, most of the recent literature on central banks has eliminated history by referring to a macroeconomic theory that identifies the behaviour of institutions (the Government, the central bank, etc.) as the only possible source of disequilibrium in these markets[59].

This approach sees history as superimposing "spurious" factors (the political and social pressures expressed by institutions) on the general mechanisms that govern the market. This in turn justifies taking these mechanisms as the starting point for logical deductions with respect to which the political and institutional factors are "exogenous variables". The analysis of central banking is accordingly bound to take one of two paths, depending whether it is the behaviour of the Government or that of the central bank that is seen to be deviant (vis-à-vis the natural equilibrium of the system). If it is the former's, it is important to assess the independence of the central bank; if it is the latter's, it is necessary to determine why an institution that should safeguard the general interest should deviate from this function.

The first path is that followed by those contemporary analysts of central banking who refer exclusively to the function of controlling the money supply and seek:

- to establish an empirical inverse relationship between the independence of central banks (assessed in terms of statutory rules and institutional arrangements) and the extent to which their monetary policies are accommodating;
- to measure central banks' autonomy making econometric estimates (usually based on reaction functions of the effects of socio-political factors, represented by economic variables such as the budget deficit, the increase in wages, etc.) of the behaviour of the central bank (represented by variables related to monetary policy).[60]

---

[59] This is the macroeconomic theory most often found in economics textbooks which is the result of the convergence of monetarist and keynesian-neoclassical thinking.
[60] See, for example: Willet and Laney (1978); Parkin and Bade (1978); Parkin (1978); Hodgman and Resek (1983); Banaian, Laney, and Willet (1983).

Such exercises are nonetheless extremely questionable. Establishing an inverse relationship between monetary accomodation and central bank independence (often determined by way of a superficial examination of the relevant law) may confuse cause and effect since it assigns the label of "independent" to the central banks of countries that are traditionally averse to inflation for other reasons (such as Switzerland and Germany). Furthermore, as has been noted, the use of reaction functions is more like eavesdropping than scientific enquiry[61].

The so-called "bureaucratic theory" of central banking follows the second path,[62] which explains the behaviour of central banks not with reference to economic policy objectives but in the light of the self-interest of the institution or of the bureaucrats on its staff. Without exception this theory concludes that, for reasons ranging from the desire to maximize prestige and minimize controls to ruthless efforts to obtain salary increases, central banks are inclined to behave in ways that conflict with the general interest.

The weak link in this chain, however, is the initial hypothesis that the function representing central banks as bureaucracies can be specified without reference to the specific political, economic and institutional context in which each bank operates. In reality, public institutions and the bureaucracies of which they are composed, reflect the role of the state in each country. Consequently, it is not legitimate to draw general conclusions about the central bank institution without considering the state of which it is a part.

The foregoing would appear to exclude the possibility of formulating a theory of central banking and to leave room only for the historical analysis of individual cases. This, however, is neither acceptable (what type of history, anyway, without any theoretical framework?) nor true, since it is both feasible and profitable to change the macroeconomic reference theory. This can be achieved by substituting the Keynesian concept of an "entrepreneur economy" for that of a system of self-equilibrating markets in the definition of the environment in which the central bank operates (Keynes 1980: 76–83).

In what follows I shall show that the approach adopted to analyze the Italian case has such a theoretical foundation and give a general meaning to the term central bank "autonomy".

Keynes defines capitalism as an "entrepreneur or money-wage economy". His synonymous use of these two terms implies that entrusting production

---

[61] See Padoa Schioppa (1983) in Hodgman (1983).
[62] See the early contributions of Acheson and Chant (1972). More recently, this approach has been revived by: Toma (1982), Shugart and Tollison (1983), and Toma and Toma (1985). It is also to be found in Friedman (1982).

and investment decisions to entrepreneurs is a characteristic feature of capitalism and that, in turn, this necessarily entails the payment of workers in money. This has two further consequences: first, that entrepreneurs must have the money for wages *before* selling their products; and second, that uncertainty is an innate feature of their activity since they do not know whether what they produce will sell.

It follows from the first point that money is primarily credit-money, i.e. an advance of purchasing power to workers. This credit is supplied by banks with the prospect of recovering their loans when spending returns the purchasing power to firms. If this occured only in part, the latter would not be able to pay off their residual debts by transferring their unsold goods to creditor banks, as they would in an economy in which money was only a means of exchange and not also a means of payment. The banking system is therefore exposed to the risk of insolvency, and consequently financial instability is an inherent feature of capitalism.

The second point means that money permits decisions regarding the use of income and wealth to be phased in accordance with the "state of confidence" in the most rational forecasts. Liquidity preference varies inversely with this state of confidence and, since it determines the level of interest rates and hence the levels of income and employment, for a given stock of money these variables can have different equilibrium values corresponding to different states of confidence. Insofar as investment also depends on the state of confidence, there cannot be a natural equilibrium value that can be determined independently of the monetary authorities and the Government.

This capsuled version of Keynes' thinking suggests that the analysis of central banking should include both the relationship between the central bank and the financial system and that between the bank and Government policy and hence, more generally, the role of the state in the economy.

This both broadens the scope of central banking analysis compared with the neoclassical-monetarist approach and makes it more *general* since central bank behaviour can be assessed with reference to the roles and strategies underlying Government and public intervention in different periods and countries.

The analysis of central banking using tests of independence, reaction functions and the theory of bureaucracy is based on a typically American concept of the state and public intervention. This sees involvement of the authorities in the economy as being justified only to the extent that it guarantees the functioning of the market as the expression of individual freedom. Government, and indeed the political sphere, are not required to draw up social and economic guidelines that diverge from those embodied in the laws of the market. Institutions are bound by the same rules as individuals – nobody is to be able to counter market forces. This explains the deeply-rooted tradition of decentralizing authority with the aim of creating checks and balances, as can clearly be seen in the history of US central banking. The approach underlying the theory of bureaucracy can be seen in the same light, since it aims to reveal the possible conflicts between institutions' particular interests and those of society, in contrast with the European tradition of focusing on the reasons of state they incarnate.

The American concept of the state and of public institutions presupposes a society already having a market organization. This has customarily been true of the United States but not of Europe, where the state is seen as an entity that expresses a public interest that cannot find expression in the market or in individual preferences. European experience stems from a concept of public institutions and bureaucracies that highlights the *grand commis d'état* as the promoter of economic and social projects of public interest. The idea of benevolent and enlightened rulers is by no means utopistic, as Brennan and Buchanan claim, but well founded in the history of European bureaucracy[63].

These disparate concepts of the state and its institutions naturally lead to central bank autonomy having different meanings. While the common American and monetarist view generates a definition in terms of ability to resist political pressure – always a factor tending to disturb the economy – the European and Keynesian view is less harsh on Governments. I would express this definition as follows: autonomy is the scope allowed to the central bank to formulate monetary policy as it thinks best (as regards both ends and means) in the light of the Government's economic policy and the socio-economic situation.

This definition includes resistance to Government-induced inflationary pressure, but does not stop there. It is more general than the US-style definition because the possibility of giving explicit consideration to Government policy (instead of treating it as given a priori) allows widely differing cases to be analyzed. Central bank autonomy can range from hand-in-glove cooperation to fierce opposition, depending on the degree of convergence on economic policy. With this framework it is also possible to envisage the case, by no means unrealistic, of a conflict between a monetarist Government and a more accommodating central bank.

The many forms that central bank autonomy can take according to the historical circumstances are well exemplified by Italian experience. Up to around 1960 the Bank of Italy's autonomy consisted in its acting as the

---

[63] See Brennan and Buchanan (1981).

trustee of the political design (which was not only or even really that of the Government since it was not shared by all the parties in the various coalitions) of opening the Italian economy to foreign competition. In the sixties, autonomy came to mean an authoritative contribution, often rendered decisive by the plurality of views in the Government, to the aim of correcting the course of Italy's economic development through planning. In this period the distinction between the central bank and the Government faded away almost completely. In the seventies the lack of success of the strategy pursued in the sixties, coupled with the need for more effective monetary control engendered by the new external conditions (the aftermath of the oil shock and the collapse of the international monetary system), made a new type of autonomy necessary. The contractual and political power that had enabled Carli to exert an almost unprecedented influence was gradually replaced by market relationships that set the Bank of Italy at arm's length from a political sphere in which planning in the public interest was giving way to fighting between interest groups, a conflict that was to lead to an attack on the central bank itself in 1979.

References

Acheson, K. and J. Chant (1972): The Choice of Monetary Instruments and the Theory of Bureaucracy, *Public Choice*, vol. 12, 13–33.
Acheson, K. and J. Chant (1973a): Bureaucratic Theory and the Choice of Central Bank Goals: The Case of the Bank of Canada, *Journal of Money, Credit and Banking*, vol. V, n. 2: 637–655.
Acheson, K. and J. Chant (1973b): Mythology and Central Banking, *Kyklos*, vol. XXVI: 362–379.
Amato, G. (Ed.) (1972): *Il governo dell'industria in Italia*, Bologna: Il Mulino.
Andreatta, N. (1973): *Cronache di un'economia bloccata: 1969–1973*, Bologna: Il Mulino.
Baffi, P. (1965): *Studi sulla moneta*, Milano: Giuffrè.
Baffi, P. (1985): Via Nazionale e gli economisti stranieri: 1944–53, *Rivista di Storia Economica*, n. 1: 1–45.
Baffi, P. and A. Occhiuto (1960): La componente esterna della liquidità e le regole di condotta monetaria, *Giornale degli Economisti e Annali di Economia*, n. 11–12: 715–733.
Banaian, K., O. Laney, and T. Willet (1983): Central Bank Independence: An International Comparison, *Economic Review*, Federal Reserve Bank of Dallas: 1–13.
Banca d'Italia (1977): *Struttura funzionale e territoriale del sistema bancario italiano: 1936–74*, Roma: Centro Stampa Banca d'Italia.
Banca d'Italia (n.d.a): *Fine dell'autarchia e miracolo economico*, Concluding Remarks of Governors Einaudi e Menichella, Janus.

Banca d'Italia (n.d.b): Concluding Remarks of Governor Carli, Banca d'Italia
Banca d'Italia (n.d.c): The Governor's Concluding Remarks for 1976 and subsequent years.
Banca d'Italia (1986): *Donato Menichella*, Bari: Laterza.
Banco di Roma (1981): *Banca e industria tra le due guerre*, Bologna: Il Mulino.
Bonelli, F. (1984): Alberto Beneduce, *I protagonisti dell'intervento pubblico in Italia*, Mortara, A. (Ed.), Milano: F. Angeli.
Bonelli, F. (1983): Speech given at the Conference on A. Beneduce, Caserta (on the occasion of IRI's fiftieth anniversary.)
Brennan, G. and J. Buchanan (1981): *Monopoly in Money and Inflation: The Case for a Constitution to Discipline Government*, London: The Institute of Economic Affairs.
Caranza, C. and A. Fazio (1983): Methods of Monetary Control in Italy: 1974–1983, *The Political Economy of Monetary Policy: National and International Aspects*, Hodgman, D. (Ed), Federal Bank Reserve of Boston et al., Boston.
Carli, G. (1962a): Deposizione alla Commissione Parlamentare di inchiesta sui limiti posti alla concorrenza in campo economico, Camera dei Deputati, Vol. II, Roma.
Carli, G. (1962b): Governo della liquidità e mercato finanziario nel quadro della programmazione dello sviluppo, vol. XVIII *Bancaria*.
Carli, G. (1962c): Struttura del sistema bancario e stabilità monetaria nel quadro della programmazione dello sviluppo, *Bancaria*, n. 2: 135–139.
Carli, G. (1966): Problemi odierni di un istituto di emissione, *Bancaria*, n. 6: 675–680.
Carli, G. (1968): Aspetti strutturali e aziendali del sistema creditizio, *Bancaria* n. 2: 168–174.
Carli, G. (1977): *Intervista sul capitalismo italiano*, Scalfari, E. (Ed), Bari: Laterza.
Ciocca, P. (1982): *Interesse e profitto*, Bologna: Il Mulino.
Ciocca, P. (1987): *Money and Economy: Central Banker's View*, London: Macmillan.
Ciocca, P. and G. Toniolo (1984): Industry and Finance in Italy 1918–40, *Journal of European Economic History*, Special Issue.
De Cecco, M. (1968): *Saggi di politica monetaria*, Milano: Giuffrè.
De Mattia R. (1963): Banca d'Italia, *Eight European Central Banks*, London: Allen and Unwin.
Fazio, A. (1969): Base monetaria e controllo del credito in Italia, *Moneta e Credito*, vol. XXIII, n. 85: 82–106.
Forte, F. (1966): *La congiuntura in Italia*, Torino: Einaudi.
Friedman, M. (1982): Monetary Policy, Theory and Practice, *Journal of Money, Credit and Banking*, vol. XIV, n. 1: 98–118.
Giannini, M. S. (1977): *Diritto pubblico dell'economia*, Bologna: Il Mulino.
Giannini, M. S. (1981): Intervento di sintesi dei lavoro, *Banca e industria fra le due guerre*, Proceedings of the Conference organized by Banco di Roma, Bologna: Il Mulino.
Graziani, A. and F. Meloni (1973): Inflazione e fluttuazione della lira, *Note Economiche*, n. 3: 46–81.
Hodgman, D. and R. Resek (1983): Determinants of Monetary Policy in France, The Federal Republic of Germany, Italy and the United Kingdom: A Comparative Analysis, *The Political Economy of Monetary Policy: National and International Aspects*, D. Hodgam (Ed.), Federal Bank Reserve of Boston et al., Boston.
Keynes, J. M. (1980): *The Collected Writings of John Maynard Keynes*, Moggridge/Johnson (Eds.), vol. XXVII, London: Macmillan.

Lunghini, G. (Ed.) (1981): *Scelte politiche e teorie écónomiche in Italia: 1945–1978*, Torino: Einaudi.
Marconi, M. (1981): Lineamenti di un trentennio di politica monetaria, *Capitale industriale e capitale finanziario: il caso italiano*, Vicarelli, F. (Ed.) Bologna: Il Mulino.
Mattioli, R. (1962): I problemi attuali del credito, *Mondo Economico*, n. 2: 27–31.
Menichella, D. (1952): Il sistema bancario italiano nel quadro interno e in quello internazionale, *Bancaria*, n. 1: 16–26.
Menichella, D. (1955): Espansione economica in regime di stabilità monetaria, *Bancaria*, n. 11: 1296–1303.
Menichella, D. (1956): Le esperienze italiane circa il concorso delle banche nella realizzazione dell'equilibrio monetario e della stabilità economica, *Bancaria*, n. 1: 7–19.
Menichella, D. (1986): *Scritti e discorsi scelti*, Roma: Banca d'Italia.
Merusi, F. (1981): La posizione costituzionale della banca centrale in Italia, *Rivista trimestrale di Diritto Pubblico*, 1081–1107.
Nardozzi, G. (1979): *Note sull'accumulazione di capitale e sulla politica della Banca d'Italia negli anni sessanta*, with an appendix by M. Grillo, UNICOPLI, Milano.
Nardozzi, G. (Ed.) (1980): *I difficili anni '70*, Milano: Etas Libri.
Nardozzi, G. (1981): Accumulazione di capitale e politica monetaria: il punto di vista della Banca d'Italia, *Scelte politiche e teorie economiche in Italia: 1945–1978*, Lunghini, G. (Ed.), Torino: Einaudi.
Nardozzi, G. (1983): *Tre sistemi creditizi: banche ed economia in Francia, Germania, Italia*, Bologna: Il Mulino.
OECD (1976): *Monetary Policy in Italy*, Paris.
Onado, M. (1979): L'attacco alla Banca d'Italia e la politica di vigilanza, *Politica ed Economia*, n. 3: 9–21.
Onado, M. (1983): Evoluzione dei criteri di vigilanza nel sistema bancario italiano, *Banca Impresa Società*, n. 2: 141–164.
Padoa Schioppa, T. (1983): Discussion, *The Political Economy of Monetary Policy: National and International Aspects*, Hodgman, D. (Ed.), Federal Bank Reserve of Boston et al., Boston.
Parkin, M. (1978): In Search of a Monetary constitution for the European Communities, *One Money for Europe*, Fratianni/Peeters (Eds.), London: MacMillan.
Parkin, M. and R. Bade (1978): *Central Bank Laws and Monetary Policies: A Preliminary Investigation*, University of Western Ontario, Ontario.
Porzio, M. (1981): *La legge bancaria: Note e documenti sulla sua storia segreta*, Bologna: Il Mulino.
Puccini, G. (1978): *L'autonomia della Banca d'Italia: profili costituzionali*, Milano: Giuffrè.
Rodano, G. (1983): *Il credito e l'economia, Raffaele Mattioli alla Banca Commerciale Italiana*, Milano: Ricciardi.
Saraceno, P. (1981a): Opening Adress, *Banca e industria fre le due guerre*, Proceedings of the Conference organized by Banco di Roma, Bologna: Il Mulino.
Saraceno, P. (1981b): Salvataggi bancari e riforme negli anni 1922–36, *Banca e industria fra le due guerre*, Proceedings of the Conference organized by Banco die Roma, Bologna: Il Mulino.
Sarcinelli, M. (1965): La creazione di liquidità e la politica della banca centrale in Italia dal 1958 al 1964, *Letture di politica monetaria e finanziaria*, Di Fenizio, F. (Ed.), Banca Popolare di Milano.

Savona, P. (1976): Introduction, *Monetary Policy in Italy*, OECD.
Savona, P. (1978): Impresa e banca nell'economia italiana, *La banca nell'odierna realtà italiana*, Camaiti, R. (Ed.), EPR.
Scalfari, E. and G. Turani (1974): *Razza padrona: storia della borghesia di stato*, Milano: Feltrinelli.
Schugart, W. and R. Tollison (1983): Preliminary Evidence on the Use of Inputs by the Federal Reserve System, *American Economic Review*, vol. 73, n. 3: 291–304.
Toma, E. and M. Toma (1985): Research Activities and Budjet Allocations among Federal Reserve banks, *Public Choice*, vol. 45: 175–191.
Toma, M. (1982): Inflationary Bias of the Federal Reserve System: A Bureaucratic Perspective, *Journal of Monetary Economics*, n. 10: 163–190.
Vicarelli, F. (Ed.) (1979): *Capitale industriale e capitale finanziario: il caso italiano*, Bologna: Il Mulino.
Vicarelli, F. (1981): Note in tema di accumulazione di capitale in Italia: 1947–1963, *Scelte politiche e teorie economiche in Italia: 1945–1978*, Lunghini, G. (Ed.), Torino: Einaudi.
Willet, T. and L. Laney (1978): Monetarism, budget deficits and Wage Push Inflation: the Case of Italy and the U.K., *Banca nazionale del Lavoro, Quarterly Review*, vol. XXXI: 315–331.

About the Authors

JEAN BOUVIER (1920–1987)
Taught history and economic history at the Universities of Lille, Paris VIII (Vincennes) and Paris I (Sorbonne). Member of the Ecole des Hautes Etudes en Sciences Sociales.
Among his numerous books: *Le Crédit Lyonnais de 1863 à 1882, les amnées de fer* (Paris 1961), *Les Rothschild* (Paris, 1967). He was the editor of the fourth volume of the *Histoire économique et sociale de la France* (General editors Braudel and Labrousse, Paris 1980).

Sir ALEC CAIRNCROSS – born 1911.
Chancellor of the University of Glasgow.
He has alternated between academic life and government service. He was professor of economics in the University of Glasgow (1951–61), Economic Advisor to the British government (1961–64), Head of UK Government Economic Service (1964–69) and master of St. Peter's College, Oxford (1969–78). He is the author of a dozen books on economics of which the latest is *The Economic Section 1939–61: a Study in Economic Advising* (forthcoming).

CARL-LUDWIG HOLTFRERICH – born 1942
Professor of Economics and Economic History at the Freie Universität Berlin, John-F.Kennedy-Institut, Berlin. Among his books: *The German Inflation 1914–1923. Causes and Effects in International Perspective* (Berlin – New York 1986)

GIANGIACOMO NARDOZZI – born 1943.
Professor of economics at the University of Florence and Reader at the Bocconi University, Milano.
Among his books: *Tre sistemi creditizi: Francia, Germania. Italia* (Bologna 1983). He is the editor of a "Report on the Italian Stock Exchange" (Milano 1987)

RICHARD E. SYLLA – born 1940
Professor of Business and Economics at North Carolina State University, Raleigh, North Carolina.
Former editor of *The Journal of Economic History*.
Among his books: *The American Capital Market 1840–1914* (New York 1975). *The Evolution of the American Economy* (New York 1980).

GIANNI TONIOLO – born 1942
Professor of Economics at Ca' Foscari, The University of Venice. Associate Fellow, St. Antony's College, Oxford.
Co-editor of *Rivista di Storia Economica* (Einaudi, Torino)
Among his books: *L' economia dell' Italia fascista* (Laterza, Roma-Bari), *Storia economica dell' Italia liberale, 1850–1918* (Bologna 1988).

FAUSTO VICARELLI (1936–1986).
Was professor of economics at the Universities of Ancona, Florence and Rome and economic consultant to the Bank of Italy.
Among his numerous books: *Keynes* (London 1980).

Carl-Ludwig Holtfrerich

The German Inflation 1914–1923

Causes and Effects in International Perspective

Translated from the German original by T. Balderston

1986. 15,5 x 23 cm. XII, 370 pages. Cloth DM 128,- ISBN 3 11 009714 1

"This is a pioneering and major work of economic history that must be consulted by anyone interested in the German inflation and the international economy of the interwar period."

American Historical Review

"... an extremely important addition to the literature ... an immensely rich and provocative book. Holtfrerich has not only provided a masterful overview of the origins and consequences of the inflation. In addition, his discussions in particular of the distributive effects of the inflation, Germany's part in overcoming the world economic depression of 1920–21, and the role of foreign capital in financing German postwar economic recovery represent major revisions of our current understanding of the German inflation."

Journal of Modern History

"His book at one stroke elevates the whole discussion of the inflation on to an entirely new level ... Holtfrerich breaks new ground in his extensive coverage of the international dimension of the inflation."

Historical Journal

Hans H. Lechner

Währungspolitik

1988. 15,5 x 23 cm. XX, 557 pages. Cloth DM 168,- ISBN 3 11 007412 5

‚Währungspolitik' „versteht sich als Leitfaden mit aktuellen Bezügen, behandelt Tendenzen und Probleme der nationalen und internationalen Währungspolitik. Lechner definiert Währungspolitik nicht klassisch eng, nämlich als Aktivitäten zur Beeinflussung der Devisenmarktgeschäfte! Vielmehr wird Währungspolitik verstanden als Oberbegriff aller das Geldwesen, die Geldversorgung und den Zahlungsverkehr betreffenden Maßnahmen der Wirtschaftspolitik. Der Leitfaden erklärt elementare Zusammenhänge wie beispielsweise die Entstehung von Geld ... Interessant ist er besonders für Praktiker ..., weil der Autor ... breit auf die Möglichkeiten der außenwirtschaftlichen Absicherung nationaler Währungspolitik eingeht."

Wirtschaftswoche, Düsseldorf, 24/88

Prices are subject to change without notice

Walter de Gruyter · Berlin · New York

James Burk
Values in the Marketplace
The American Stock Market Under Federal Securities Law
1988. 15,5 x 23 cm. X, 207 pages. Cloth DM 98,- ISBN 3 11 011714 2
(de Gruyter Studies on North America, 2)

A sociological study of the American stock market, this volume traces the effects of federal securities law on the ethical and structural development of this central financial institution. It provides an institutional analysis of this stock market's strategic ability to adapt to its new regulatory environment. The book departs from usual studies of market regulation in at least two ways: First, the assessment of the consequences of market regulation is focused on the changes it has brought for the market as a social institution. Second, it emphasises an analysis of strategic conduct that assumes market participants act purposively in the pursuit of their own interests, but that they do so on the basis of limited knowledge within a complex institutional structure. The imperfect integration of such a structure hinders deliberate efforts at social control.

Economic and Strategic Issues in U.S. Foreign Policy
Carl-Ludwig Holtfrerich, editor

1988. 15,5 x 23 cm. XVI, 297 pages. Cloth DM 98,- ISBN 3 11 011793 2
(de Gruyter Studies on North America, 3)

Has the American economy become the Achilles heel of U. S. foreign policy? While the U. S. pursued a policy of military build up and thus asserted its leadership position in the strategic field, its international position in the economic field deteriorated dramatically. Will the international commitments and claims of the U. S. to a leadership role in the Western world falter under pressure from economic constraints? Or is the imbalance in America's foreign economic position merely a passing phenomenon that will fade away as soon as the current mixture of diverse international economic policies has been adjusted?

Such key economic and strategic issues in U. S. foreign policy are discussed in this book by a group of European and American scholars, among them Rachel McCulloch, I. M. Destler, Donald Avery, David P. Calleo, Hanns D. Jacobsen, and Helga Haftendorn.

Prices are subject to change without notice

Walter de Gruyter · Berlin · New York